HERE'S LOOKING AT YOU, KIDS:

Michael Curtiz and His Hidden Families

Other works by Ilona Ryder

MA Thesis: "The Influence of German Romanticism in Anna Brownell Jameson's Winter Studies and Summer Rambles in Canada" (U of A. 1994)

Snowflake (2011) ISBN 978-0-9877224-0-9.

HERE'S LOOKING AT YOU, KIDS:

Michael Curtiz and His Hidden Families

Ilona Ryder

HERE'S LOOKING AT YOU, KIDS:
Michael Curtiz and His Hidden Families

Published by Ilona Ryder, Beaumont, Canada

ISBN 0-978-0-9877224-1-6

About the Cover:
Michael Curtiz sent this 8 x 10 glossy print to his five-year old son Michael Vondrak in 1930 with the inscription, "For my dear Michael with great love and hope that I will see him soon. Hollywood California, 1930, Michael."

Publication assistance and digital printing in Canada by

PAGEMASTER
PUBLISHING
PageMaster.ca

DEDICATION

Dedicated to my father, Michael VonDrak, late of Seattle, Washington.
"Creativity … changes familiar things into new form and meaning."

ACKNOWLEDGEMENTS

In the more than twenty years since I began this project, I have had the privilege and luck to meet countless people – family, friends, archive and library staff, writers and readers – all of whom contributed with information, advice and support. I thank all who have lent a hand, an ear or their eyes, all who have given me a place to stay, accompanied me on some wild research trip, or accepted my often unexpected visits and inquiries.

Without James Eadie, who in 1995 said to me, "No one has written a biography of Curtiz. You must do it," this book may never have been started.

From a guestbook entry on my artist father's website I discovered the Hill family who, incredibly, had lived in Edmonton almost the whole time I've lived here. Curtiz's late daughter Sonja even knew my mother, but neither of them knew their connection! Duncan Hill was one of the first "cousins" I met on this journey. Thank you, Duncan!

Early on, another cousin Michelanne and her husband visited all the way from New Zealand and we began to collaborate on her Dad's story. With her help, I was able to visit him, my own "Uncle Mike Forster" in Santa Barbara.

While my father Michael VonDrak was alive, he freely shared his own story but also showed me how sensitively I would have to treat the information. His daughter Lisa first copied for me the dozens of letters that our grandmother had received from Curtiz and kept! Without those letters, I may not have written this book.

I received some of the most valuable family information from my cousin Anikó Szanto who lives in California. And I owe much to the late Kitty Curtiz who lived in Krems, Austria. She shared her poetry and clippings, and after she died her friend Helga gave me access to personal letters.

Beyond the family, I wish to thank friends and acquaintances far and wide. From the Hungarian film historian, Gyöngi Balogh, I received articles written by Curtiz early in his career. Emil Sandi, right here in Edmonton, translated these from the Hungarian. During my visits in Vienna, Guenter Krenn and Armin Loacker of the FilmArchiv, and friends Daniel Kazan and Heinz Kempel have given their support.

I visited James Robertson, the author of *The Casablanca Man,* at his home in Kent, England. His research was done largely at the Warner Bros. Archives in Los Angeles, where I also obtained access to legal and film files when my friend Ursula travelled there with me. Ned Comstock at the UCLA library supplied us with newspaper clippings, as did the Academy of Motion Pictures. A major piece of the puzzle surrounding Curtiz's arrival in the U.S. was solved with the help of staff at the National Archives in New York.

Closer to home, friends and family members have read and taken interest in this book. These include colleagues Karl Homann, Jannie Edwards, and Greg Randall; Laurie Allen and Caterina Edwards; my friends Ursula and Robin Hedley-Smith; and my sister Theresa who was the first to read the completed manuscript. Taking part in a three-week writing workshop at the Banff Centre earned me confidence and advice from professional and aspiring writers.

Last but in many ways most importantly, I am grateful to the family members who populate these pages for allowing me to tell their stories. Out of the hidden corners of memory and documents, our stories shed some light on the man to whom we owe our lives.

CONTENTS

A JOURNEY BEGINS

Where and when does the story of someone's life really begin? Certainly it could begin with a place and date of birth, a brief sketch of ancestral roots, and a statement about the biographer's involvement. For me, the story of my grandfather's life starts on the side of a dirt road in Northern Alberta on a spring day in 1962.

On the morning of April 12, 1962, the news came over the radio that Michael Curtiz, Hollywood film director of such well-known movies as Casablanca and White Christmas, had died. I was just leaving our farm home to go to school. As I waited there along the dusty road for the bus that would take me the three miles to Perryvale, I thought about the man who was understood and felt by me as Grosspapa, about my grandmother Fränzi Omi who had told me many stories about 'Mischka' as she called him. I thought about my real father Michael Vondrak. [1] I thought about what my life might be like if things had been different: if Fränzi and Mischka had married. If my mother and I had been able to follow my father (their son) to Hollywood, I might have been a fourteen-year old movie star instead of standing here on this dirt road!

My daydream was cut short by the school bus coming toward me, bright yellow against the drab grays and browns of an Alberta pre-spring day. I went to school. Life went on.

*****

As the years went by, however, I found that the memory fragments could not be so easily erased. How could I forget about my childhood in Vienna? The times Fränzi Omi would tell me about my grandfather? Even as a child I could tell that her way of saying his name was filled with great love. I heard her pronounce it Mischka, but Anikó [2] my Hungarian-born second cousin and

one of the first new relatives I found on this odyssey of mine, reminded me of the correct spelling in Hungarian, Miska.

If Fränzi Omi and I were walking down the street and a film
of his was playing at the local Kino – perhaps the recent German
release of *Der Jazz Sänger* (*The Jazz Singer*) 1952 – she would point
out to me that her Miska had directed that film. She would remin-
isce at length, but I was probably more concerned about getting a
cone at the Italian ice cream shop nearby.

I became aware, even as a child, that some family members
talked in hushed tones about the man who was my father's father.
The fact that he was a famous film director gradually sank into my
consciousness, but it just made the scandal that much more of a
secret, something not to be talked about. That my grandfather was
Jewish seemed to be less of a problem than the fact that he had not
married Fränzi, that my father was born out of wedlock.

For me, a little girl starting kindergarten, there was a more
pressing dilemma: why didn't I have a Papa like the other kids?
I didn't know that a plan had long been in the works to send my
father Michael Vondrak to the U.S. to be with his father Michael
Curtiz, to live and work in Hollywood. I didn't know that three
years after the end of World War II, this plan had finally come to
fruition. Curtiz had sent the affidavit and had paid for the passage. Fränzi decided not to tell him that his son had married and
had a child. Curtiz knew only that his son was finally ready to
make a new life in Hollywood. The best way – she thought – was
for him to be a single man. So, less than a year after my parents
were married, they allowed themselves to get divorced on false
grounds. My father, at the age of twenty-two, embarked on his
long journey. Promises were made; reality happened.

After years of waiting, my mother realized she and I would
never follow Michael to America and that their marriage was really over. In Philadelphia, my father remarried and in Vienna, my
mother remarried. In 1956 when I was nine years old, my mother,
my stepdad and I emigrated to Canada, and it seemed that even
the little I knew about my father and my grandfather was to be
wiped from my life. We never spoke of Michael Curtiz, and I was
not allowed to correspond with Fränzi Omi.

****

So it was that, even after the strong sense of connection I felt
to my grandfather that day in 1962 on the road near Perryvale,

the stories and vague information about Michael Curtiz that were part of me would remain in hibernation for many more years—almost forty years, actually. I was busy growing up, creating a career, getting married and having my own children. I did begin to exchange letters with Fränzi Omi, however, and I appreciated the opportunity to keep up my German. I also gained more interest in my roots, including the story of my grandfather.

In the 1980's I came across Sydney Rosenzweig's *The Major Films of Michael Curtiz*. This book introduced me to black and white movies long-forgotten and those few that are considered classics by historians and die-hard film buffs. The book had black and white photos—stills from those films, and some speculations about Curtiz's private life.

After all those years, I had found a new source of information about my grandfather. For the first time, I had a few real details about his life and a whole lot of ideas about his work. I felt embarrassed that I had little knowledge of the films he made. When did I ever pay attention to his name on the credits? Had I even seen *Casablanca*?

Suddenly here he was: his name in print, some pictures of him at work. Here were details about his methods and his ideas. I was so excited that I remember jumping up and down with glee, in my kitchen. I knew for the first time in my life that I would, I could, I had to know his life story, the story of how he became my grandfather, the story of how his life is intertwined with mine.

More years elapsed until I told bits of this story to a dear friend, a drama teacher and film buff, who said, "You know, of course, you must write his biography. It has not been done." The most exciting discoveries came early on: I was not alone in calling him grandfather: while still in Europe, Kertész had fathered at least three other children. How naive I had been! The first was a daughter, with his Hungarian wife and actress in 1915. In Vienna there were two other children beside my father. All three 'Vienna children' had different mothers. In California – after his death – a little girl was declared by a court to be his child also. Besides myself, there are eight other grandchildren, and by the time I started writing this book, there were already several great-grandchildren. If he could see us all now, he'd be looking at us with eyes wide open.

In my journey I've also become acquainted with film historians and writers who know more about his work than I had ever imagined, Hungarians who are proud to translate articles by and about him, and many others who have a general or specific interest in Michael Curtiz as a film director and a person. I've read and heard all the popular stories about him: in Hollywood he killed the English language and he fought with actors. He was a womanizer and an intensely private man. I was sad to find out that he died miserably of untreated cancer.

But something kept nagging at me: beneath all the facts, the semi-truths, the fictions, there had to be a man who felt pain and joy, triumph and disappointment: all the emotions that make up a human life. My quest became to round up the 'Usual Suspects' and some not-so-usual ones, and to get to know this man of many names: born Kaminer Manó, changed to Kertész Mihály in Hungary [3], written as Michael Kertész in the rest of Europe, nicknamed Miska, and finally anglicized to Michael (Mike) Curtiz in America.

Budapest, 2000

So now I can start with the place where he began. It is July 2000, and I am standing in front of a house in Budapest – Number 12, Jokai utcá [4]. The house is taller than those on either side—could be an addition, a renovation. Above the mezzanine windows, a façade that includes a panel of relief-sculptured figures — possibly a theatre troupe — hints at turn-of-the-century Nouveau Art. But I'm too excited to care about such architectural details right now. Behind one of those tall double windows, on a cold night in December 1886, my grandfather was born.

I've come to Budapest by train from Vienna, where in the previous two weeks I had spent more time in in archives and museums than with my relatives. They were becoming a little skeptical of my research, but a local journalist, Georg Markus, interviewed me over coffee at the Sacher Hotel [5].

Now it is time to walk the streets that my grandfather walked as a child, to see the first city that he saw.

As my early morning train left the Vienna hills behind and struck east across the plains, precursor to the famous Hungarian Steppes, I was briefly homesick for Canada, for the wide open skies of Alberta. I wondered what Michael Curtiz might have thought about on this stretch of track in 1931 when he came "home" from America for the first time? What would my grandmother have

Number 12, Jokai utcá

thought on this train in 1933 when she was taking her son to meet Curtiz's family in Budapest? The corn fields waved me on.

My train pulled into Keléty Railway Station two hours later, and I was nervous. Will my contact, a relative of a Hungarian friend back home, be there to meet me? Then I saw my name in capital letters printed on a white piece of paper. An elderly gentleman was holding the sign high above the white cap on his head. He looked friendly. I sighed with relief: István.

Our first communication was halting; he apologized for his rusty German. "But it's better than my English," he explained with a laugh. István was tall and thin; his tanned face and hands adding to his healthy appearance. A retired bank employee, István liked to walk, but explained that to get to my hotel we have to take the subway. He produced tickets, and we descended into the bowels of the Budapest subway system. I was astonished at how steep and how long the escalators are. After taking two sets of these steel creepers, we arrived at the platform.

Far beyond the older part of the city, we emerged into the brightness of mid-day, and I checked in at the Hotel Stadion. István told me about the preparations he had made for my research visit. First, however, he wanted to show me his city. We had lunch around the corner from the National Bank where he used to work. Then we toured the historical palace hill on the Buda side of the Danube and sipped orange juice on a terrace overlooking the river and the Parliament Buildings on the Pest part of BudaPest. Later, we viewed the same sights from a different angle. A Danube boat tour was on our 'do not miss' list. A stroll along the upscale shopping street, Váci utcá, completed our day.

All along, I tried to imagine what Budapest looked like a hundred years ago, when my grandfather was a child and a young man here in the last days of the Austro-Hungarian Empire. Many of the public buildings and apartment houses you can see today already existed at the beginning of the 20th century. They probably looked cleaner, painted in pastel pinks, yellows and greens. Many street names were in German, and instead of the steady stream of cars, horse-drawn carriages, wagons and streetcars dominated. The broad sidewalks along the main boulevards were lined with market stalls. There might be street entertainers - an organ grinder with a monkey, perhaps. Today, the wide pavements seem strangely empty but for the occasional set of restaurant tables or racks of merchandise spilling from store fronts.

Early the next morning, István picked me up at the hotel and we made our way to the Jewish Community Archives in the Seventh District. We had an appointment at the records office at eight o'clock. As we pushed through the morning crush on the subway, he told me to hold my satchel in front of me and close to my body – there are thieves on the train. Most people seem busy getting to their workplace, I thought to myself, but then I saw a group of young men who were eyeing people intently. The escalators, full to capacity, seemed endlessly long this morning. István explained that during the Cold War in the mid 1900's, the extra deep tunnels were built for use as fall-out shelters in the event of nuclear war. Let me out, please!

We walked along the inner ring street, the Károly körút, until we came to the Central Synagogue. One block along Wesselény utcá, we turned right onto the narrow, cobbled Sip utcá to a blackened building with a huge, steel-girded double door. We stepped inside the dark entrance hall; the door slammed shut behind us, the echo reverberating off the stone walls. Temporarily blinded by the bright morning sun outside, I blinked to see a guard cubicle to the left. A young man sitting in front of a small computer monitor waved us to his station. István explained in Hungarian why we are there; I showed my passport, and the young man gave us directions to the office where we were to meet with the records people.

It's the usual Old Europe city building – I recognized the style from Vienna. The plain façade against the street is deceiving, for once you pass through the entrance hall, the courtyard might contain gardens, or as in this case, a parking area. A broad marble stairway flanked by wrought iron railings winds gently upward. I hardly noticed the small elevator in a corner. Peering through the barred windows facing the courtyard, I imagined horses being harnessed, metal-shod hooves resounding off the cobbles and carriage hardware grinding and clanking.

István and I climbed to the third floor and approached a set of large whitish double doors. A woman's rough voice answered our knock and we entered a square room that held her massive, cluttered desk. She stubbed out a cigarette in an overflowing ashtray and rose to direct us through another set of double doors into

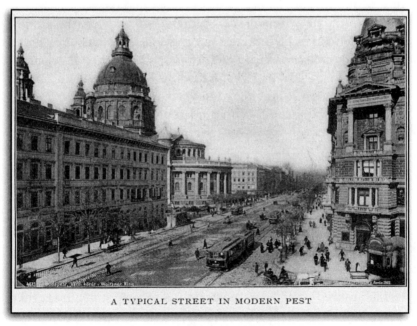

A TYPICAL STREET IN MODERN PEST

1903 travel book on Budapest

a larger, darkly furnished room dominated by a big table piled high with old books and registers.

We were introduced to the main record keeper who already had the huge birth record book for 1886 open at the page for December 25. He wasted no time in pointing me to an entry near the bottom of the page, the entry for **Manó,** a male child born to **Ignácz Kaminer,** and his wife **Golde Natt.** [6] The beautiful slanted writing in record Number 2328 disclosed to me, in the original, all the details that I had been waiting to see with my own eyes. In the far right column, a notation in tiny handwriting confirms Manó's name change from Kaminer to **Kertész** on December 27, 1905 just after his nineteenth birthday. I touched the heavy yellowing paper and noticed the worn and bent corners. The secretary handed me two sheets of paper – photocopies! I placed the treasure in my folder.

Then, with the help of a translator who appeared out of no-where (did my guide arrange this as well?) we talked about what other records I am searching for: the birth of Ilonka Kovács – my grandfather's first wife, their marriage and the birth of Katherine (Kitty), their daughter. What about the death of Ignácz Kaminer? I knew about these events, but what are the dates? They shook their heads and muttered to each other in Hungarian. I showed them the 1903 family portrait and a list of names and dates.

Their advice droped like so many precious pearls: an ad-dress on Dob utcá, directions; try City Hall, the Jewish Museum. There is a promise for further effort on their part, and they asked me for my e-mail address. This room, this building, felt incompat-ible with modern technology, but the computer monitor among the piles of papers and files reminded me otherwise. With much hand-shaking, smiling and thanking, we took our leave, retraced our steps down the stairs, past the guard in the entrance hall, and out into the bright sunshine.

After several false leads for more information, we decided to look for the house. The street and house number where my grand-father's family lived at the time he was born is documented on the birth record: 12 Gyár utcá. The district should be another clue: VII Ker (7th District). The name of a midwife, Klein Fánni, suggests he was born at home, in that house. That was in 1886, though, and over a hundred years later, the current Budapest street index that I brought with me showed no such street in the seventh district.

Gyár is Hungarian for factory, a common word. In 1886 any street might have had a factory or led to a factory of some kind. Any street might have been called Gyár utcá. After the collapse of the Austro-Hungarian Empire with World War I, the political tides washing over the city, then World War II, Budapest endured many changes. Street names could have been altered several times: Gyár utcá—or whatever its name is now—may not even exist. But now I was thinking like a person from North America, where in almost any city, rows of houses can be razed to make way for a freeway. This is Europe, so there is more hope that the street still exists. After trying at several antiquarian dealers and used book stores,

"1901 Neuester Plan der Haupt- und Residenzstadt Budapest" [7]

István and I were lucky enough to find a Budapest street map from 1901. Close enough. And there it was: Gyár utcá!

A quick comparison with the current map confirmed the street does, in fact, still exist. It is now called Jokai utcá. From where we were on the Inner Ring near the city centre, Jokai utcá was at least fifteen blocks away, so it was back down to the subway. We emerged on the large square facing the Nugati Railway Station. A modern glass building flanked the corner where Jokai utcá is supposed to start. Finally, I saw the sign for Jokai utcá, and as we moved away from the square I was relieved to see the numbers decreasing from the high 80's. We were looking for Number 12. The street looked like so many others in Budapest, like so many streets in other European cities. Thousands of four-storey houses were built during the urban expansion in the latter part of the nineteenth century. By 1886 this was a typical upper middle-class neighbourhood.

On every corner, there is a sign showing the range of house numbers in that block. Finally, there it is: 10 - 14 Jokai utcá. This is the block. And here is the house. Here is Number 12, at last. On December 25, 1886, Kaminer Manó, who the world would one day know as Kertész Mihály and Michael Curtiz, was born in this house.

Ancestral Congregations

Twenty years before Manó Kaminer was born in that house, his father Ignácz had come to Budapest from his birthplace of Delatyn, Galizia. This town, now usually spelled Deylatyn, is located on the northern slopes of the Carpathian Mountains that divide present-day Hungary and Ukraine. The region Galizia was known in the late nineteenth century as the Karpatenländer (the Lands of the Carpathians), a province of Austro-Hungary. Today, it is part of the Ukraine. The capital of Galizia was Lemberg (now L'viv). Delatyn is situated on the Pruth River above the larger center of Kolomea (Kolomyya). Foothills surround the town; agriculture and forestry are the main industries. Galizia (named after a region in Spain) was known as a historical gathering place for Jewish people who had been ousted from various parts of Europe.

Ignácz Kaminer was born in Delatyn ca. 1850. His father, who was born in Poland about 1820, went by the surname Kohn, and his wife Rachel's maiden name was Aszodi. Ignácz was the youngest of three Kohn brothers. Moricz was the oldest, and Benjamin (Báchi) was the middle son, born in 1840.

By 1850, the Austro-Hungarian Empire had taken its ultimate shape. The March Revolution of 1848 against Chancellor Metternich's policies signaled the beginning of the long reign of Emperor Franz Joseph I (1848-1916). Continuing military struggles with Prussia required more and more soldiers. Eventually, lack of volunteers forced the conscription of all able young men from all regions of the empire, including Galizia, populated largely by Jews.

There was a loophole in the law, however. The army did not conscript an only son in a family, and the three Kohn brothers took advantage [8]. Two of them changed their surname: Báchi changed his to Katz, and Ignácz changed his to Kaminer. Only Moricz remained Kohn. For these three brothers, the deception worked, because in 1866, they left Delatyn, traveled over the Carpathian Mountains and down into what is now Hungary. This was already a well-traveled route and modern maps mark it as a main highway. Their destination was the bustling twin cities of Buda and Pest.

In another part of the Austro-Hungarian Empire, the family of Golde (Aranka), Manó's mother, was living in the city of Grosswardein on the banks of the river Koros. The Hungarian name for this ancient city at the edge of the lowlands or steppes was Nagyvarad, and today we know it as Oradea, Rumania. Aranka Nathan was born there April 12, 1862.

It's interesting to note that Aranka is the literal translation for "gold," so the familiar name Golde is both a nickname and simply another form of the name. Aranka was the younger of two sisters. Their mother apparently became ill and bedridden for ten years before she died, still a fairly young woman. Their father had also died early. The two sisters eventually migrated to Budapest to make a living.

Around the same time, the families of the women that my grandfather would become involved with – the mothers of his children born in Europe – were also taking shape. Most of these other families had also migrated from smaller centres to larger cities. Ilonka Kovács, his first wife and the mother of Katalin (Kitty) was an exception; she grew up in a well-to-do and conservative Protestant family in Budapest, possibly with government connections. Lucy Doraine was the stage name she took in her teens. Mathilde Förster who gave him his first son in Vienna in 1920, was born into a Jewish family whose most recent migration was from the area north of Budapest, not far from Curtiz's own roots. There was some Italian in Theresia Dalla Bonna's family background, and my grandmother Fränzi Wondrak traced her family roots to Bohemia.

The Austro-Hungarian Empire was the political force that choreographed the economic and social dance that the players of this human drama acted out on the Central European stage during the latter decades of the nineteenth-century. Numerous cultural crossroads and intersections touched these people's lives.

A hundred years later, scholars are studying these phenomena. They are very interested in the transference of cultural influences that escalated in the nineteenth and early twentieth-centuries among the Central European countries that we now know as Ukraine, Czech Republic, Hungary and Austria. These studies are largely based on family histories just like the ones that emerge in the story of my grandfather.

The cultural mosaic that characterizes large cities such as Vienna and Budapest originates in these family stories, in their culture, art, music, literature, and daily lifestyles. When I look at my grandfather's young life as Kaminer Manó, his rise to fame as Michael Kertész in Austria, and his work in American film as Michael Curtiz, I need to remember these roots: Jewish spiritual and family traditions, Kaiserlich und Königlich (K & K) sensibilities [9], the clash of modern and traditional values, and uncertainty about personal safety.

History tells us that as a direct result of wars with Prussia, Emperor Franz-Joseph I of Austria transformed the unitary state of Hungary into an equal partner in the Austro-Hungarian Dual Monarchy which consisted of "independent territorial entities with equal rights, united only by the person of the ruler, common military and financial systems and a common ministry of foreign affairs" [10]. It was the beginning of a liberal, economically stable era which saw the population of Budapest swell from 178,000 in 1850 to 370,800 thirty years later.

During the 1870's and 80's, the young Ignácz Kaminer would have found it easy to get work as a room/house painter, his occupation as listed on Manó's birth record. In a city booming with new construction, all trades were in demand and commanded high wages.

In Budapest, Ignácz met and married a young woman who had come to the capital from Grosswardein. They had two children: a daughter Etel in 1882 and a son Antal, born in 1885 [11]. It is possible that their mother died in childbirth, for very shortly after, Ignácz married her older sister Golde (Aranka), [12] who bore Ignácz seven more children. Their first son was Manó, my grandfather.

The Empire's residence city Vienna was also in economic boom during the last decades of the nineteenth century. People streamed from all the corners of the empire, and the city annexed a number of surrounding municipalities. According to official census tallies, the population exploded from 726,000 in 1880 to 1,365,000 in 1890, and by 1910 the city reached the highest figure in its history, with 2,083,630. [13]

These two vibrant cities, Budapest and Vienna, would share the main stage for some of the most dramatic scenes in my grandfather's life.

PART I

CHILDHOOD AND ADOLESCENCE: 1886 - 1912

Creating Identity

When Manó (Emmanuel Michael) was born December 25, 1886 in the family apartment at Number 12, Jokai utcá, it was also around the beginning of Hanukah, the Jewish Holiday of Lights. Although the family was probably not Orthodox Jewish, this was still a good omen for an anxious family awaiting Aranka's first baby. Klein, Fánni was the midwife that helped Aranka with the birth. The godfather was Aszódi Mór, possibly Ignácz's employer or co-worker, of Dob utcá Number7. On January 2, Dr. Jakob Weinberger performed the brit milah. This birth record, Folio 2328 in the book for the year 1886, was prepared on a wintry Budapest day soon after. The following excerpts from the book of birth records are from the treasured photocopies I obtained.

Other details – the baby's size, weight, exact time of arrival – all the vital statistics that parents love to share with family and treasure for themselves – these I can only guess. There were no digital camera images in 1886, no e-mail to share them. As soon as

Folio	Given Name	Date		Gender

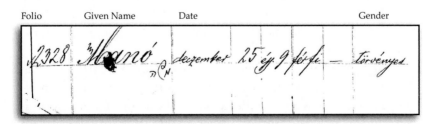

Father	Mother	Address	Midwife	Doctor

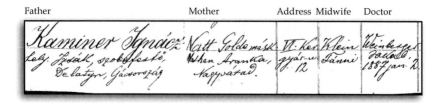

Witness (Godfather)	1905 Notation (name change)

the twenty four year-old mother was able, she would have sent off notes to her own family and friends. Cards and gifts would arrive at Number12 Jokai utcá during the first few months of 1887, by post. There may have been some visitors.

Interesting things were going on in the world that little Manó entered: Robert Louis Stevenson was publishing *Dr. Jekyll and Mr. Hyde* and Sir Arthur Conan Doyle was working on the first Sherlock Holmes story, "A Study in Scarlet." Karl Marx's *Das Kapital* was being translated into English; Franz Liszt had just died in July. The Canadian Pacific Railway began transcontinental railway service, and Vincent Van Gogh was busy painting in and around Paris; his "Self Portrait as an Artist" is a major work. Verdi was writing opera in Milan, while Gilbert and Sullivan were working on another operetta in London. Bruckner was composing "Te Deum," and Emil Berliner was spending time improving the phonograph's sound quality. Perhaps most significant of all, the American H. W. Goodwin had invented celluloid film! Talk about serendipity: Michael Curtiz was born at the moment his future artistic medium was born half a world away! [1]

In presenting the director Michael Curtiz's birth date as December 25, 1886, I am correcting one of the main pieces of misinformation that were circulated about him throughout his life and, indeed, until very recently. Even Kati Marton in her book The

Great Escape still says that the date of his birth is "subject to debate" [2]. The actual record also makes it clear that he changed his name on December 27, 1905, just after his nineteenth birthday.

In the public papers that I've found, Curtiz's birth date is most often given as December 24, 1888, a minor discrepancy of two years, and at least one source gives the birth date as 1892 [3]. Interestingly, the 1929 Warner Brothers biography of their new director gives no birth date. It seems my grandfather didn't worry too much about what he told reporters and employers, but when he dealt with government officials, he was more careful. On ship passenger lists, on naturalization papers, and on his marriage license, for instance, he gives his correct age.

Far from such worries as the date he was born, little Manó grew into a toddler and first consciousness in the late 1880's, surrounded by an ever-growing family. His older sister and brother Etel and Antal were the first to share their toys with him, and he in turn shared his toys with baby sister Regina "Denda," born October 26, 1888 when Manó was barely two years old. During his elementary school days, Manó gained two more brothers: Deszö (David), born March 24, 1893, and Lajós came along on April 12, 1895. Later on, there were two more sisters and another brother. Margit (Margaret) was born May 29, 1897 and Kornellia arrived March 18, 1901. When she was forty, Aranka bore her husband one more son, Oszkár (later Gabor Kertész and still later Gabriel or Gabe Curtiz) born October 16, 1903. The Kaminer children – with a range of twenty-one years between the oldest and youngest – eventually numbered nine!

Large families were certainly not unusual, but it's always somewhat of a mystery as to how they made ends meet. Here, too, what my grandfather told people wasn't necessarily the whole truth. Manó's birth record shows his father Ignácz Kaminer as room painter (szobafostö) and his mother Aranka without an occupation. There is one other early document, from 1901, about Ignácz – it's a Statement of Citizenship issued by the Budapest Mayor's office which, unfortunately, does not confirm his occupation. In 1929, the Warner Brothers biography that Michael Curtiz must have helped to prepare says his father is an architect and his mother an opera singer! But in other sources, notably Frazier's article of 1947 and Martin's article and book of the same time period, Curtiz is quoted as saying that his father was a poor carpenter. [4]

Let me stay with Ignácz for a moment. He migrated to Budapest about 1880, a time when the city was booming. Tradespeople would have been in great demand, and in the thousands of apartments in hundreds of city blocks being built, a room painter would have been both respected and well paid. When Manó was born, his father was thirty-six and already had two children. Being a room painter would allow him to feed his growing family over the next years. It is, of course, possible that the work situation changed as a result of economic or personal reasons. The work could have dried up; Ignácz could have been injured. Any number of circumstances could have brought him down to be a "poor carpenter" at a crucial time to create those memories for my grandfather.

As a grown man, Michael Curtiz could have constructed illusions about his father's occupation and status for his own convenience and purpose. The "poor carpenter" image might solicit reactions of sympathy. The label "architect" usually creates a perception of privilege and wealth. We are left with the question, why? By the way, I've found no other source created during Curtiz's lifetime that shows Ignácz as an architect.

For a young man with a growing family, the logistics are almost impossible. Ignácz would have had to gain the necessary education before Manó was born in 1886, would have had to take up room painting for a while and then gone into the architect profession later on. Curtiz's sister Margit, called it a rumour. The idea that Ignácz was an architect "is a great exaggeration: He was a house painter!" she told her granddaughter Anikó [5].

Aranka, Manó's mother, presents a similar puzzle when it comes to work or intersts outside the home. Anikó admits the family doesn't really know, but they think the idea that she was an opera singer also comes from the 1929 Warner Brothers biography of Curtiz. In that document, Aranka is said to have "gained prominence as a concert singer in Vienna." The article by Frazier in 1947 picks up on this theme by suggesting that she "had operatic ambitions." Later sources repeat the idea with a bit more reserve: Rosenzweig uses the word "claimed" and Robertson suggests it's "generally accepted" that Aranka was an opera singer.[6]

That she had aspirations to the theatre and encouraged artistic interest in her children is not impossible, though. Aranka was born in 1862, in Nagyvarad, a culturally vibrant city in eastern Hungary. Other circumstantial evidence suggests Aranka's possible involvement in the theatrical arts. The usual sources have Curtiz mentioning several times that when he was eleven years old, he got his first taste of the stage in a production in which his mother was involved. The opportunity may have been very close to home, for according to Anikó's grandmother Margit, the family was living in a house on the corner of Weselény and Akácfa utcá around the same time, 1897. In the same building there was a restaurant, and on another corner of the intersection was the Magyar Szinház, the Hungarian Theatre. According to family story, there was always a peacock around the house and garden, and Manó used the bird in a play [7].

Manó, Etel and Antal, circa 1898

One tantalizing bit of evidence is a picture taken of three oldest Kaminer children taken about 1898, when Manó was eleven.

The photo shows Manó, Etel and Antal, dressed in what appear to be special outfits. What about the basket and the flowers? The girl's dirndl, and the sashes and medals the boys are wearing? Notice the Austrian-style hats they are holding. Given that Budapest was still very much a part of the Austro-Hungarian Empire, the children may have been dressed for a school pageant on the occasion of a national holiday, or they may be on the stage for a theatre production.

A further set of family information helps me better understand the Kaminers' standard of living. Sometime after Manó's birth in the apartment house on Jokai utcá – perhaps as late as 1901 – the family moved to No. 23 Weselény utcá and it is possible that Ignácz owned that one-storey building. The date is significant, for on April 12, 1901, Kaminer Ignácz was officially recognized as a Citizen of Hungary. The document issued by the office of the Mayor of Budapest qualifies him and his family as legitimate residents of Budapest.

Around 1903, the family moved again, north of the Erzsébet körút (Elisabeth Ring) to a two-storey building at No. 32 Szovetség utcá. According to the family, Ignácz owned the building. Did he perhaps help to build it? And is that why Curtiz called him an architect? Regardless, Ignácz would have been pleased. This house was also his last home, for he died there on March 23, 1923. His widow Aranka and the remaining children at home, including married couples, occupied various parts of this house until Aranka emigrated to the U.S. in 1939, at which time Michael Curtiz apparently bought the property, renting out its apartments. Ultimately, no proceeds were realized by the family. [8] Quite recently, another twist in the story of this house emerged, and you will read about that further on.

All of this material, along with my grandfather's statements about his parents – whether inflated, deflated, or fabricated to a certain extent – seems to confirm that the family enjoyed a comfortable, perhaps even well-to-do middle class lifestyle in those early years. Without getting into details at this point, the fact that the Kaminer family was Jewish carried no special significance: while separate religious and educational facilities were used, integration and assimilation was the dominant policy and practice.

At School

Working within this frame of social, cultural, and personal probabilities, especially regarding time and location, I was anxious to know about my grandfather's school experience. Using his correct birth date of 1886 on the one side and the reliable information about his first contract as a theatre actor in 1908 on the other side, I have tried to construct what I believe to be a plausible sequence of events.

Up to now, I've been using Manó, short for Manuel (Emmanuel) and actually my grandfather's middle name, or rather one of them. It's now time to move on to Mihály, Hungarian for Michael, because this is the name by which he became known in Hungary and beyond. Kertész Manuel Mihály would have been his full legal name. It's interesting to note that when my own father was born in 1925, Michael Kertész as he was known in Austria at the time wrote to my grandmother, "He should have two given names like me, Manuel Michael." [9]

When Mihály was ready to go to elementary school, he would have gone with his two-year older brother Antal to a school in the neighbourhood, perhaps just a few blocks down the street, past the park on Jokai utcá. Mandatory education from age six to fifteen was introduced by the Hungarian Education Act of 1868 after the control of public education was transferred from Vienna to Budapest in 1860. The state, however, did not administer the lower level of schools. For example, elementary schools could be "opened and maintained by any fictitious or natural person, denomination, state, society or individual" [10]. The Seventh District of Budapest where the Kaminers lived was mainly a Jewish community, so I can assume that Mihály's first few years of schooling were at a neighbourhood Jewish school.

There were two streams of elementary school, a three-year and a six-year program. Parents could choose to keep a child in elementary school for six years in the "day-school" program; this would be followed by the vocational stream of secondary education, known as "Realschule." Children who showed academic promise could spend as little as three years in elementary school, in the "continuation school" program, and then go directly to the eight-year secondary school, the "Gymnasium," where they would prepare for university [11]. From the evidence available, I can only conclude that Mihály took the latter route.

It's been a struggle trying to piece together my grandfather's higher education, and some contradictions will remain. The most pervasive but also mysterious references are to the post-secondary Budapest institutions that he supposedly attended: Markoszy University and the Royal Academy of Theatre and Art, from which he had to graduate in order to get a theatre acting contract. The available literature – articles, books, indexes, electronic sources – perpetuates his attendance at these schools to an absurd end. First, Markoszy University seems to exist only in the realm of biographical information about Michael Curtiz. And second, the literature tends to muddle the dates or ages when he supposedly attended that institution.

The 1886 birth date is useful in trying to get a picture of Mihály's educational path. In order to get to university, Mihály would have attended the nearest "Gymnasium" school, beginning in the fall of 1895, just before he turned nine years old. This next level of schooling was subject to the same loose government guidelines and community privileges as the elementary schools, but the secondary school system in Budapest mirrored the Austrian and indeed the Western European dual systems of the time [12]. The 1883 Secondary School Act required only the Gymnasium schools to teach Latin and Greek as well as Hungarian, but reforms in 1890 allowed all secondary schools to drop Greek. By the time Mihály entered the Gymnasium school, then, he would have taken Latin, but maybe not Greek. It's difficult to know what level of schooling he was referring to when, in Pete Martin's 1948 book Hollywood Without Makeup, he is quoted as saying that he studied three languages [13].

If education was mandatory until the age of fifteen, Mihály had to attend at least until sometime in 1902. At the end of the eight-year Gymnasium program he would have written his "Matura" (Matriculation) exams, possibly in spring 1903. Again there are conflicting reports of what he did during those years. According to Hungarian film historian Gyöngyi Balogh, he joined a traveling circus as an acrobat sometime between 1899 (age thirteen) and 1902 (age fifteen) and began acting with "traveling stages." Frazier's article, on the other hand, has him joining the circus at age sixteen, and the biography in World Directors follows Pete Martin's lead about Mihály joining a traveling circus at age seventeen. The exact age details may be immaterial, but it's reasonable to conclude that Mihály made these excursions on the side, perhaps during summer holidays. His own testimony (in Frazier) indicates he was with the circus for three years, a statement that – if taken literally – completely throws the constrictions of a formal education out of whack. But there are so many obvious mis-statements in Frazier's article that I refer to it only as a comparison benchmark.

Mystery also surrounds Mihály's extra-curricular activity. Some sources say he appeared in these entertainments as a strong man, while elsewhere he "insisted that he was on the trampoline". Pete Martin quotes him regarding his athletic abilities: "I was a good athlete in school … Runner, jumper like that; so I work on bars and rings." Pantomimes and juggling were also part of his repertoire [14]. One thing seems certain: Mihály may have had early and multiple opportunities for being closely involved with the physical aspects of entertaining an audience. The effects of movement and action would become important aspects of his success in directing films.

Toward A Career

Another treasure of my research, and one of the first items that my cousin Anikó was kind enough to share with me, is the Kaminer family portrait of 1903. Aranka the matriarch is seated in the center, with her youngest child, Oszkár (Gabor) propped

The Kaminer Family, 1903

up against her. From left to right on the photo, back row, we have Regina (Denda) with her niece (Etel's daughter Ilonka Szücz) on her lap; then the father Kaminer Ignácz; Deszö (David); Aranka as mentioned; Antal, Ignácz's son from his first marriage; Mihály; and Etel, Ignácz's daughter from his first marriage. The three children in the front row, left to right, are Lajos in what has been suggested is a school uniform [15]; Margaret (Margit), and Kornellia.

Within two years of this family portrait, my grandfather undertook an important step. Just after he turned nineteen in December 1905, Mihály changed his surname officially to Kertész. A notation on the birth record confirms this move. His brother Antal did the same about a year later when he was twenty-one.

In their father's generation name changes were done to avoid military service, so why would these young men change their name now? For Mihály, the name change may have been a pre-career move. Kertész is a very common name in Hungary –literal meaning "gardener." When Imre Kertész won the Nobel Prize for literature in 2002, we thought that maybe here is another relative. But it turns out he is not.

An interesting example of the practice of Hungarian Jewish families changing names is portrayed in the film Sunshine [16]. There is a scene where the three Sonnenschein siblings are flipping through a dictionary to come up with a name. They stop at the page for words starting with "so.." maybe wondering if Sonnenschein is listed. They see the word sör, which means beer: a round of laughs. But then the word sors stands out for them: sors, Hungarian for fate, fortune or destiny. This becomes their choice, and the three young people chatter merrily as they make plans to become successful players in Budapest society. Watching that scene, I can visualize the Kaminer brothers and their sister having fun with their choice.

With his new name, Kertész Mihály followed his interest in acting and resolved – perhaps also in the same year – to enroll in the Royal Academy for Theatre and Art. As he confirmed later, in order to get a theatre contract in Hungary, one needed to graduate from this school [17]. The research of Hungarian film historian Gyöngyi Balogh indicates Kertész won his first formal acting contract in 1908, so I can assume that he attended the Academy for two years, graduating in 1908 at the age of twenty-one.

Over his long career, my grandfather reported quite consistently that he went to university and then to drama school, and it makes perfect sense that he attended The Royal Academy of Theatre and Art – or The Academy of Dramatic Art as he sometimes called it. Getting through the Academy was tough, he admitted. Out of a class of 182, only 16 achieved the diploma; he was one of them [18].

When people hear that someone has gone to university, has taken higher education toward his or her profession, they create an image. Higher education lends credibility – in this case, to the early articles Kertész wrote about his vision for film, to the scripts he wrote and worked on, to the decisions he wanted to make as a director, and ultimately, to being involved in the business end of the fledgling film industry in Hungary.

So when I read material such as Martin's article calling Michael Curtiz the "Champion Language Assassin," naming him the harsh taskmaster who disregarded the safety of actors, and so forth, I am dismayed that such dramatic material (even where it is true) tends to color the world's perception of the man and demean his overall contributions to the film industry. His success in the film industry is no doubt at least partly due to that formal education.

*****

While he was building his professional identity, Kertész worked as an actor in live theatre in Pécs, a vibrant city south of Budapest [19]. However, according to his roommate Lajos Bàlint during the 1907-08 theatre season, Kertész was dissatisfied with his acting abilities. In fact, he was already thinking about directing, already thinking about film [20].

Nevertheless, Hungarian film research shows that he worked on the stage for some time before he moved over to film [21]. In 1908, when Kertész was already twenty, he signed a short-term contract with the theatre in Szeged, a city about 150 kilometers south-east of Budapest, before coming back to the capital to sign a three-year contract with the Budapest theatre company Magyar Szinhaz. But his friend and confidant Lájos Balint explains that Kertész's feelings about acting were waning: "He was indeed one of those rare actors who did not complain if he did not get a role to play..." [22]. Instead, he had had his eye on directing for some time:

> He said, very sincerely, that he does not think he can become
> a really good actor. "Something is missing in me," he said. "I

can only achieve a fraction of what I feel is necessary in acting. I would rather be a director..." [23]

Balint agreed that Kertész did not have the "multicoloured talent"
that an actor needs, but he also commends him for having recognized that lack in himself. Changing his career was indeed the
right move for Kertész, a move that led him to realize his dreams,
not only about himself, but about the new medium, film:

> What is your opinion about films? [I asked him] "I can see
> fantastic possibilities in this field. It offers huge perspectives
> never achievable on the small stages of a theatre. I think I
> could work very well in this field." [24]

And so it was that by 1910, at the age of twenty-two, Kertész began
working with Projectograph Film Company while continuing his
work in the theatre until his one-year acting contract ran out in
1911. Then in 1912, he met Ivan Siklósi, film title writer, who may
have encouraged Kertész to act in the film Utolsó bohém (The Last
Bohemian, 1912). The same year, Kertész acted in and probably
directed Ma Es Holnap (Today and Tomorrow), the first feature
film made in Hungary. A sign of his ongoing drive for perfection is
seen in his disappointment in the product: "This film is not satis-
factory even as a first production – I and my technicians do not
know enough about this trade. But I have decided to learn it" [25].

To learn more about the trade, Kertész traveled to Denmark
where Nordisk was at the leading edge of European film; the company was well-funded and staffed with professionals. He learned some important lessons about film making there: to succeed,
you need good people – lots of people, and lots of money. Indeed
when he returned to Hungary, Kertész took on the film industry
in all seriousness and proved that he "could work very well in this
field." [26]

Bryan Burns describes these vibrant beginnings of film as
"cross-fertilization between Hungary's rich theatrical world and
the new medium." [27] The tendency in Hungary to see film as an
equal to, and not as a "poor relation" to literature and drama,
made it more respectable for educated young men like Kertész
to consider the cinema as a rich artistic field of endeavour. Some
of that cross-fertilization occurred in the famous Café New York,
located right in Kertész's back yard. The café was part of the imposing Palais New York, originally built as a flagship head office

for New York Life Insurance and now a luxury hotel, on Erszébet körút (Elizabeth Ring). This boulevard runs along the edge of the 7th District where Kertész and his family lived. He is known, in fact, to have been a regular at the café. A popular story from this era concerns the already famous dramatist Molnár Ferenc (1878-1952), who apparently threw the keys to the café into the Danube, so that it should always remain open for him and his friends [28]. Molnár had penned several plays that Kertész would turn into films over the next few years. It's quite possible that they met and discussed ideas about such projects. Cafés were also the first places that moving pictures were shown, and the new medium would have been just the thing for the disenchanted theatre actor to get interested in.

The café as a European institution is still very much alive in cities like Budapest and Vienna, and the regular patrons who can afford the time will spend hours there. Besides the coffee which is usually served on a little tray along with a glass of water, a tiny bowl with lumps of sugar under silver tongs and a small creamer, you can order baked goods or even a light meal depending on the time of day. The pace in the European café is slow: it is a place where you can read the paper, think, work in solitude, or meet friends. Today as always, students frequent the cafés, but their notebooks are connected to electric outlets instead of pocket-chains. I have spent several hours on several occasions in Vienna's Café Prückl which, although not nearly as posh as Budapest's New York in the early 1900's, is for me still a place to stimulate the mind.

The regular patrons of a café then, as now, would lay claim to their own tables or corners in the high-ceilinged rooms. Then, as now, the current day's newspapers are threaded on bent bamboo holders with a handle at the bottom, so that the reader can flip pages easily and prop the paper up against the edge of a table for easy reading. Lighting is provided by huge windows on the street side, sconce light fixtures on sometimes ornately decorated pillars, and by a variety of chandeliers hanging from the very high ceilings. Around the room there are coat racks that also accommodate hats at the top and umbrellas at the bottom.

It is known that important men in theatre, film and literature frequented the Café New York, including the "king of operetta" Imre Kálmán, and the future great director Alexander Korda. Given the equality of stature that Korda and Kertész were to gain in the world of film, I have wondered whether they were acquaintances in those early days. But as Kati Marton points out, there is "no record of interaction" between them. And when it came to work, Kertész and Korda were rivals rather than friends. [29] Korda spent several years as reviewer and critic, and it would be interesting to know what he might have written about Kertész's early films. Much later, in America, their relationship was rekindled.

*****

This may be the juncture at which one may say, "and the rest is history." Mihály Kertész / Michael Curtiz the director is born, and we should concern ourselves primarily with his work from this point forward. But I say that this is exactly where our interest in him as a person surely must continue: A man does not cease to be a private person, a son, a brother, a lover, just because he has chosen a demanding career. Nor does the career prevent him from becoming a father, uncle and grandfather. And beyond family, there is still the role of being a friend, a confidant, a business partner, or a rival.

Most of what has been written about Curtiz concentrates on his career, a career that spans two continents, fifty years, and over a hundred films. But what does a twenty-three year old, a forty-six year old, a sixty-four year old man of the world do behind closed doors, in his spare time, on his holidays, with his friends, family and children? What are his personal hopes, dreams, and disappointments? What are his habits and idiosyncrasies? And is it possible that as an artist – for that's what a director of his caliber must be called – infuses his work with threads from his personal life – past and ongoing?

I want to know my grandfather as the man he was in his heart, so I will follow him through what I have discovered about his career and his personal life and what I can infer from some of his films.

PART II

LIFE AND WORK IN HUNGARY: 1913 - 1919

Early Career

In 1913 Mihály Kertész was an ambitious, good-looking young man of twenty-six. He cast his eye about and saw what was available, both professionally and personally. Traveling to Denmark, Kertész acted for and learned the craft of director from the renowned August Blom. Although the available information of his activities in Denmark is ambiguous, it's generally accepted that Kertész acted in the film *Rabelek* and both acted in and directed *Atlantis* (Balogh, Caanham). He also observed other actors and directors at work. In an article he wrote the same year for the Hungarian film magazine, *Mozgófénykép-Hirado* (Movie News), Kertész recalls an important lesson he learned about the responsibility of the director.

> One must be very careful, that if the filming must be interrupted and continued on another day, that the clothing of the actors should be the same on both days, otherwise the forgetfulness of an actor may lead to a ridiculous situation. It happened at the filming of the Atlantis, that in the scene filmed on the ship Tetgen, the principal actor Olaf Froens wore a cloth cap. I happened to be present in this scene, as an actor. Because it was getting late and too dark to continue, we had to finish the scene on the next day. But Olaf Froens forgot that he wore a cloth cap on the first day, and put a straw hat on his head. When the filming was finished . . . according to

custom, it was shown to the board of directors. Ole Olsen . . .
observed the mistake. Who was to blame? The director.

But the error had to be corrected: the ship Tetgen had to be
leased again, for 5000 Danish crowns a day, and the scene
had to be filmed again, all for a straw hat. The director must
be very careful, because the responsibility is all his. [1]

Several years later, in another article that appeared in *Mozihet*, he
recalls a lesson about the power of the director over the actor:

I had once an opportunity to see for myself how closely
an actor must follow the director's orders. A few years ago
I was in the huge atelier of Nordisk in Copenhagen, when
Psilander, the celebrated actor, had to play an episode in a
jail. Richard Davidson, the excellent Danish director, was
showing him step by step in minute detail the whole scene,
and Psilander was following him very carefully, all the way.
I was watching them from the corner of the stage and I was
amazed to see that the director was shouting at him, pushing him, and the famous film actor was obediently following
him in everything....

When the episode was finished Psilander told me: "Sie dür-
fen darüber nicht staunen. Ein Kinoschauspieler muss so ar-
beiten. Er muss das tun, was ihm das Wissen und das Herz
des Regisseurs diktiert." (You should not be astonished. The
film actor must do what the director's knowledge and heart
dictates.) [2]

From these two observations, based on his 1913 experiences in
Denmark, it's easy to see how some of Kertész's own work habits
developed. He took his role as director very seriously.

The increasing popularity of moving pictures, in Hungary
as elsewhere, was the happy accident that gave Kertész the opportunity to continue with this work. By 1913, Budapest boasted
114 operating film theatres[3.] Aside from the economic and professional power of the director's role in this new industry, Kertész
no doubt also learned about the personal power that comes with
being a director. A most memorable scene in which this power is
demonstrated occurs in one of his early American films, *The Mad
Genius* (1931). A theatre director lures a young girl into his office
for sex in return for letting her act in the production. The director

gets what he wants, and the aspiring starlet gets a chance at what she wants – without guarantees, to be sure. After 2017, the #MeToo movement would have something to say about this.

Kertész understood both sides of the power struggle. He continued acting but also began directing a series of films: *Házasodik az uram (My Husband's Getting Married)*, *A Tolonc (The Exile)*, *A Kölcsönkért csecsemök (The Borrowed Babies)*, *A Hercegnö Pongzolaban (The Princess in a Nightrobe)*, and *Az Ejszaka rabjai (Prisoner of the Night)*. He also made *Az Aranjásó (The Golddigger)* the first of a number of films based on plays by Molnár Ferenc.

It's interesting to speculate whether or not Kertész knew Molnár personally – the ambitious young film-maker collaborating with the established playwright to adapt drama for film. Even if that was only his dream, there's no doubt in my mind that Kertész and his colleagues looked to the current popular entertainment – theatre and opera – on which to base at least some of their projects. After all, the public would be interested to see what this new medium would do with their favourite pieces.

Kertész made another brief sojourn to Scandinavia where he worked at Svenska Biograph Studio under Joseph Sistrom – more training for what was beginning to look like a career. What he had learned about acting and directing culminated in the film Bank Ban (Lord Bank), considered Kertész's first commercial success as a director [4]. The film was made in Kolozsvár (Klausenburg), Transylvania (now Cluj-Napoca, Rumania) and released in 1914.

Kertész was only twenty-seven years old.

World War I

On June 28, 1914 Archduke Franz Ferdinand, heir to the Austrian throne, and his wife Sophie were assassinated in Herzegovina while on a military inspection tour. They were riding through the streets of the capital of Bosnia Herzogovina in the third car of a six-car motorcade; the car the royal couple rode in was an open sports car with its top down. The circumstances of the assassination are about as dramatic as they could be – the stuff of movies! After a botched bombing attempt on the motorcade, a planned reception at city hall went ahead, and it was only through a coincidence that one of the assassins suddenly saw himself near the car as it was leaving that event, and took the opportunity to fire the two fatal shots.

The events of that day – the Empire's formal response known as the July Ultimatum, as well as its rejection – spread through the European media like wildfire. Everyone would have known the reported details. The aftermath and consequences of the assassination were the hottest topic of conversation for the weeks leading up to the actual beginning of World War I on July 28, the day Austria-Hungary declared war and mobilized its army. Russia and France joined the action immediately, having obligated themselves to do so under treaty with the Triple Alliance. Soon all the Great Powers except Italy had chosen sides and joined the war.

I have tried in vain to pin down documented evidence of my grandfather's involvement in World War I. As we will see for other aspects of his life, there are several versions. By far the most detailed description is offered by Pete Martin in his book, *Hollywood Without Makeup* (1948). This version has Kertész sign up for the 24th Howitzer Regiment, the mounted Austro-Hungarian artillery, where he served two tours of duty. He advanced to the position of captain, was wounded, returned to duty, and was wounded again. At this point, the government assigned him to the Italian front, and then to Constantinople to film war news." [5]

George Frazier, in his 1947 article "The Machine With a Rage" published in *True* magazine focuses on another angle. He writes that Kertész joined the "mounted Austro-Hungarian artillery where he mastered the horsemanship that in later years has won him a two-goal polo rating. Wounded on the Russian front after three years' service, he was assigned to work on propaganda films." [6]

Kingsley Canham, Norman Keim and Sydney Rosenzweig all say that Kertész served briefly but returned to civilian life and filmmaking by 1915. Film historians Büttner and Dewald writing in the book *Elektrische Schatten* add to that a note that he may have been wounded. Their Hungarian counterpart Gyöngi Balogh makes no mention of the war service of her country's celebrated director.

In his memoir *Eighty Odd Years in Hollywood*, John Meredyth-Lucas mentions his stepfather's service in the Austrian artillery only briefly, but goes on to recount in more detail his alleged involvement in the Communist government propaganda films. However, one must remember that even if Meredyth-Lucas's version is correct, this political development came only after the end of World War I.

The filmography does help with some of this, but ultimately the films Kertész made during the war years also reflect on his private life. Early in 1915, Kertész acted in and directed *Akit Ketten Szeretnek (One Who is Loved by Two)*. As his stature as a director grew, Kertész found his popularity increasing. Around the sametime, he met Ilonka Kovács, a fifteen year old girl with stars in her eyes.

Exactly how they met is not known, but Ilonka was probably already studying ballet at the Budapest Theatre School, whereupon she had several engagements in theatre productions. [7] Another source suggests that she also took piano lessons and attended the acting school known as Association of Hungarian Actors. [8] At some point, she took the stage name **Lucy Doraine**. Christian Viviani has another version of the girl's background, and what happened next. Lucy had been "adamant about wanting to become a comédienne. The family did not look favorably on these aspirations and the young director who encouraged them. Lucy nevertheless triumphed; she married Kertész who put her in his 1916 film, *A Farkas (The Wolf)*. [9]

Whatever the story, when Lucy rolled her big eyes and smiled that temptress smile, she would have been hard to resist. The twenty-eight year old director did not resist. They fell in love, ran away to Bratislava and married when Lucy found herself with child. On November 25, 1915 their daughter Katalin Ilona Eva Kertész was born in Budapest. The baby was baptized in the Protestant faith. Katalin is Hungarian for Katherine (as Ilona is Hungarian for Helen), and her birthday is also her "Name Day" which honors Catherine of Alexandria. [10] Eventually, however, the nickname Kitty suited her best, and she went by Kitty Curtiz for most of her life.

His Own Family

Although there is a strong possibility my grandfather had other liaisons and that he may have fathered other children even before he married Ilonka Kovács, I will consider Kitty his first child. She was definitely his only legitimate child. She was also my aunt.

In 2000, the year I was doing research for this book in Vienna and Budapest, I also discovered that Kitty was alive and well at the age of eighty-four and living in Krems, Austria, a short train ride from Vienna. It had been a long journey for her from her birthplace Budapest, to Vienna as a young child, and then to America where she grew up and spent the better part of her life. After traveling widely during middle age – including Spain and her beloved Cyprus – Kitty had returned, close to her roots once again.

I didn't meet her the day I took the train to Krems on a gamble. Dr. Krenn at the Filmarchiv Austria had given me her address but there was no telephone number. I found out later that she preferred not to receive phone calls. The apartment building where she lived was right across the square from the train station. It was a thrill to see her name on the register at the door. But before I rang that bell, I wanted to be prepared, so I walked around the corner to a flower shop. With a modest but suitable bouquet in hand and with my explanations and apologies for the intrusion practiced, I returned to the apartment building and rang the bell. No answer. I rang again, waited, and tried a third time. No answer.

Now what was I to do? Suddenly, the ever-vigilant *Hausmeisterin*, the apartment caretaker whose job it is to watch the comings and goings around the building, came toward me through a dimly-lit hallway. *Wem suchen Sie?* Who are you looking for? I explained briefly and she replied that Kitty was in Vienna, in the hospital.

After I told this friendly woman about my quest, she invited me into her own apartment and offered to phone Kitty to let her know of my visit. She dialed the number of the private room and I could heard Kitty's response, loud and clear, from across the table: "I do not want to see her, do not let her into my rooms," and the rant went on. Frau Hausmeisterin could feel my shock and discomfort, so when she hung up the phone, she calmly continued to chat about Kitty, what she was like and what she did. Among other things, she was a writer – of poetry mainly. Unfortunately she could only tell me about Kitty's most recent book, *Blut und Liebe (Blood and Love)*, but I resolved to purchase it as soon as I could. With a wad of notes and mixed feelings, I gave my hostess the flowers, thanked her and returned to Vienna on the next train.

Kitty's book was not easy to find. I placed an order, and when I received it, the poetry left me with more mixed feelings. A profound sadness came through her lyric verse, and I knew instinctively that she had suffered much. Some six months after my trip to Krems, I wrote her a letter and to my surprise, she wrote back. Over the next few years, we corresponded and I got to know Kitty's sometimes charming, sometimes abrasive personality. She wrote me many letters and sent me many clippings and articles about herself, as well as several volumes of her unpublished poetry. Alas, she did not share with me her unpublished autobiography.

Kitty's poems did help me to better understand the times and events that affected everyone in those years when Kertész and her mother first started out. For example, Kitty suggests that the year she was born,

> Milk was scarce, and it was dear,
> it was winter and we had
> only very little coal for a fire,
> and almost nothing to eat.
>
> And I cried and was hungry ...   [11]

Kitty laments her mother's inability to give her what she needed most, a mother's care and love. Even though one source suggests that Doraine gave up acting for three years, her list of film credits include *A Farkas* released in 1916, so she must have been in front of the cameras soon after the birth of their child. She also starred in the Hungarian film *A Napragorgós hölgy (The Lady with Sunflowers)* released in Hungary December, 1918 and also directed by her husband.

Even as war raged in Europe, Kertész Mihály celebrated his twenty-ninth birthday on December 25, 1915 as a husband, a father, and a rising film director.

Work Comes First

Kertész's passion for his chosen career seemed to grow even as conditions in the industry became more and more difficult. In 1916 he made at least four films, at first also as an actor, but increasingly only as a director. He acted in *Az Ezust Kecske* and *A Medikus.* He directed *Doktor Ur,* a comedy about lawyers, and the drama *A Farkas,* already mentioned. These last two films were once again based on plays by Molnár Ferenc, the popular Hungarian playwright who would also emigrate to America and become internationally famous.

This connection between Molnár's plays and Kertész's films supports the popularity of "Film d'art" in Hungarian and indeed European cinema of the time. The term originated in France, 1908, where a group of filmmakers formed the Societé Le Film d'Art in the hopes of attracting the new film audiences to higher forms of art. This attempt to marry the popular and the intellectual encouraged "a new, more educated audience, while convincing producers that there was popular appeal in highbrow entertainment" [12].

Both aspects of the movement, I believe, appealed to Kertész, and the early influence of the values and vision of "film d'art" would determine choices he made about his work and how he thought about directing for the rest of his life. In Hungary, he made no less than five films based on Molnár plays, including the playwright's first commercial theatre success, *Az Ordog (The Devil)* in 1918. In 1919 Kertész began work on *Liliom* which unfortunately remained unfinished when he left for Austria. Late in his career, in 1959, he returned to Europe to direct *Olympia (A Breath of Scandal)*.

At Phoenix Films/Projectograph, the main film studio in Budapest during and after World War I, Kertész quickly became a force to be reckoned with. His insistence on the best actors, the best scripts, huge crowds of extras in his epic films, and the most exacting set details perpetuated his ongoing fight for money, as evidenced in the articles he wrote in 1916. In July, his lengthy article "The Direction of the Film" was published in *Mozgófénykép Hiradó*, the official newsletter of Hungary's film industry. In this essay, Kertész suggests that besides having enough capital to produce good films, the most important ingredient is an excellent director who has "the professional experience, good literary knowledge, and artistic capability." He then outlines the most important qualities of the man at the helm.

> A film director must know the art of the scenario, the art to transform the theme into action, to fill the action with good movement, in a way that the spectator should always remain under the impression that he is looking at real life. The director must be familiar with every nuance of the technical side of film making. He must know how to shorten each action to prevent it from becoming boring. In collaboration with the cameraman, he should know how to bring the picture into focus, and prevent too much brightness ruining the quality. He is also responsible for the proper presentation of the scene: if the actor is in the background, his movements should be broad and ponderous; when he is closer, his mimics should be more delicate and discrete. When these technical conditions are met, there comes the artistic part of the director's work. The play among the actors, the building up

of the scenes: this can be achieved only if the director has the real qualities of the actor himself. [13]

In another article, Kertész derides his country for not providing sufficient capital to the film industry: "It is incomprehensible why the big capital is not willing to help the film industry," he writes in "The Future of Hungarian Film" which appeared in *Mozihét* [14]. If the financial help were provided, he writes, they could include the special effects that made American and other European films so popular.

Despite this lack of financial backing, Hungarian films in 1916 were, according to Kertész, of very high quality. In his opinion, this was achieved through the commitment and passion of those involved in the industry. He sums it up eloquently in a rousing, patriotic article that appeared in *Kino-Riport* in October of that year:

> In times of gloom, of superhuman torment, of blood and sorrow, in the confusion of war, the Hungarian motion picture industry rose mightily …. Those who did not study it do not understand how much care, how much devoted love and untiring sense of duty is needed to reach this level of recognition in our country…. [15]

Kertész's vision of success also involved him in the business aspect of film. In 1917, he became Director of Production at Phoenix. [16] In the same year, ten of his films were released: E*gy Krajcar Tortenete, Az Arendas Zsido, Az Ezredes, A Fold Embere, A Halalcsengo, A Kuruzslo, A Szentjobi Erdo Titka, A Senka Fia, Tavsz A Telben, Zoard Mester,* and *Tatarjaras.*

Over the next two years, the ambitious director may also have begun to travel again. In his 1947 article in *True* magazine, Frazier indicates that Kertész went to Berlin to work with Ernst Lubitsch as well as Fritz Lang, possibly on an episode of Lang's famous series *Die Spinnen (The Spiders).* In doing so, he may have directed Lili Damita, the French star whom he would meet again. Another source indicates Kertész may also have traveled to Sweden and participated in two films: *Wellington Rejtely* and *Odette Et L'Histoire Des Femmes Illustres.*

Armed with new ideas, he returned to Budapest where he made eight more films to be released in 1918: *Kilencvenkilenc, Judas, Lulu, A Napraforgos Holgy* (with Lucy Doraine), *Alraune, A*

Vig Ozvegy, Varazskeringo, Lu, A Kokott and *Az Ordog,* the latter
based on the Molnár Ferenc play whose central idea derives from
"Faust," but with a twist. Here, the devil manipulates other characters and can anticipate their thoughts.

In November 1918, World War I was finally over, and as
Europeans breathed a collective sigh of relief, Kertész was just
about to turn thirty-two years of age. No doubt he thought his
plans and ambitions for the Hungarian film industry would finally
be realized, but the success of Phoenix / Projectograph was dashed
when the Communists rolled in. The reign of Bela Kun and his
Republic of Councils was established March 21, 1919 and lasted
until August 1, 1919. One of the regime's goals was to nationalize
all property and industry. The film industry was not immune.

Lajós Balint, Kertész's room-mate from his early acting days
in Pécs, had this to say about the film work during that short inter-
val:

> During the time of the Bolshevik republic [in Hungary]
> Kertész directed one short film on the theme of a poem of
> Antal Farkas: "The return of my young brother." I remember
> only vaguely the theme of this film, but the most promin-
> ent moment of it was when a flag appeared from behind a
> hill carrying the symbol of the sickle and hammer, carried
> by a young man returning from Russia, where he had been
> a prisoner of war. This scene was intended to express the
> message that we [Hungarian Bolsheviks] should achieve the
> same glorious revolution ... [17]

Balint is referring to the film listed in Curtiz filmographies as My
Brother Comes. Others have corroborated this with slightly different details. John Baxter lumps Kertész in with the "leftist filmmakers who had participated in the ill-fated nationalized cinema" in Hungary [18]. According to Baxter, this group which also
included Alexander Korda, Laszlo Vajda [19] and Bela Lugosi among
others, ran the short-lived Hungarian nationalized film company.
After the fall of the Hungarian Republic of Councils, the filmmakers fled – Kertész to Vienna, Korda to England, and Lugosi to
Germany.

How did the nationalized film company come into being in
the first place? John Meredyth Lucas, the stepson who heard and
overheard many stories while my grandfather was married and
living with Bess Meredyth in Hollywood in the early 1930's, re-

peats a fairly convincing tale. In the time of the Red Terror, the popular name for the Bela Kun regime, Kertész, like the other soldiers and officers of the defeated Austro-Hungarian forces, was especially worried. Meredyth-Lucas dramatizes the events from the viewpoint of a young boy being told a scary story:

> ...one night [there] came the dreaded pounding on the door. Red Army Guards were there for him. He said a quick good-bye to his mother and family, expecting it to be his last.

> He was taken down to a former palace of the old regime, ushered through long corridors to massive doors, which were pushed open and Mike thrust inside. In the far corner of the enormous room, a man sat working at a desk, his back to the door. Mike waited uncertainly, not knowing whether to speak or simply wait. After what seemed an eternity, the man turned toward the light and jumped up, throwing his arms wide. "Mishka!" (sic) After a stunned silence, Mike drew his first easy breath. It was Korda.

> "Mishka," his friend repeated, "Come over here. We've got it made." [20]

Korda had somehow become Minister of Propaganda according to Meredyth-Lucas, and decided then and there to appoint Kertész Managing Director of Phoenix Studios. The film The Red Banner would be his first assignment: he was to start the next day, without a script, just a detachment of Alpine troops for "charging through the snow, Red banners flying. No scenes, just footage." [21]

This adventure story ends in an unlikely way. When the Communist regime fell apart, recounts Meredyth-Lucas, another friend and colleague Gabriel Pascal "found Mike and was able to sneak him aboard a train and out of the country." [22] At least the flight part of the story appears to be true: in her poem "Die Flucht" (Flight) written decades later, Kitty vividly remembers her three year-old self at the border crossing.

> Never will I forget
> how the two border guards
> laughed because I cried
> as they bayoneted
> the overstuffed bags,
> just for fun and spite. [23]

Balint takes a different view of the events: "I do not say he had to leave Hungary because the Bolshevik regime collapsed there or because of the production of the mentioned small film," he suggests, "since he went to Vienna already in May, 1919." [23] Kertész had been invited to the Austrian capital by Alexander (Sascha) Kolowrat, and there he stayed because, as Balint points out, he would no longer be welcome in Hungary.

Regardless which version of his exit from Hungary is true, it is a fact that my grandfather and his immediate family took up residence in Vienna's 4th District, in a sumptuous apartment in Karlsgasse, in 1919. In Budapest, he left behind his parents, siblings and their families. He left behind an unfinished film, *Liliom*. He had worked tirelessly to help establish Hungarian cinema, and he is duly recognized by his country as one of the early forces of that industry.

PART III

KERTÉSZ IN VIENNA: 1919 - 1926

At Sascha Films

The deal that Kertész Mihály of Budapest made with the wealthy film producer in Vienna proposed ambitions plans, a grand vision for the Austrian film industry. In 1918 Kolowrat had traveled to the United States to study American films and film making. After he saw D.W. Griffith's *Intolerance*, he wanted to emulate the epic film genre in Austria. He may have already envisioned the basic concept for *Sodom & Gomorrah* when he invited Mihály Kertész to Vienna. Griffith's blockbuster of 1916 combined four parallel stories through the ages to develop the film's main themes of sin and punishment, *Sodom & Gomorrah* – in its reconstructed form – presents no less than three parallel stories. Two years of preparation work were set to begin in 1920: Kolowrat and Kertész would be busy.

His full name was Count Alexander Joseph Kolowrat-Krakowski. He was an interesting personage and highly regarded as a pioneer of the film industry in Austria. Kolowrat was born into both old and new money: his father hailed from a long line of Bohemian nobles, and his mother was an American heiress. His father had chosen America for the place of exile for participating in a duel, and there he married and saw his son born in January, 1886. Eventually, he was pardoned and the family moved back to Europe. The young Count's well-documented adventures – racing motorcycle and cars, flying planes and balloons – already would make a fascinating story. But after 1909 his interest turned to film, and he threw all his passion and resources into the business until his untimely death in 1927 at the age of forty-one. Sascha Films became an Austrian national treasure.

Sascha is the pet name for Alexander or Alexandra, originally coined in Russia, and for Kolowrat it became synonymous with his lifestyle and his work. In 1919, when Kertész brought his family to Vienna, Kolowrat's film venture bearing the nickname Sascha, had already created its own history. What had started in 1914 as the Count's personal Sascha Filmfabrik (Sascha Film Factory) became an Austrian-Hungarian partnership during World War I – the Sascha-Meßter Film GMBH. [1] In 1917, Germany's recently established mega film producing company UFA (Universum-Film Aktiengesellschaft) bought the Meßter interest in Kolowrat's company. At the end of the war, the shifting political and financial winds made a new corporate structure necessary, and Kolowrat drew on his influence with important people in both fields to create what he expected would be a sustainable entity. Now he could set about producing films in a new, uncensored climate that ushered in the roaring Twenties. In 1919, Sascha Filmindustie Aktiengesellschaft (Sascha Film Industry, joint-stock company) was established.

Kertész, with his Germanized first name Michael, quickly became acquainted with the company's directors, including Alexander Korda, an old friend, who had arrived in Vienna around the same time. A number of films were already under production in 1919, and Kertész's first Austrian film *Die Dame Mit den Schwarzen Handschuhen (The Lady with the Black Gloves)*, released in November, completed the list. The film starred his wife Lucy Doraine.

Budapest was less than a day's train ride from Vienna, and no doubt Kertész journeyed back and forth several times in the first part of 1919, to establish himself in Vienna and to personally bring Lucy and their daughter Kitty to their new home. Along with Fräulein Rosa, the governess that Kitty remembered fondly in all her writings, they joined "Papa" in the large apartment in Karlsgasse, just a few blocks from St. Charles Church and surrounding parks. They had reached their "wonderful new homeland."

Kertész and Kolowrat collaborated easily on their common vision for the future of film. You'll remember that Kertész's had

said to Lájos Balint a decade earlier, "I can see fantastic possibilities [for film]. It offers huge perspectives never achievable on
the small stages of a theatre...." [2] There may still have been some
skeptics about the artistic value of film, but gradually it became
clear that film would not go away. The Austrian novelist Joseph
Roth wrote a series of articles in the magazine Die Filmwelt (Film
World) between March and October 1919, and I can well imagine
that my grandfather pored over these – on the one hand to improve his German, and on the other hand to gauge the current
climate for his work. Roth's articles definitely influenced the way
film would be received in the ensuing years; Kertész and Kolowrat
rode the wave.

Lucy Doraine starred in her husband's films, and Kitty was
taken care of by Fräulein Rosa while her parents worked. Papa
Michael – or Miska as he often introduced himself – enjoyed the
power that comes with being the first director of a country's major
film studio.

At thirty-two, Kertész took to his professional and personal
status with gusto. The film industry in particular embraced the
lifestyle of what came to be known as the Roaring Twenties. The
reality of three children born to Kertész over the next five years
shows that directing films was not his only passion. When I first
started thinking about my grandfather, while I still believed that
my father was his only child from the Vienna years, I concentrated
on my grandmother's stories. But before Fränzi there were two
other liaisons.

Thilde Forster: Bank Teller or Aspiring Scenarist?

Imagine my surprise when I read in James Robertson's book
The Casablanca Man that in 1923, an "Austrian court decided that
[Kertész] was the father of a boy born in November 1920" [3]. This
boy was not my father, and the details – that the mother pursued
Curtiz in the United States for maintenance in the 1930's – did not
fit with the stories and the evidence about my grandmother's dealings with him.

How did Robertson know this? When I met him in England
in 2000, he told me he had found the American court documents
while doing research for his book at the Warner Brothers Archives.
The bulk of *The Casablanca Man* deals with the Hollywood films,
and Robertson makes a good case for re-assessing the director's
artistic vision, but he didn't have the information he needed to

delve into Curtiz's private life. For me, those few hints were like a challenge. Robertson laments that, "no Curtiz family member has expanded out knowledge of his European life" [4]. I know a little about that, I thought.

And these tantalizing bits about another "Vienna" boy, another Michael – well, I just had to know more. So I wrote a letter that Robertson forwarded to the daughter of the man who is my uncle. She had already contacted Robertson after reading his book, and now he acted as our go-between. It was a protracted business at first as we were still using snail mail. But two years later, I received an e-mail from Michelanne Forster in New Zealand and the missing pieces began to fall into place.

The ease with which we began to exchange information got me hooked on this new technology. Our first flurries of information shot through cyberspace with amazing speed. My new cousin and I chatted about each other's family and our connections with Curtiz. We both had questions to ask, assumptions to correct, and above all, a great wish to meet. We shared fathers who were both sons of Michael Curtiz, and we shared grandmothers who had both dealt with and won, each in her own way, the struggle of single mothers to raise their children.

In chronological terms, the story of Mathilde (Thilde) Förster is the first one of these women, because she was the mother of Kertész's first Vienna child. She must have met him soon after his arrival in Vienna in 1919 because their son was born in November, 1920. It's possible that she went to Sascha Films to pitch a story idea or even submit a film script because writing for film was what she had dreamed of and ultimately how she supported herself. In fact, once she gained entry into the industry, she was a successful screen writer for many years.

Thilde's first credited screen writing effort was for *Venus im Frack (Venus in a Tuxedo)*, produced 1927 in Germany. Another version of the title, *The Ideal of Woman in Our Time*, suggests a lively, modern theme. Co-writer was Ladislaus Vajda, the Hungarian playwright who had also worked with Kertész to write *Sodom and Gomorrah* in 1922, two years after Thilde had her child. This suggests Thilde's connection with Kertész helped her professionally, at least in the beginning.

Regardless of how they met, there was also a historical family similarity between Thilde and Kertész: the middle-class Jewish family she was born into also came from Galizia. Her father, Dr. Markus Förster, was born in Lemberg (now L'viv, Ukraine) in 1866. When you look at a map of the Austro-Hungarian Empire, you'll notice that Lemberg is not far from Delatyn, the birthplace of Ignácz Kaminer, my great-grandfather. Förster's wife Helena (Hinde) Margulies, two years his junior, came from Krystynopil (now Chervonohrad, Ukraine) a small city north of Lemberg. They were married in late 1895 or early 1896 and lived in Lemberg. Their first son Ludwig was born there in October 1896. The young doctor and his family soon moved to Brezezany, a village east of Lemberg, where their daughter Thilde was born April 25, 1899.

When Thilde was about eight years old, the Förster family moved to Vienna – not to Budapest as had the Kaminer boys twenty years earlier. The doctor and his family settled in Ottakring, Vienna's 16th district, where he became a fixture among his people. Michelanne kindly shared her grandmother's memoir with me. In it, we can see Thilde the writer as she describes her father's day-to-day routine from a young girl's viewpoint:

> …Usually, Papa makes his house calls on foot, back and forth through the crowded streets, up and down the broad stairs to the apartments of the well-to-do and the steep, narrow steps to the cellars and garrets of the poor. The sick must be helped. The well-to-do pay. The poor don't.

> Today, perhaps because the number of calls is larger than usual, perhaps to give his little daughter a special treat, Papa has hired a carriage to take him on his round. The carriage is a little shabby, the upholstery threadbare in spots. The driver is an old derelict with a red nose, one of Papa's rogues' gallery or nonpaying patients. The horse is an elderly mare with her ribs showing, but the little girl has not yet acquired the sharp, merciless sight that reveals such details. To her a carriage is still a carriage, a coachman a coachman, a horse a horse.

> The mare trots along on her thin, knobby legs. From time to time, the driver cracks his whip smartly in homage to his illustrious passenger. On the faced velvet of the seat, between father and daughter, rests the black leather bag, the proud symbol of Papa's profession.

As they enter the street where they live, the driver slows down. The street is a neighborhood market in the morning with stalls lining it on both sides. The people surround the carriage. "Guten Morgen, Herr Doktor." "Guten Tag, Herr Doktor." There are quick progress reports and sidewalk consultations. "That medicine did the trick. My pain is gone." "Little Mitzi is coughing again. What shall I do?" Papa is holding court from the height of his seat in the coach, and dispensing advice, gratis. The little girl looks on, her heart swelling with pride.

She, too, gets her share of the prevailing affection and good will. "An apple for the pretty little girl?" "A bag of nice ripe Bosnian plums?" "A basket of wild strawberries?" My how she's grown. I hardly recognize her."

Thilde went to public primary school, where being the doctor's daughter was more important than being the only Jewish child in her class. The only way she experienced the difference – then – was that she went for instruction in reading Hebrew prayers while the other children went to catechism, the Roman Catholic elementary teachings of church doctrine that I also remember from my own childhood.

In his unpublished autobiography, Michael Forster [5] remembers his mother's early passion for reading and writing. She excelled in Latin, he says, which means she went to Gymnasium (matriculation high school) where that was a core subject. Living in Vienna in the days of the Empire was special for many Viennese, and Thilde had a closer brush with royalty than most people can boast.

...she is one of a group of children who have been chosen to dance before the Emperor. The occasion is an anniversary.... Twice a week, the little girl is taken to the splendid old city hall to practice with the other children the simple dance they are expected to perform. She is doing neither better nor worse than the others as they hop and skip and curtsy and get in each other's way.

On the appointed day, dressed in Biedermeier style – white dressed with lace-edged pantaloons sticking out below the hem – the children are transported to Schönbrunn and lined up on the lawn in front of the palace.

At last, the band strikes up. The Emperor appears, a shrunken old man almost lost in the splendor of his entourage. The children gape. They have never seen such uniforms and dresses, such silks and velvets, plumes and medals, such sabers.

The Emperor separates himself from the group and walks slowly along the rows of little girls in white. Perhaps our little girl stepped out of line. Perhaps the old man stumbled or lost his balance. Whatever the reason, the Imperial boot lands with its full weight on the child's foot.

For a moment, their eyes meet. The old man looks at the child absentmindedly, not unkindly, with his tired, washed-out eyes that are embedded in folds of pale, loose skin...

"Pardon," he says and walks on, forgetting the little girl even while he is still looking at her, and thinking of God knows what.

Thilde wrote this memoir many years later when she was living in Hollywood, California, working for the County Sheriff's department. But writing stories and scripts was obviously an interest from her youth. Because she was from a traditional family, there may have been opposition to her interest the new medium – film – which became popular in Vienna during her youth. Going to a movie was the newest family treat, but Thilde probably had to fight to get her way and pursue a career in the film world.

It's true that a Vienna residency record, as well as various court documents give her occupation as being a bank employee. Thilde could, of course, have worked in a bank at some point – but the question is, for how long? The label that followed her is just a word.

*****

Thilde's affair with Kertész in the early days of 1920 resulted in the birth of his first Vienna child, a boy, born November 20, 1920. The event is recorded at the Jewish Registry in Vienna. When I went there to verify the documentation, I found the bureaucratic barriers quite daunting. After several phone calls, I secured an appointment with Frau Weiss. On the day and at the time I was told I should come, I made my way to a nondescript building in a rather unfriendly corner of Vienna's 1st District. Once inside the imposing double-door entrance, I was motioned to come forward by a man behind a wicket surrounded by iron bars. He asked me my business and also whether I had any knives or sharp objects on my person. I handed him my pocket knife which I used to carry with me everywhere before 9-11. I was then allowed to pass through an iron grate doorway, up several stairs and through more double doors. Frau Weiss took me to the room where the birth records are kept and had me wait by the table while she retrieved the volume for 1920. Together we flipped through the pages until we found the entry for November 20, for Michael Förster. A photocopy was provided, and I went home to my little apartment to translate it.

The infant was apparently placed in the Schönbrunn Infants' Home, although I have not found records to corroborate this. Thilde remained his official guardian, and two and a half years went by without any evidence of legal action. Then two things happened: Thilde's father passed away in 1922, and she discovered that Kertész had a new mistress. In 1923, she took him to court to solidify his responsibility to support her son.

The defendant Michael Kertész was ordered to pay two million Austrian Kronen (200 Schillings) per month, in advance, to the "mother and guardian" of the child. During the proceedings, Kertész admitted to being the father of the child. His income was shown to be four million Kronen (400 Schillings) per week or sixteen million Kronen (1600 Schillings) per month. [6] Court documents do state other obligations: "his mother [in Budapest] as well as a legal child, 7 years of age." Testimony also indicated that Thilde's son was of "sickly condition." Kertész was ordered to pay "such amount which is required by a suitable institute of first class." [7]

Kertész paid this support until he left Austria for the United States in 1926. Then the payments became intermittent and gradually stopped. This period was a time of great financial hardship for Thilde and her son, remedied only when Thilde was finally able to secure work as a scenarist for UFA in Berlin. The 1923 Judgment would become the basis of Thilde's continuing effort to obtain reasonable support from Curtiz ten years later, in California.

A Pattern Created

As an adult, Kitty Curtiz knew about Thilde Forster and the boy – her half-brother Michael – and she believed that her father's affair in the winter of 1922/23 aggravated the relationship between her Papa and her Mama Lucy Doraine. Kitty was, however, painfully aware that it did not affect his work. In fact, in the face of personal troubles, Kertész may have thrown himself harder into directing. He immediately made the film *Dame mit dem schwarzen Handschuh, (The Lady with the Black Gloves)* released in 1919. He directed three films in 1920 and four more in 1921. Some of the titles (given only in English here) reveal themes that intersect with matters of the heart: *The Star of Damascus, Boccacio's Nights of Love, Miss Tutti Frutti, Duchess Satanella, Mrs. Dane's Confession, Labyrinth of Horror, The Lady with the Sunflowers, Cherchez la femme, The Scourge of God.* In other words, the threads of my grandfather's life and work – even at this stage – are being woven into a tapestry of connecting scenes and patterns.

In 1922, work on the monumental film *Sodom & Gomorrah* began in earnest. This film is perhaps the most telling in terms of what was becoming of Kertész's life. Everything about the huge project – the story, the actors, the massive preparations, the filming itself, as well as the circumstances of its release – everything can be seen as a model for Kertész's own life.

First, Kertész was totally involved with all aspects of the project, from co-writing the script with Ladislaus Vajda, to planning the monumental scenes, to casting. One of the photos I have shows Kertész in a white shirt and tie standing before the partly finished Temple to Astarte at the Laaerberg outdoor film factory. And the story of how he launched Walter Slezak's film career will echo time after time: he told the young man that he had seen him in his "vision" for the part. In short, Kertész wanted to have a say in all aspects of the films he directed.

Second, the film's subtitle *Die Legende von Sünde und Strafe (The Legend of Sin and Punishment)* suggests subject matter that might resemble a chapter out of Kertész's own life. A contemporary description of the film's story line is enlightening:

> A young woman, exposed from childhood to bad influences, is forced by her mother into engagement to an older, wealthy man. This drives her previously established fiancée to attempted suicide. During the engagement party and in

> a confused state, she is about to seduce the older man's son
> when she experiences a terrible dream that lets her see the
> consequences and brings her back to her first love who is
> slowly dying. [Embedded in a priest's warning to her] the an-
> alogous biblical events and motifs reinforce the moral crimes
> and the inescapable punishment. [8]

The power of money, the opportunity for seduction, the moral
low-life, juxtaposed with the Christian recognition of sin, retribu-
tion and the possibility for redemption – these are all aspects of
Kertész's life and relationships. Is this coincidence, or not? One
does wonder about the attraction of certain subjects in one's work
at a deeper psychological level, especially when one's life moves
in similar spheres.

Exactly how the story of *Sodom & Gomorrah* really ends in the
film remains enticingly confusing because of production decisions
made between its first, full three-hour showing and subsequent
screenings in 1923. Furthermore, the variant footage eventually
found many years later in Russian film archives suggests a different story line altogether. The version available now, reconstructed
by the Filmarchiv Austria in 2002, does, however, reinforce the
Legend of Sin and Punishment in which Kertész was first absorbed
in 1922.

Finally – and we have seen and will see this side of him again
– besides doing the work of directing films for Sascha, Kertész also
became involved in the business politics of the Austrian film industry. The Union of Stage and [Movie] Theatre Personnel was
founded in 1918, a Directors' Guild followed in 1919, along with
a number of other associations for those who worked in film. In
December 1922, these bodies merged to form the Association of
All Filmmakers of Austria, the *Filmbund*, and Kertész was on the
executive.

According to a historical overview of this umbrella association, the most successful years for Austrian film industry are
concentrated in 1921 and 1922. Besides the leading film factories
that included Kolowrat's Sascha Films, about twenty other film
producers in Vienna contributed to a national output of more than
seventy feature-length films and more than fifty short films. It was
thought that Austria could become the future of European film.
Despite the *Filmbund's* political, financial and social power, however, a crisis was brewing, a crisis that would see the downfall of

Austrian film production and a veritable exodus of film makers over the next few years [9].

These events also affected Kertész's personal life. His close involvement as an executive member of the *Filmbund* may have given him the opportunity to meet his next mistress. Even though the association held its formal meetings in the Café Dobner free of charge, [10] the men of Sascha Films no doubt met frequently at the company's headquarters at No. 31 Siebensterngasse. A young woman named Theresia Dalla Bonna lived just around the corner.

This crisis in the Austrian film industry also had far-reaching consequences for Kertész's career. Over the next few years, he would begin working elsewhere in Europe. Often this was by way of a partnership production between Sascha and another studio in Berlin or Paris, even London. These periods of travel in turn affected his private life, as we will see most clearly in his correspondence with my grandmother, Fränzi Wondrak, beginning in 1925. In the interim, however, Kertész divorced Lucy Doraine and had a two-year liaison with Theresia Dalla Bonna which resulted in the birth of baby Sonja in 1923, around the same time that he also made the acquaintance of my grandmother.

Theresia Dalla Bonna

One spring day a number of years ago, I received in my mailbox a plastic bag containing an envelope that was badly ripped, and inside, a very thick wad of photocopies. I examined the package and found that a woefully inadequate envelope was used by someone at the Vienna City and State Archives to send me the Family Court files on Sonja Dalla Bonna, the child born August 11, 1923 to Theresia Dalla Bonna and Michael Kertész. "They don't know how to deal with overseas mail," I thought, and I was thankful the quality of paper I was used to here – our North American excesses.

When I'd calmed down from my indignation about the way the package arrived, I sat down at the kitchen table and spent the next two hours skimming through the four hundred or so photocied sheets of 8 x 12 inch paper. Some were reproductions of documents the same size while others pages had huge swaths of black below a short communication. Many, many of these memos and lists were handwritten in various styles of German script. Oh this will be fun, I thought. Little folds and nicks picked up by the

copier are a tell-tale sign of carbon copies and thin paper, moul-
dering away in file boxes for over eighty years.

But it was the contents of it all that shocked me the most. The
archive file number includes the date it was created. The first sheet
indicates September 1923 and the last date is April 24, 1942. If I had
been under the impression my own family's story was tragic, that
assumption changed dramatically as I read these court files.

I had known for a while that Sonja was my aunt. That new
wonder of technology, the Internet, had given me the clue. Duncan
Hill, one of Sonja's sons, had posted a blurb in the guestbook on a
Michael Curtiz website. When we talked on the phone in 1999, an
avalanche of information poured out from each of us to the other,
and soon I knew that Duncan's mother Sonja Dalla Bonna had
met British officer Jack Hill in Vienna in 1945, that they had married and started a family in England and eventually emigrated to
Canada. Altogether there were four children, all living in Western
Canada. They had even met their grandfather twice, in 1955 and
1959, and I envied their personal contact with the man I knew only
through stories and pictures. Ultimately, however, Sonja was disappointed by the fact that Curtiz had not included her name in
the Last Will and Testament whereas the two sons are mentioned
– just mentioned.

But back to Sonja's beginnings. Her mother, Theresia Dalla
Bonna, born September 29, 1907 was the middle child of Felix
and Leopoldine Dalla Bonna, she a native Viennese and he from
Northern Italy (then a part of Austria). Felix had been a mail man
during World War I and the couple brought up their three children in an apartment at No. 9 Mondscheingasse, in Neubau, the
7th district of Vienna. Theresia met Michael Kertész when she was
fifteen, in 1922, and gave birth to their daughter Sonja Theresia on
August 11, 1923.

Theresia's occupation is most often given as *Heimarbeiterin*
(home-worker) but it's unclear if she ever worked outside the home
as well. A home worker would take in sewing and needlework, a
fairly common way for women to earn money in the those days.
Girls would be taught the basics of needlework early in their
schooling – I remember my own experience of learning how to
crochet and cross-stitch in my Viennese Grade 1 school room, so
these skills were still on the curriculum in the 1950's. Theresia
might have expanded her skills in *Handelsschule* (Trade School) –

the same kind of school where my mother learned to be a seam-stress.

At the Trade School she could also have learned secretarial skills. The family believes that Theresia did not come to Sascha Films as an extra for a film production like my grandmother did, but that she may have worked as a secretary at the Sascha Film head offices at Number 7 Siebensterngasse, just around the corner from Mondscheingasse. If this is true, she could have met Kertész there.

I went to that neighbourhood and walked down Mondscheingasse to the former Sascha headquarters, a building now covered in pastel pink stucco, and I was surprised when the huge double front doors yielded. A wide set of marble steps led up to the next set of glass inset doors – locked. And as I stood in that vestibule, I could almost see him and perhaps some of the other men, each with a secretary on his arm, strolling out for a drink at the corner bar after work….

✳✳✳✳✳

So here I was with four hundred pages – a mere snapshot of family history that could be traced back and followed forward through time. But after a quick survey of the archive file, I knew Theresia had suffered, and little Sonja – what an introduction to the world she'd had! And then I thought about Sonja's children, my cousins, and how they would both treasure and be upset by this new information.

A brief summary of the archive file covering the three years between the girl's birth and Kertész leaving for America begins to tell the story about this newest responsibility in his life and how he 'directed' its unfolding script. The first document in the archive file on Dalla Bonna is a formal Report dated September 5, 1923, barely a month after Sonja was born. It was filed in the jurisdiction of Theresia's home district Neubau (7th District of Vienna), to get the ball rolling, so it seems, and obtain some kind of support for the child. The father of the child is not named and therefore can-not be asked to appear at court.

A few months later, in October 1923, "Miss Theresia Dalla Bonna, Private Person" makes the following statement in front of the court:

I am the legitimate daughter of Felix Dalla-Bona, Municipal Employee, XIII Linzerstrasse No 114. I do not wish to name the Father of my child. He is providing sufficient support for the child. He has also acknowledged paternity in writing, but I also do not wish to present this writing to the municipality.

I suggest Mr. Michael Kertész, Director at Sascha-Film-Company, Vienna IV, Karlsgasse 15 as guardian of my child. The child is in my care.

Signed "Dalla-Bonna Therese" [11]

There is also a notice to change jurisdiction because the father of the underage Theresia lived in the 13th District, Hietzing. This reflects the family's belief that Theresia's parents were separated, and that the fifteen year-old mother was now living with her mother and the baby. Clearly Theresia's father's domicile mattered and Theresia names Kertész as a potential guardian of her child. The underaged, single mother could not be guardian.

In the early 1920's, child welfare laws as they applied to unwed mothers and their children were in the process of revision throughout Europe, but the fact that a male was named as guardian in this case – rather than Theresia's mother, for example – reflects the reality of a time when women had little real power. In Austria, women had gained the right to vote in 1919, but many other rights and privileges came much more slowly.

*****

Kertész was obviously involved in the case of Theresia and the child, but two other events upset Kertész's life at this time. In March 1923, his father passed away in Budapest at the age of seventy-three years. Also in 1923, research indicates that Kertész and Lucy Doraine were divorced, although obtaining definitive documentation was a challenge.

I have found no details about the events surrounding the death of Kaminer Ignácz, but I expect Kertész traveled to Budapest frequently during the time. Ignácz is buried in Rákoskereszturi izraelita Temetö, one of the largest of the many Jewish cemeteries in Budapest. His grave is Number 1A, Section 43, Row 37. Maybe on my next visit to Budapest, I will finally look it up!

The situation in which Kertész found himself the summer of 1923 – his family in mourning, his marriage on the rocks, Theresia Dalla Bonna about to give birth to his second Vienna child, and two-year old Michael Förster to support – did set a pattern, I believe, for dealing with his private life. He would keep it absolutely separate from his work life; he would avoid the press, and sometimes even make deals not to have stories about him or them published. Inquiries would be met with courteous half-truths, evasive semi-fictions, or outright lies. No wonder very little was written about his private life – in Europe and later in America: too much is contradictory or unsustainable.

Not only did my grandfather keep his private life from the eyes of the world, but he also kept the different parts of it separated, hidden from each other. Except for rumours, the families of his children out of wedlock did not know of each other. Much later on, the truth may have emerged here and there, but in the mid-1920s life for Kertész fit the decade's label: Roaring.

Franziska (Fränzi) Wondrak [12]

If my grandfather practiced elusive ways and has remained an elusive figure in my life, then my grandmother was the opposite. She was real and familiar, so real and familiar that my own perception of her was all that mattered to me for a long time. To me she was and will always be Fränzi Omi, my grandma Fränzi with whom I lived as a very young child. Hers was the hand I held while my mother was at work. Hers was the voice I can still hear, telling me stories or laughing at some silly notion of mine.

For a long time I took for granted all that I knew about my grandmother. Her unusual past was nothing out of the ordinary for me. I didn't question how she came to have a child with a famous film director; I didn't question why she hadn't married him. When she talked about him to me, and later when she wrote me letters about him, Michael Kertész/Curtiz was always Miska. Now I know that in my total acceptance of my Omi, I didn't really know her at all.

By 1988, when my interest in Michael Curtiz surfaced so dramatically, Fränzi was already eighty-two years old, and although we corresponded regularly, she was no longer able to tell me her whole story in detail. I became painfully aware that I had lost precious time and missed unique opportunities through the years. Still, bits and pieces of her life and her memories trickled down to me. Her letters to me, some pictures, a few documents, details mentioned by relatives and friends: the threads began to gather. She passed away in 1990, and I inherited those items. There was one great treasure, however, that I had to wait for. It was a packet of some sixty letters, letters that Michael Curtiz had written to her over a period of some twenty years from 1924 to 1947. These letters she had given to her son, my father. When I gained access to those letters, I knew that at the center of their lives there was a love story.

*****

Franziska (Fränzi) Anna Wondrak was born January 12, 1906, at the home of her parents, apartment Number 6 at Schulgasse 7, Vienna XVIII, and baptized at the district church, Weinhauserkirche. Both her parents hailed from the north-western region of the Austro-Hungarian Empire, the Bohemian provinces. Her mother, Anna Richter was born 1866 in Kaaden, a small city on the Eger River and in the shade of the mighty Erzgebirge (Ore Mountains). The town is now called Kadan, the river is the Ohre, and the region is now part of the Czech Republic. My great-grandfather August Matthias Wondrak was born in Vienna 1876, but his parents had recently migrated from the same part of the empire as his future wife. According to August's birth record, he was domiciled to Kosnitz/Tabor, a town south of Prague where his father Anton Wondrak, a tailor, and his wife Catharina (born Warnicek), had lived before they, too, migrated to Vienna.

The young Anna loved her native city and surrounding countryside. Her diary, a tiny leather-bound volume with very faint pencil notations, is filled with romantic descriptions of outings into the mountains. [13] When she was about twenty-five years old, the "beautiful Anna" as her friends called her, moved to Vienna along with her mother Teresia Richter.

The two women were among the thousands who migrated to Vienna to seek work in the 1890's when the empire's capital was booming economically. Anna soon found work using her skills in cooking. Through some acquaintances, she met August (Gustl), who worked as a waiter at the Sacher Hotel. The young man was smitten by her mature beauty, courted her actively, and married her in November, 1900. They had four children in quick succession: Auguste (Gusti), Anna (Anny), Franziska (Fränzi), and Eduard (Edy).

Early in 1908, when little Fränzi was only two years old, her father received an offer from one of his regular clients at the Sacher Hotel. Count Peachevich of Slavonia needed a manager for his chateau and estate, Schloss Retvalo in the south-eastern regions of the empire. When the young man replied despondently that he had a wife and four children to support, as well as his mother-in-law, the Count simply said, "Well, then, just bring them all."

It was an offer the ambitious waiter could not refuse, and so the family packed their belongings and made the long train journey, first east to Budapest and then south through the towns lining the Danube to the point where the Drau (Drava) enters the larger river. Just a short distance up the Drau was the small city of Esseg (Osijek) on whose outskirts stood the baroque Schloss Retvalo surrounded by sprawling grounds.

The young family had a good life in the company of the benevolent Count, who was also a favourite with the surrounding inhabitants. My grandmother Fränzi, as a normal two year-old, committed to her memory some vague, general feelings, maybe some smells and a few images. As she grew, however, more details took hold. Eventually, she shaped these memories into a few distinct stories from that time: stories about her own fairy-tale grandmother Teresia Richter, and of the Gypsy bands that would come through the region with their horses. She shared some of those memories with me, and it appears, with Miska.

ozdrav iz Osieka.
Gruss aus Essegg.

Dvor grofa Peachevich'a.
Schloss Graf Peachevich.

"Your Kertész Grosspapa wondered that I still knew everything," she wrote to me once, "but how can one forget such
things? He said, 'Franzl, you must write down your childhood memories.' He also told me that 'in no event must you
forget your grandmother.' —She was unique in all ways.
Today, he explained, there are few such grandmothers, and
least of all in the U.S.A. 'America is a land without soul.'"

"As for me," her letter continues, "I always felt myself more
of a kindred spirit with my grandmother than with my own
mother. Some of my most vivid memories of childhood are
about my grandmother, who was a master at storytelling.
She would tell stories about her own life, or she would make
up stories for me and my brother and sisters, her grandchildren."

"In the evening, in the glimmer from the embers in the tiled
stove, I would imagine the characters in my grandmother's
stories. There wasn't a story she didn't know, but the favorite amongst us children was 'Genouvesa and Rosa von
Tannenberg.' She also taught us how to pray; when we knew
one prayer, she would go to the next." [14]

Fränzi's grandmother is also the one who got the horseshoe. One
fine day, a troupe of Gypsies came through the area to entertain
the people and sell their wares. Everyone went out to see these
wild people on their wild horses. Standing near the edge of the
race course that day, Teresia may not have realized the danger she
was in as the horses flew past. Suddenly, a horseshoe came loose
and almost hit her. She bent down and picked it up for good luck.
That horseshoe has found its way down the generations and half-
way across the world to my house where it hangs above a doorway.

The children were spoiled in this life at the Count's chateau.
There was always enough to eat, and they played with the Count's
children. Wearing fancy hand-me-down clothes, they look a little
out of place in the picture taken in 1909 on the next page.

Less than a year after he had taken his family to Esseg,
August Wondrak struck upon a path from which his marriage
would never recover. One day he was simply gone. The children
didn't know where. His wife may have known more, but she kept
it to herself. Was it that he sought adventure, or did he go to seek
better opportunities away from an increasingly fragile political

and economical situation in Europe? Several months after his disappearance, Anna received a long letter from him, postmarked New York. The original of that letter is fading with time, but it tells a familiar tale.

Plied with stories of a booming economy in America, a man leaves his family and sails to New York, only to learn the hard way. Oh yes, between 1904 and 1908, ninety-two hotels had been built, but there were also 250,000 unemployed in this city alone. People will work for next to nothing. To work in the hotel business, a person has to know both English and French, and he needs references. August was lucky: he met a friend he had known in Vienna and who got him a job at the St. Regis Hotel. Today, this

The Wondrak children, left to right: Fränzi, Edy, Gusti, Anny

original Beaux Arts classic landmark built by Colonel John Jacob Astor IV in 1904 on Fifth Avenue at 55th Street is one of the luxury hotels from that era.

But in 1908, the $25 per month salary that August received for a fourteen-hour work day barely covered his living expenses. He shares this list in the letter.

Rent per month	13 Dollars
Laundry per month	5 "
Shaving, haircut	2 "
Diverse items	2 "

That adds up to 22 Dollars per month which leaves me 3 dollars. I have to be careful not to do or buy anything else. I don't even buy the newspaper, just some tobacco for my pipe for 5 cents once a week.[15]

Of course, I can imagine that much of the "poor me" content in this letter was designed to assuage his wife's anger and worry. He also tries to explain how the whole thing happened; the letter is full of remorse and concern, particularly about their son Edy who may have started to show the signs of his future crippling illness.

Even though August seemed to be sincere about coming back, it was not to be. The Count begged Anna to stay, but she decided to return home with her children and her mother. The Count told Anna to take whatever furnishings she might need. A modest chest of drawers is still in the family's possession.

Back in Vienna, Anna took an apartment on Schopenhauerstrasse in the 18th District, the same apartment that Fränzi lived in for most of her life. How the two women and the four children crowded into the *Zimmer-Küche-Kabinett* space we can hardly imagine nowadays, but many apartments were built on this model. I well remember my grandmother's, which did not change much over the years since I was there as a child in 1950, a teenager in 1966, and an adult in the late 1980's. The large room (*Zimmer*) measured about 200 square feet and had a large window overlooking the courtyard of the apartment block. The kitchen (*Küche*) had a stove, an icebox, a stand-alone cupboard, and some surfaces including a table. Finally, the small bedroom (*Kabinett*) may originally have held more than the single bed that I slept in. A cold water tap and basin were in the hallway outside the entrance doors opposite which was the door to the toilet. This particular apartment was at the split-level position from the main building, so the toilet wasn't shared with neighbours. Thank goodness for small miracles.

When August finally did return to Europe, to Vienna, Anna took him back but the reconciliation didn't last. After another failed try at emigrating to America, he took a small apartment a few blocks away. Eventually they divorced. Anna worked as a housekeeper for a family of bankers, so the children once again enjoyed high-class hand-me-downs and a sense of well-being. August worked at various positions and tried his hand as an entrepreneur. Among his ventures was a mushroom-growing enterprise that he set up in the cellar of a house nearby. Manure was a ready commodity, for in those days and for many years to come, horses were used for transport, and it was still common for people to keep farm animals in the courtyards of the apartment blocks. In fact, I remember myself as a five year-old in 1952 walking many blocks, under the protective eye of my older cousin Wolfgang, to take vegetable scraps to a woman who raised chickens. We walked back very carefully with a few fresh eggs.

Fränzi in 1912 – forty years earlier – may have done the same, and when it was time for her to go to school, I can imagine her quite vividly, clutching her grandmother's hand on the walk down the hill, through the park on Aumannplatz and up the hill on the other side, where the chestnut trees signaled the school yard. Forty years later it was I, clutching Fränzi's hand, walking the same route to the very same school for my first Kindergarten days. The chestnut trees under which I played during school breaks were probably the same ones she saw, and they were still there in 2000 when I walked down that street – a sentimental moment. The old brick school building, however, has now been replaced or refurbished into a modern structure.

In May of 1915 Fränzi along with her young brother Edy received their first communion in the Weinhauserkirche, the neighbourhood Catholic church that still beckons when you travel up the Number 41 *Strassenbahn* (tramway) along Währingerstrasse and then Gentzgasse. During the World War I year of 1915, the streets and the church may have looked and felt desolate, but the documents commemorating the children's communion make up for it. The narrow 7 x 11-inch parchment is dominated by a large image of Jesus administering the host to the apostle John the Baptist. The muted reds and greens of the figures' robes and the elaborate border create a sharp contrast and draw the eye to the vivid gold halos, Jesus' beige shirt and the white host. At the bottom of the document is the information, with name, date and signatures set out in neat handwriting.

The Weinhauserkirche holds similar memories for me. It was in this church that I attended Sunday school, learned the basic Bible stories, and experienced the cool and mysterious interior of this house of God. The wooded garden that stretches up the hill behind the church introduced me to the holiness of nature. I was baptized and had my first communion there, although I have no such elaborate certificate. My mother's family did not attend church regularly, but Weinhauserkirche was nevertheless a fixture in our lives. In 2000, I spoke with Frau Dauner, the secretary in the church offices. She remembered Fränzi very well and even visited her grave occasionally. She made a photocopy of my grandmother's Birth- and Baptismal Certificate for me, cut it meticulously with the largest pair of scissors I have ever seen, and carefully applied her official stamp and initial to the document.

*****

World War I did not affect the eight-year old Fränzi at first. She was busy doing what young girls do: making friends, continuing school, and absorbing the environment around her. But life was getting more and more difficult for the family. By the time she was fifteen, Fränzi was looking around for work to help support the family, but there were few opportunities even for apprenticeships. She and her friends spent more and more time together, going to movies when they could afford it, smoking when they could get away with it, and dreaming—dreaming of the good life.

When her friend Grete found out that Sascha Films was looking for extras, Fränzi did not hesitate. Together, the two young women prettied themselves up as best they could and hopped on the tram to the Sascha Film Factory in the 19th District. They were hired on the spot.

Kertész Becomes My Grandfather

One of the first productions in which Fränzi and her friend were cast was the comedy series *Cocl & Seff*. Two 8 x 10 black and white production stills that were among her memorabilia are from the episode "Seff as Reporter," dated July, 1922. The setting is fake-Egyptian, and Fränzi is one of several attendant 'beauties' surrounding the pharao, his priests, and Seff in a Charlie Chaplin outfit, writing on a notepad. In one shot each of the attendants is holding a garland of huge white (fake?) flowers. In the other picture, the flowers litter the floor and the attendants appear to be gyrating, their hands clasped palms up abve their heads – rather uncomfortable, I'd say. Their baggy costumes are made out of dark colored crêpe material; it hangs from thin shoulder straps, and is drawn in loosely at the waist in the popular 1920's style. Metal breast plates stand out brightly against the dark cloth, and the girls are all wearing wigs of dark hair in ringlets bound low on the forehead with a sash that ends in a garish white bow over each ear. The light-colored flat sandals on their feet do not match the outfits at all. This rather unflattering attire is mirrored in the disenchanted look on the faces of these extras.

It's obvious that this series of short films followed the tradition of slapstick comedy. This was a time when seeing the human body in action was still a relatively new visual experience for audiences. Displaying the human body in grotesque ways has always been a way to make people laugh, and silent film made the most of it.

My grandmother and her friends would have come to work in their finest clothes. Looking smart to go out in the street was one of Fränzi's lifelong principles. She would have prepared carefully the morning of shooting – getting up early, making sure her hair was perfectly combed under a summer hat, and putting on her best shoes. Fränzi used to tell me that stylish shoes and a good haircut were of ultimate importance for the whole impression a woman made. She might have worried about her outfit, which was more than likely a hand-me-down. Going to work in film, you have to look your best, you have to look like a lady. But as we see from the production stills, it really didn't matter after she arrived at the studio. Once she put on that horrid costume, her carefully chosen outfit hung lifelessly on a hook in the dressing room.

The faces also reflect a certain confusion about what the young women are doing. It looks as though they were not quite used to being told how to stand or move just like this or just like that. They soon learned from the director of these comedies, which was not Kertész, however.

When Fränzi and her friend became extras at Sascha, Kertész had already been working with the Austrian film giant for three years. He had come to Vienna in 1919, and by the summer of 1922 he was working on the monumental epic *Sodom & Gomorrah*, the last film he would make with his wife Lucy Doraine. The story about Kertész and Doraine discovering Walter Slezak, the "beautiful young boy" and aspiring actor who also stars in the film, tells us a bit about the freedom that directors had in those days. It was at the Sacher Hotel bar late one evening, and here it is in Slezak's own words:

> I strolled into the bar, ordered a scotch & soda – not because I like scotch & soda, but because it's a fashionable drink. I smoked a long cigar and portrayed the image of a blasé, elegant rake. At the next table sat two gentlemen and a lady. When the woman gestured towards me, the men turned around and looked me up and down. I recognized the woman … Lucy Doraine. She smiled at me and I smiled back (discreetly, for I was a man of the world). And then one of the men got up and sat down beside me. "Your permission, but I had you in mind." He spoke this sentence in dead seriousness and with a thick Hungarian accent. I must have looked at him stupidly, for he continued: "Please understand, you are my vision!"

> For a minute, I thought an escaped mental patient had just sat down beside me, and I was determined not to be annoyed: "Of course, I understand completely," I answered.

> "No, you do not understand," he said with sadness, "but I will explain, if you please. My name is Kertész, Mischka. I am preparing Sodom & Gomorrah, legend of Sin – and I need a young man as beautiful as a picture --, and you, if you please, are beautiful as a picture!"

> Slowly I grasped his meaning… [16]

The filmography in James Robertson's *The Casablanca Man* does also credit Lucy Doraine as being responsible for casting, as indeed she had been for most of the films she made with her husband-director. But Kertész' part in "discovering" actors and then shaping them for his films was one of his hallmarks for the rest of his career. Doris Day is a famous Hollywood example.

There are many – hundreds if not more – who he approached but did not, after all, cast in his films. One of my newly-discovered cousins, Duncan Hill, was eleven years old in 1960 when our grandfather asked if he would like to play the young Huck Finn in *The Adventures of Huckleberry Finn*. By that time, however, there was a totally different method of casting. Eddie Hodges, and not Duncan Hill, ended up with that role.

For *Sodom & Gomorrah*, Kertész was also involved in writing the script. Together with co-writer Ladislaus Vajda, he created the basic elements of the story. Filming was done in two out-of-town locations: Erzberg in Styria, and the beautiful seventeenth-century palace at Laxenburg near Vienna, still a favourite place today where city folk stroll around the grounds or rent a boat to glide over the lovely ponds. The garden house where the main character Mary Conway has the dream of her punishment is situated in the gardens at Laxenburg. Other scenes were shot in Vienna's inner city, at Schönbrunn and at the Hermes Villa, the former imperial hunting villa of Lainz on the slopes of the Vienna woods.

The outdoor scenes for Part 2 were created at the Sascha "dream factory" on the Laaerberg, which in 1922 was essentially a gravel pit. Today, this is a large public park attached to a rehabilitation facility of the same name. The torn-up landscape gave shape to the present abrupt hills and deep ponds. A cone-shaped hill has been cultivated into a rose garden, and many paved and gravel paths crisscross the terrain. Some vestiges of the 1920's film city activities are still in evidence, such as a three meter high metal clock and several stone carvings that came, no doubt, from one of the many sets that were built here. Unfortunately, these objects are not labeled, nor is there any historical signage.

Fränzi Wondrak was one of the thousands of extras that were hired for *Sodom & Gomorrah*, and although I've watched the reconstructed film several times, I've not been able to spot her in the crowds. In other words, neither the camera nor the director got close enough to her, but she is there somewhere because she told me that she took the tram all the way to the Laaerberg for shooting.

One morning in 2000, I also took a much more modern tram, transferred twice, and when I found the location, let my imagination reconstruct massive temple to Astarte, ancient Syrian goddess of fertility, beauty, love, and war. At the steps through that rose garden planted on that perfectly round hill, I closed my eyes and saw Kolowrat, Kertész and their crew busily planning the scenes.

The film's Part 1 "The Sin" had its debut October 13, and Part 2 "The Punishment" was premièred October 20, 1922 at the

Löwen-Kino, Vienna, III. After the film was released, a court case was launched on behalf of a number of extras who had been injured during the scene in which the temple is destroyed – a few were even killed. The defendants were Kertész, the assistant director Arthur Göttlein, and Otto Wannemacher in charge of pyrotechnics. In its decision to assign liability, the court found the technical man to be mainly at fault: judgment was a fine of 500,000 Kronen and ten days in jail to Wannemacher. [17]

During 1922, Kertész also directed Die Lawine (The Avalanche), and then moved on to two more films based on stories from the ancient world: Der Junge Medardus (Young Medard) and Samson und Delilah. This latter film he co-directed with Alexander Korda who would go on to fame in Britain. A third film, Namenlos (Nameless) also appeared in 1923. One major difference was that Lucy Doraine was no longer Kertész' leading lady and that their marriage had finally ended. After many false leads, I finally found the evidence: documents to commence proceedings were filed in the District Court Margarethen, Vienna on May 18, 1922. It appears the divorce was uncontested because Lucy may have already moved to Munich in 1922 to star in Opfer der Liebe (Victim of Love), released by Münchner Lichtspielkunst AG (Emelka). By 1923, the year that her divorce from Kertész became official, she had already founded her own production company, Lucy-Doraine-Film GmbH, and released her first film, Die Suchende Seele (The Searching Soul). [18]

Their daughter Kitty had been exposed to the joys and the sorrows of growing up a child of celebrities. In her poetry she explores a particularly poignant memory:

> My mother whom I loved,
> was for me just like the sun –
> a radiant beauty, but unreachable.
> And often I slept in the closet,
> in with her expensive dresses
> and the many heavy furs,
> or upon her satin sheets,
> rolled up like a little puppy,
> happy to breathe in the scent
> of mother and to dream,
> that she caressed me tenderly. [19]

Surrounded by material wealth, Kitty was alone much of the time. She had only Fräulein Rosa in a world that must have been confusing for a little girl.

*****

In the fall of 1923, Kertész began work on *Harun al-Raschid* (released March 21, 1924). And it was here that he met my grandmother. Fränzi had been cast as an extra in this film. My grandmother told me many times about the moment of meeting. She was positioned somewhere on the set – I could see Kertész prowling around as a good director would – when suddenly he approached her and said, "You're very pretty, a little too fat, but pretty." Then he put her in the front row.

So it happened that in a production photo dated November 22, 1923 she is in full view, sitting on the floor in what looks like a comfortable position. The contemporary set is a ship's deck and a group of men and women are lounging on huge pillows and eastern rugs, watching exotic dancers. A tuxedoed man is playing a small banjo-like instrument. One of the other female onlookers is wearing a safari hat, but Fränzi is bareheaded with chin-length hair. She is wearing a dark dress, and her bare arm supports her. A wistful expression on her face appears to match the general mood. No doubt he had told her exactly how to pose and what expression her face should wear.

He was thirty-six, she was sixteen. I have no reason to believe Fränzi aspired to be an actress – there is no evidence of acting lessons, for instance, and she never talked to me about her roles, her prospects in film. Instead our conversations focused on Kertész, her Miska.

So if Fränzi was not an aspiring starlet, how did an affair start up between them? If she did not go to him in hopes of advancement, then why did she go? From everything I know about my grandmother's life, I can only deduce that for her it was love, a love that lasted for her lifetime. Something must have struck Kertész about her too, because he voluntarily supported her and their child – my father – keeping her impossible dream alive, for better or worse.

Personal and Industry Crisis

The year 1924 was tumultuous for Kertész. It was perhaps the last good year for him at Sascha Films as problems in the

Austrian film industry became serious. He directed three less important films, *Ein Spiel Ums Leben (A Game for A Life), General Babka,* and *Der Onkel von Sumatra,* and then he made *Die Sklavenkönigin (Moon of Israel)* which was an immediate hit with Austrian audiences. After it was released in Germany and the United States, this film also caught the attention of international film makers.

In February, 1924 he wrote a postcard to Fränzi from Bad Gastein in the Salzburg region of Austria where he was working on location: "Dear Fränzi! I am already here 3 days and not a single shot. Bad weather. Hope to be in Vienna in 5 – 6 days. ... Many Greetings, Kertész." A second, hand-colored postcard from Salzburg let her know he was on the way home.

They were obviously seeing each other regularly, and I know that Fränzi played as an extra in *Moon of Israel* which was filmed during the summer months for a release date of October 24. Among my grandmother's treasures was a business card identifying Kertész as First Director of Sascha. On the back is written "2 tickets." It's tempting to think that this refers to two tickets for the premiere of this, her last film. Is it possible that he might have taken her, his current mistress?

The premiere is described as a lavish affair staged in the Eos-Kino, an imposing movie theatre in Vienna's 3rd District. The entrance hall was decorated Egyptian style, complete with images of gods and statues of ancient warriors. On the stage, an altar was bathed in mystical bluish-red lighting, and the 60-piece orchestra performed a long overture. Toward the end, the music mingled with muffled choir song to set the mood for the drama about to unfold. [20]

If Kertész and Fränzi attended the premiere together, the loose style of dress would have hidden any tummy bulge – she was three months pregnant. Kertész had suggested she get an abortion. She took his money for the procedure, took the tram to the doctor's office but could not go in. When she told Miska what had happened, he was not angry. Instead, he vowed to help her. This short letter written near Christmas is the first of many with the same message.

My dear Fränzi!

Received your dear letter, and I also wish you a happy Christmas and New Year. About your wishes I will make them come true after the holidays. I trust you, and you will also not be disappointed in me.

Many Greetings, Kisses. Miska

Kertész could not have known that his promise would be irreversibly affected by the impending changes in the Austrian film industry.

Post-World War I inflation in Austria had spiraled out of control between 1922 and 1924. Austrian National Bank historians explain that Austria, along with Germany and Hungary, did not succeed in stabilizing its currency after the war. The decline in industrial production and poor harvests had further devastated the economy. Moreover, Austria, which had been used to a large economy under the monarchy, now had to struggle with the structural problems of a smaller economy. This imposed a great burden on the budget, which already had to cope with war debts. [21] The cost of living and doing business increased dramatically due to repeated devaluation of the currency. Just imagine the effect on the population when, in August 1922, the cost of living was 14,000 times higher than before the war! The young Republic eventually succeeded in beginning a process of stabilization, which included conversion of Kronen to Schilling.[22]

Unfortunately, these efforts did not help Sascha Films to remain a viable enterprise. To exacerbate matters, film theatre operators took advantage of cheaper imported films to fill their Kinos. Kolowrat tried his best to lobby the government for stricter controls on foreign film imports, but to no avail. In January 1925, the film industry moguls tried a more direct approach, and Kertész was with them. Sascha Films had planned a demonstration with the other branches of the film industry union, and that morning a group of about forty men and women met in the small square in front of the head office on Siebensterngasse, marched through the busy market street Neubaugasse, down the broad arterial Mariahilferstrasse, onto the Ring, and finally toward the Parliament Buildings. Unfortunately, the outcome of that confrontation yielded nothing beyond excuses and promises. Clearly, Socialist (Red) Vienna was beyond its peak influence, and economic and cultural globalization was spreading. [23] By mid-February, Kertész was in Berlin and spent some time with the film company Fellner & Somlo. Was he representing Sascha, or himself?

Whatever other promises he might have made to Fränzi as these events unfolded I do not know, but I do know this: He kept his word about helping and supporting her through her pregnancy and beyond. She never took him to court, never sued him for financial support. They corresponded for close to thirty years, and even though I have only one side of the exchange – his letters to her – they tell a story of commitment. Here is one of the first, written in his distinctive hand, with some mistakes in his German, but demonstrating a close personal relationship, trust, and love.

Fellner & Somlo   Berlin March 5 lll 25

My Dear Fränzi !

Don't be angry that I haven't given a sign of life so long, but I am already 20 days in Berlin. At Sascha company I had many difficulties and the company has material problems, so I went to Berlin to find another contract. Probably I will come back to Vienna after all on May 5 and work it out with Sascha so I can still work in Vienna this year.

The money that is needed for the birth and infants' home (per month) you must write me punctually because I didn't understand it from your letter. And I have to ask about it here in Vienna and if it is less expensive here then we will keep the Baby here. You know, Franzel, I have to be so frugal because right now there is such a crisis in our work. Of course you shall have what you need, but with modesty. I hope, later there will be better times and we won't have to be so thrifty. Write soon to Vienna.

Tell your Mama she should be calm, I will provide so that you don't have any worries.

Greetings to your sister and brother-in-law.

I kiss you many times

Miska [24]

Kertész was torn between finding a new contract and continuing on with Sascha-Films in Austria. As it turned out, he did go back to Vienna but directed only two films during 1925, both collaborative projects among Austrian, German and British film companies:

Das Spielzeug von Paris also titled *Célimène, la poupée de Montmartre (Red Heels)* and *Fiaker No. 13 (Cab No. 13)*.

It's interesting to note that later in the year (sometime between September and December, 1925) Sascha Filmindustrie of Austria created a corporate partnership with Fellner & Somlo that included sharing the administrative offices of the German company in Berlin. Kertész's letters to Fränzi dated December 2, 1925 bears the letterhead imprint Sascha-Filmindustrie at the same address: Berlin SW 48, Friedrichstrasse 224.

As Ralph Hoppe writes in his book about this famous Berlin street, by the end of the 1920's Friedrichstrasse was teeming with film companies which would eventually include a German branch of the American studio Metro-Goldwyn-Mayer (MGM). Friedrichstrasse also had numerous cinemas, some of which dated back to the earliest days of film. For example, in 1879, the Apollo-Theater on this same street offered a mixture of live and photographed performances, albeit not moving pictures at the time. When motion pictures were invented in 1895, the German company Bioskop won a patent for Germany and presented the first movies to the public at the Wintergarten-Varieté on Friedrichstrasse. This was on November 1, 1895, almost two months before the Lumière Brothers brought film to the Parisian public at the end of December. [25]

By the time Kertész took part in Berlin's role in film history just as he had in Budapest and in Vienna, Friedrichstrasse was well connected through electric transit lines, above and below ground, with all parts of the city, the train stations and even the Tempelhof airport. [26]

A New Responsibility Arrives

For Fränzi, who was eight months pregnant, Kertész' letter from the bustling film world of Berlin deals with much more urgent matters: the birth of their child, arrangements, and money. The letter reached her in Abbazia, Italy (now Opatija, Croatia) where she was staying with her sister Anny and brother-in-law Franz Palka. Palka, a veteran of World War I, was employed as Director of the Casino in the Palace Hotel. The Palkas, with their three-year old boy, rented a spacious apartment in the Villa Niri on the slopes overlooking the town.

Abbazia had long been a favourite resort for Europeans, situated as it is on the warm Bay of Quarnero near Rijeka (Fiume).

Here, at the north end of the Adriatic Sea and sheltered on the west by the mountains of the Istrian peninsula, Abbazia was – and still is – a lovely place to be. It's easy to imagine that despite her condition, Fränzi dreamed of the future while she enjoyed long walks along the promenade with her sister and nephew.

Fränzi no doubt gained hope and personal comfort from Kertész' communication, but the text presents realities to come. For me, looking through the long lens of known outcomes, some issues are already apparent. His excuses may have been real and the promises sincere, but we will see how Kertész tended to direct aspects of his personal affairs in a similar manner over the years. The statement about "a crisis in our work" can be substantiated in 1925, and much later there were real work slow-downs in Hollywood.

His work, and therefore his income, was not steady or secure, but it was always a lot more than most other people could even imagine earning. Family expectations echoed formal documentation of his director's salary. My feeling is that Fränzi trusted her Miska unconditionally. She knew little if anything about his other obligations, and in fact, she had no other choice: she was dependent on him.

The next subject in the letter – what to do with the baby – also reveals the director's touch. He will make the decisions. For Kertész, whether or not she should bring the baby back to Vienna is also about money, about practicalities. The suggestion to place the baby in an infant's home is not out of line with common practice at the time. One of the main achievements of socialist Vienna, along with special cultural and educational policy, and municipal housing, was *Fürsorgepolitik* (communal welfare). Under the new policies for family care, the number of infants and toddlers who were raised in infants' homes doubled from before World War I, [27] but it was not only the needy or homeless who took advantage of the facilities that sprang up throughout the city. People associated the practice with a safe and healthy environment. Kertész also had first-hand experience, for his first Vienna child, Michael Forster, had been placed in such a home for at least two years after his birth in 1920.

Kertész visited family in Budapest in the spring of 1925 as he was in the habit of doing as often as he could. But he also wrote to Fränzi several times before the baby arrived. As these two short letters show, he was keeping his promise.

Dear Fränzi :　　　Received in Abbazia March 15, 1925

I arrived today from Berlin and I've now received your letters. I will arrange everything as you wish in 3 - 4 days. I'm writing only a few lines because I have much to do, and you should be calm. God will help to bring everything in order.

Many Kisses, Miska

Dear Fränzi　　　　　No date (addressed to Abbazzia)

I have come to Vienna from Budapest today, and I am sending you 1 ½ million Austrian Kronen. Divide that up so that you can buy what you need in the meantime. Write to me then and tell me your plans.

I greet you in this hope that [you] are well.

Miska

In his travels during 1925, Kertész probably met another woman, one of the most important women in his life. Bess Meredyth, his future wife in the United States, was in Italy with the 1925 MGM production of *Ben Hur: A Tale of The Christ*. Meredyth was one of the writers on the project. In an interview for Hungarian film magazine *Mohezit* in 1931, she said that she had met Kertész during the location filming, which took place in Anzio, south of Rome and in Livorno, the Tuscan seaport not far from Pisa.

Although her son John Meredyth Lucas says in his book *Eighty Odd Years in Hollywood* that they "were introduced" in about 1928, [28] it's possible he just didn't know about the earlier meeting. Could one of the trips Kertész took from Vienna, or some of the work he was involved with in 1925 include a jaunt to Italy? Was he weaving a new thread into the scene, even while he was writing these words to Fränzi?

Dear Fränzi !　　　　(Received)　Abbazia 22 April 1925

I am as I was to you, <u>and don't think</u> for a moment that there will <u>come a time when I will leave you or the little one in a lurch</u>. I am sending you today 1000 Lire, and [then] to Merano if you will write me your address, I'll send 500 Lire as you requested. I can't send the whole amount at the moment but you can go without worrying to Merano.

I know you are a good and decent woman and want to keep
the little one with you. I didn't understand your letter very
well. Just calm down. I am not against your giving birth in
Fiume because in a hospital where there are doctors, care
will be taken.

Do as you think best. If you want, you can leave the little
one in an infants' home in Fiume for 3 - 4 months or until he
takes milk, and I will pay what it costs, because during this
time you can get some work, and then after a few months
or a year, you can take the little one to live with you. I think
that's the smartest way to do things, because in an infants'
home in Fiume the little one will be well taken care of, and
protected against sickness.

I stand beside you in every situation, and will write again
soon.

Kisses Miska

I have sent 1000 Lire by express today. On the first or the
third, I will send the 500. Waiting for news from you, how
you are.

Despite the confusion about locations – Fränzi and the Palkas had
already decided she should have the baby in Bolzano [29] – his commitment is clear from this and subsequent handwritten letters. He
underlined those words of encouragement, forcefully.

When I first read the pack of sixty-some letters that my
grandmother had kept for more than fifty years, my heart went
out to both of them. These early letters in particular confirmed my
understanding of the how the relationship between them played
out over the years. He may have left Fränzi and my father in
Europe, but he did not abandon them. Keeping his promise meant
that he had to script and scenarize the manner in which he supported them to fit many different situations.

It's almost certain that Fränzi did not receive this last letter until much later. Bolzano (Bozen in German) is a small city in
the mountains of Northern Italy (then Southern Tyrol, a part of
Austria) where she could get proper medical attention, and the
baby would be placed with the Maurachers, friends of the family.
Fränzi would be in a German-speaking city, and people there
would address her as Frau Kertész.[30]

When and where she did get this letter, Fränzi must have been tremendously relieved. Her confinement was no doubt weighing on her, both physically and psychologically, so the money would certainly be welcome, and the Palkas would have given Kertész credit for coming through.

And yet, as I consider the issues and decisions that Kertész repeats here, it may be just as well she did not read it in a highly vulnerable state just before giving birth. While he acknowledges her reservations about placing the baby in an infant's home, at least at the beginning – "I know you are a good and decent woman and want to keep the little one with you" – he keeps pushing the point, citing commonly-held beliefs about protecting the infant. Judging from Kertész' letter, Fränzi was not expected to breast-feed her baby; instead, she could be looking for work.

This suggestion might also have upset this young mother-to-be. Is he telling her in a roundabout way that he intends to support the child but not her? In the court decisions regarding his first two Vienna children, this was indeed the intent: Kertész was to pay for the care and upbringing of the children, but he had no obligation toward the mothers. He knew that Fränzi had basic training as a secretary, and that she had worked for Sascha Films as an extra. But the nineteen year-old from Vienna may not have had market-able skills in Bolzano.

****

It was long and arduous trip from Abbazia to Bolzano by steam train – Rijeka to Trieste, past Venezia, Padua, Verona then north through Trento and finally Bolzano. Although I have no proof, I will assume that her sister accompanied Fränzi and helped her to get settled in. One or more representatives of the family Mauracher might have been waiting for them at the station. Mrs. Mauracher, a long-time friend of the Vondrak family, had been engaged to take care of the baby. She lived in a small mountain vil-lage, *Kastelruth* (now Castelrotto) about twenty kilometers north of Bolzano, and that's where the baby would be taken. Nice people, very reasonably priced, healthy air, out of the way: everything the situation demanded.

In the meantime, arrangements for a hotel room had most likely been made in advance, and Fränzi would soon be settled in comfortable surroundings where she could rest and wait. What might the evening before the birth of her baby been like for her?

She would have read and re-read Miska's letters. And while his words may have relieved some anxiety, she would have wanted him to be there with her. Her sister was a poor substitute.

To still her nervousness, Fränzi's might have needed some comfort food. Let's imagine she ordered a favourite dish, one that reminded her of home: *Mohnnudeln*, wide egg-noodles topped with a ground poppyseed mixture, quite sweet. Of course they wouldn't make it like her Mami did, but at least here they make it— she couldn't get it in Abbazia. The young servant girl who brings the tray is a round-faced, red-cheeked farm girl. Schatz'l she calls herself. But the noodles don't taste right tonight, and Fränzi hardly touches them. The honeyed milk that came along with them feels soothing, though, and she drinks the warm liquid greedily. Soon weariness overtakes her and she retires to the lounge again, too lazy to go to bed.

The next few days blurred into each other. Then on April 29, Fränzi began her labour, was admitted to the Bozen General Public Hospital, and with no apparent difficulties gave birth to a healthy baby boy, my father.

The Paper Trail

Every scrap of paper I've been able to find on this important event is a treasure. I know from the hospital's invoice, for example, that my grandmother's stay was eleven days, at 30 Lire per day, and that a midwife assisted at the birth – the fee 150 Lire. This document, soft paper wanting to stay folded as it had for so many years, bears only her name Wondrak Francisca, "private person" from Vienna, as the patient. But on the back, there are two notations in pencil, each in a different handwriting. One says "Kertész Michael junior" and the other "Kertes Berlin Friedrich str 124 bei Fellner und Somlo."

In the next letter from Kertész, which arrived in Bolzano on the day the baby was born, he brings up the subject of coming to visit.

Vienna / Received April 29, 1925 Bolzano

Dear Fränzi

I hope you are well? God will help you get through everything. I sent the money to Abbazia and the second portion I will mail on Thursday to Bolzano General Delivery. Please

> let me know immediately when it arrives and inform me by
> telegraph when everything is over. Be calm I will stand by
> you, if God will help that I can work.
>
> I hope to be finished with my work at the end of June so I
> can come to Italy and visit you and the little one. The best is
> that you put the infant in an infant's home for now because
> they understand it better to raise the little one until the little
> one takes reins, like you. Write to me ... and I will send you
> money ...

But there is much to be done before he can come to Italy, work that
Kertész is thankful for. He is probably referring to the film *Das
Spielzeug von Paris*, the first collaborative effort between Austria's
Sascha-Films and the Germany's UFA (Universum Film AG).
Filming was done in Germany and Paris, and that meant more
traveling for him that spring. The film was released in Austria on
October 16, 1925.

Another matter was also pressing on Kertész, however. For
months, the Youth Welfare authorities in Vienna had been trying to work with him on the matter of Sonja Dalla Bonna, born
August 11, 1923. The child's mother Theresia Dalla Bonna had
finally allowed the authorities and the district court to pursue
Kertész on the matters of paternity and financial support for the
child. Hearings had been postponed time and time again during
1924 because Kertész was supposedly not available. Finally, just
as Fränzi was giving birth to his next child in Bolzano, the Dalla
Bonna case was being heard in Vienna. These proceedings no
doubt impacted his promise to come to Italy after the end of June.
In fact, the judgment in the Dalla Bonna case is dated July 2, 1925.

The document can be summed up with a few words: Kertész
is judged to be Sonja's father, and he is to pay 120 Schillings per
month from July 1924 up to and until Sonja is self-sufficient.
Theresia's evidence is that she had sexual relations with him at
the crucial time. His defence is that he broke off sexual relations
on September 1922 when she allegedly stole items from his apartment. At one point, he apparently tried to pay her off with 5 million Kronen, but she refused after she consulted a lawyer.

The courtoom drama continues: his lawyers bring evidence
against her character – an alleged arrest, other men. They also
try to show that Kertész was ill at the crucial time. The document
then summarizes his employment status and income, but acknow-

ledges that he has debts, including back taxes and obligations to his divorced wife, a legitimate child (Kitty), an illegitimate child (Michael Förster), as well as his 74-year old widowed mother in Budapest. The 120 Schillings support for Sonja Dalla Bonna is found to be appropriate and a request for an increased amount is denied. It's interesting to note that two years earlier, in the judgment granted in favor of Thilde Förster, maintenance was set at 200 Schillings per month!

After the Dalla Bonna hearing, a newspaper article titled "The Self-experienced Film of the Director Kertész" appeared in Vienna's Illustrierte Kronen-Zeitung (Illustrated Crown News). The article juxtaposes Kertész as both victim and victimizer: he fell into the trap of a "little girl" whose favours he demanded. But ultimately he is portrayed as a nice guy: he stood by her through all of this. The media judges that he "must pay for his own love story" [31] Once again, today – after 2017 in the face of the #MeToo movement – things would have gone differently for Mr. Kertész.

*****

When my grandmother left the hospital in Bolzano on May 9, 1925 no amount of sun and warmth could dispel the dark cloud hanging over her. She was about to hand over her baby to Frau Mauracher, who would take him kilometers away to the mountain town of Kastelruth to be nursed. My father believed – perhaps because he was told – that his mother actually had a physical impairment so she could not nurse him. However, in those days breastfeeding by the mother was not seen to be as important as it became later in the twentieth century. On the same day, Kertész was posting a letter in Vienna, addressed to Fränzi in Bolzano:

> (To Bolzano   Mailed Vienna   May 9, 1925)
>
> Dear Fränzi
>
> Here I send 2,000,000 Austrian Kronen. Hope it's enough for now. Write soon, how you are – you haven't answered yet. I am working a lot and have little time, that's why I'm writing so little. Many greeting and kisses
>
> Miska

A month later she finally received the letter acknowledging the birth of the child.

My dear Fränzi !   Vienna, June 4, 1925

I congratulate you on your baby boy and for you, that everything went well and without danger. I am happy that you
have a baby boy, but I am sorry that I couldn't be there. I
think it would be best to put the little one in an infants' home
for the time being until he takes milk and then you can take
him to yourself.

You will think about that yet—tomorrow morning I will send
you again 2 million Kronen [32]. —Hope that everything continues to go well—*the boy should be called Manuel Michael
and in the writing it should say his father is Michael
Kertész.* He should have two given names like me, Manuel
Michael. About the religion we still have time to talk.
   Many greetings and kisses

   Miska

Fränzi would have felt a mixture of emotions: thankfulness for
the money, disappointment that Miska had not come to visit, and
some confusion over the instructions regarding the baby. She did
follow through with the naming for the most part: my father's
given names are **Michael Emmanuel Franz**. But the family name
would legally remain Wondrak until it was changed to Vondrak in
practice many years later.

   For years, except for the hospital invoice and these few letters – along with other documents that indicated my father's birth
place and date – there was no conclusive proof that he was the
son of Michael Kertész. That is, until about five years ago, when
my father found a long-misplaced document, folded so many
times and for so long that it had almost fallen apart. Scotch tape
almost ruined this all-important document – his official Baptismal
Certificate. It not only corroborates the dates but also names the
"natural" father of the child as "Kertese Michele of Budapest."
Vondrak Francesca, the mother, is shown as *nubile* – unmarried.
The baptism took place on May 4, 1925 in the parish church
Prepositurale, a Roman Catholic church in Bolzano, the Reverend
Don Vittorio Wurzer presiding.

   How the next weeks and months played out for Fränzi,
Kertész and their new son cannot be known. The money kept
coming, as per letters of June 13, July 26, and August 11. And by
all accounts, it was plenty. My father told me that Fränzi did even-

tually work in Bolzano as a seamstress making household items such as curtains. Her wish to remain near her infant son may be a reason why she did not go back to Vienna to see Kertész. Clearly, however, she expected him to come and see her and the baby.

But according to Kertész's letters, he was "involved in very heavy work" (June 13), and out of the country several times. "I arrived back in Vienna… after 3 weeks out of the country with my film and now it's finished" (July 26). "I was in Berlin for 6 days and returned today" (August 11). In an undated letter he notes, "I have very much work and problems."

Indeed, film history tells us that production of the last two films he made in Europe had been chaotic. The first of these, *Fiaker No. 13* was filmed in the winter months 1925-26 in Berlin's UFA-Atelier am Zoo (Studio at the Zoo) as well as in Paris, France. [33] But of course it wasn't all "very heavy work" in which he was involved. I can easily imagine Kertész writing a letter and sending money to Fränzi in Bolzano one day, and the next day sitting in a Vienna courtroom defending himself against the paternity suit brought by Theresia Dalla Bonna.

Leaving Them and Europe Behind

On January 21, 1926 Fränzi wrote a postcard from Abbazia where she must have gone to visit the Palkas, perhaps over Christmas. It is addressed to her father August Wondrak in Vienna. The postcard is made from a snapshot of herself strolling along the seaside promenade in Abbazia, flanked by thick greenery on the one side and metal railing on the other. She's a bit chubby, but her round cheeks complement a natural smile. She is wearing a dark skirt and jacket open at the neck and framed with a white collar. Light-colored stockings and dark, buckled pumps complete the outfit.

The postcard tells us a little bit about her state of mind at the time. She thanks her father for his good wishes, especially as they were unexpected. Fränzi's parents were separated. She mentions that, at the time of writing, she and the baby were quite ill with a cold. When she writes, "It would be wonderful if my dearest wishes would come true. Let us trust in God," I believe she is referring to her dream of making a life with Kertész. Little did she know that even as she wrote, things were about to change forever.

Between January and May, 1926, Kertész was busy with the very last film he directed in Europe, *Der Goldene Schmetterling (The*

Golden Butterfly). [34] This was another collaborative effort, this time among Austrian, German and British film companies. Some of the filming took place at the UFA studios in Berlin, but most of it was filmed in London. [35]

This information corroborates the undated postcard he sent to Fränzi from the Cecil Hotel, London, on which he writes, "I've been working in London two months already." In his 1947 article in *True* magazine, George Frazier suggests that Kertész was working with Gaumont-British films when Harry Warner spotted him. [36] His last European film was released in Germany on August 30 and in Finland on October, 1926.

Both films starred Lili Damita, a French film star who eventually also came to America, where she became Mrs. Errol Flynn. Several sources suggest that Kertész had a relationship with her – and was "fleetingly" married to her – during this time. So far, I have not found any evidence to support these statements.

While in Germany, Kertész was burning the candle at both ends. He apparently made a deal with Stefan Markus of the German company Markfilm, but he eventually got out of it with the help of the Warner Brothers legal team a year later. It was the Warner Brothers standard contract, however, that Kertész signed in Berlin on May 10, 1926. Typewritten on ten pages of legal-sized paper, the contract is a legal work of art.

For $15,600 US in the first year and certain expenses, Kertész would direct films exclusively for and according to the wishes of the producer (Warner Brothers), would relinquish any and all rights to individual benefit for the work, would conduct himself according to moral standards as set, and could be relieved of his duties if the work did not satisfy the producer. The clauses regarding moral standards were, of course, included to satisfy strict morality laws in place in America at the time, but it is ironic nonetheless to think of this in light of my grandfather's conduct in Europe. Can a leopard change its spots?

As director for Warner Brothers, Kertész could be suspended without pay, and he could be lent out to other studios. Nevertheless, the option to extend the agreement for three years – each time with substantial increase in salary so as to more than double the amount by the end of 1930 – was an attractive carrot to dangle before someone like Kertész, hungry for work and security. There was an extra $2000 US – albeit only a loan – for out-of-pocket expenses in Europe and passage to Hollywood set at a maximum $600. It was his responsibility to arrange for legal passage and entry into the US, and he had less than a month to do it. Article 1 of the contract required him to be ready to work in Hollywood June 1, 1926. [37]

*****

Before he left Europe, it seems reasonable that Kertész got in touch with family. He tried to see his ten year-old daughter Kitty who was living in Berlin with her mother Lucy Doraine. Doraine was doing well as a silent screen star in Germany, acting for the company we now know as the Bavaria Film GmbH, and producing films under her own name, Lucy Doraine Film GmbH. [38]

Kitty herself told me in one of her letters that she had been very ill with pneumonia that spring. On the day her father came to see her, she was asleep and Fräulein Rosa would not let him disturb her. It's heartbreaking to think that a father's efforts to visit his child were unsuccessful. By the time Kitty found out what had happened, they were separated by thousands of miles.

Kertész also traveled to Budapest to arrange final travel documentation and visit his family in Budapest. A photo of him on Travel Day is dedicated to his sister Margit. I imagine that he might have boarded the Orient Express at Budapest to its western end-point, the Gare de L'Est, Paris. Perhaps on some unfinished business, he made a stop-over in that city before carrying on Cherbourg for the ocean passage.

I'm not surprised that he did not stop in Vienna, although the mandatory resident records for Vienna show that Kertész did not de-register (he is listed until February 2, 1927). He may have intentionally kept the apartment or perhaps that detail of bureaucracy was simply forgotten. But he did send a letter to Fränzi from the Hotel Prince des Galles (Prince of Wales Hotel) in Paris.

1926- Paris (no date)   Hotel Prince deGalles (sic.)

Dear Franzi

I was in such a situation that I could not write you. Please don't be angry. Now I have also sent the letters to Mr. Mathias in this letter. I am travelling today Wednesday to America, will send from New York immediately the birth documents by express. I think the best is if you don't stay in Vienna too long. I think the lawyer can complete everything even without you. Hope all is in order. Dear Franzi don't be sad but this was a difficult question. Hope it is solved in good order.

I am very nervous whether or not you have enough money? But I can't send any until I arrive in America. You also cannot write to me except to Hollywood at Warner Brothers Studio. Be assured that I will do everything so you are happy and satisfied.

I hope Buby is better already, and I remain with love and many greetings.

Michael

Send the letter(s) to Mathias

The hotel is just a few steps from the Champs-Elysées on Avenue George V. When I went there in 2006, I was taken aback by the modernized façade but enchanted by the lobby that looked unchanged from that earlier time. I went into the bar just to the side and paid nine Euros for an espresso that came with a little tray of treats. I sat there soaking up the atmosphere and to pondering the contents of this letter, which I had brought in my research satchel.

Mr. Mathias was a lawyer in Vienna who, even at this early stage, had been retained to begin the process of Kertész adopting my father. The birth documents mentioned are those of Kertèsz himself. Years later, this had still not happened and whether by chance or by design is not my place to judge. Problems, promises, assurances – the same pattern.

What about Thilde Förster? Theresia Dalla Bonna? Neither the Forsters nor the Hill family members have any evidence that Kertész got in touch with the mothers of his other two Vienna children. Where and how were these women and their children situated at the time of Kertész leaving Europe?

Recognizing the realities of life as a single mother, Thilde Förster began early on to expand her opportunities in the film industry. She continued to write stories and tried to sell them to film producers throughout Europe. She may have had access to some money from her father who died in 1922. With that and payments from Michael Kertész as prescribed in the Court Judgment of 1923, she took her son out of the Schönbrunn Infant's Home and they lived in an apartment at Dapontegasse 2/2, in the 3rd District of Vienna. But in the same year that Kertész left for America, she also left Austria for good. The residence registry shows that Thilde, her widowed mother and the boy "left for Italy during 1926." She also persuaded her brother Ludwig to join them on this journey. Ludwig would accompany his sister around Europe and become a father-figure to the child for the next ten years.

These travels affected her young son. As an only child, without a permanent home, little Michael had a lonely childhood. Conscious of the need to earn her own living, Thilde would sometimes settle the boy and "Uncle Ludwig" in cheap out-of-the way places while she traveled to writing assignments. However, she was generous and ready to live it up when money was available.

Thilde's independent spirit and resourcefulness gave her a good start, but her fight to bring up their son was only beginning. Herself a Jew and the mother of a Jewish boy, she would face some trying times.

Theresia Dalla Bonna, the mother of Kertész's second Vienna child did not fare as well. As noted, the Court handed down its Judgment on Theresia Dalla Bonna's paternity suit on July 2, 1925. By the time Kertész left for America in 1926, he was already in arrears on the support payments for his daughter Sonja. The court managed to get his Berlin address – there is a note on file from April 1926 – but no communication seems to have been attempted. It would take two years to track him down in Hollywood and renew the formal request for payment. Whether he paid in the meantime is questionable. Over the years, he did respond to these formal prompts at least some of the time, but Theresia's private efforts seem to have failed.

*****

When Kertész finally arrived at Cherbourg, France, his mind was most likely on the imminent voyage and what he would find in America. Cherbourg is across the Baie de la Seine from Le Havre, another important French sea port, one that I also sailed from in 1967. I had been in Austria for a year and a half – my version of the grand tour after completing high school – and was returning to Canada with my mother who had come to Vienna for a visit. We were on the SS France, and at the time I had no idea that forty years earlier, my grandfather had boarded the SS Leviathan just across the bay.

My October voyage across the Atlantic was pleasant enough: sunny, calm days prevailed, and the huge ship rode the waves smoothly. I managed not to be seasick as I had been on my first crossing at age nine. Six days later, we arrived in New York, gliding noiselessly past the Statue of Liberty and docking on the Hudson River side of Manhattan. The impressive skyline was nothing like today, but much more built up than it was in 1926.

Kertész sailed in early June, so the weather was likely pleasant also. The *SS Leviathan*, a much smaller ship, took a full ten days to make it to New York. On June 6, 1926, he walked onto American soil.

SS Leviathan in New York harbour, mid 1920's [39]

PART IV

AMERICA, THE FIRST YEARS: 1926 - 1930

An Immigration Story

Multitudes of people from all parts of the world have long considered America as the land of opportunity. Many have come to escape political persecution. Others hope to find meaningful work so they can offer their children a chance at education and a better life. And many seek adventure and opportunity that their homeland does not seems to offer.

Michael Kertész's decision to come to America probably included bits of all these factors. Professionally, he had been extremely active in Europe. His stints in Denmark, Germany, Italy, France, and his six-year residence in Austria had polished the directing skills that he first developed in Hungary. He had experienced first-hand the horrors of World War I, and he was there for its political aftermath. In Hungary, he had seen the birth of the film industry, and had witnessed the threats of political and economic trends. Things had been rosier in Austria at first, but by 1924 Kertész saw the beginning of decline even there.

With his multiple personal responsibilities and obligations, Kertész was always looking for job security. Already in 1925, he was concerned about the state of his work in Vienna. In his letter to Fränzi, he hinted that Sascha Films "has material problems" so he had gone to Berlin "to find another contract." As the story of his last two films in Europe suggests, there was no security to be gained there, so the opportunity to go to America under contract to Warner Brothers Studio was an offer he couldn't refuse.

Regardless of the financial security, however, the decision to leave the Old World could not have been easy – it never is. Although I was just nine years old in 1956, I remember the adults discussing immigration to Canada. After my father Michael Vondrak left Vienna in 1948, the intention was that I and my mother would follow and we could be a family again. However, circumstances and time were to make that impossible. When they had resigned themselves to the reality, each looked for and found a new relationship. My father married Frances Burke in Philadelphia, and in Vienna my mother married Frank Sobernig when I was six.

One of the greatest gifts I received from my stepdad was his dream to own land, a near impossibility in Austria for him. So he set his sights on Canada, and my mother must have shared the dream because for two years, it became the sole focus of their lives. There were endless plans, official steps, financial considerations, personal doubts, family opposition or encouragement depending on mood. In my stepdad's case, a close friend first agreed to come along only to back out at the last minute.

Finally in 1956, our little family of three and a half (Mom was expecting Frank's first child) undertook the journey that would change our lives forever. Frank went first, in June. My mother eagerly read his letters: reports on the voyage, decisions he made along the way and his excitement when he finally settled on Edmonton. He found work and rented an apartment. Four months later, she prepared me and as many of our possessions as we could, and we followed.

For me, a nine year-old, it was a big adventure. My cousin Wolfgang – three years older and already a fan of the Karl May books about the Wild West – had plied me with stories. Like other children in Vienna, we were buying American-made bubble-gum that came with collectible cards of cowboys and Indians. As we surveyed our little stash of images, my imagination formed what I could expect to see in Canada. After the long train ride from Vienna to Hamburg, crossing the Atlantic by steamship to Quebec City, I eagerly awaited the train ride across the prairies, where I searched in vain for those elusive creatures. I did see lots of cows, though, and – just north of Calgary on the last leg of our journey – my first coyotes.

Every immigration story has its own unique twists and turns, and the adults are concerned with much more important matters than looking for cowboys and Indians. Every day, every hour, there's something new to deal with, from the logistics of where to go and who to ask what questions, to the worry about the luggage, the language barrier, and the immigration authorities. I remember Mom being confused about what food to order on the train in Canada – the tomato soup was so salty! Immigrants have to get used to so many new things.

*****

My grandfather's immigration story is just as unique, just as filled with personal and work-related expectations and feelings. As the SS Leviathan plied the Atlantic Ocean, he must have had many things on his mind. I have a photo of my stepdad on board the Ascania of the Cunard Line, his back to the camera. Kertész would have spent some time on deck the same way. Who knows what went through their heads as they looked out over the waves.

Kertész had begun his ocean voyage on June 1, 1926 from Cherbourg, France. Far from being an immigrant ship like the one on which Frank crossed, the United States Lines' SS Leviathan was marketed as "the largest ship in the world" at the time. Photographs in the 1922 booklet "The Story of the Leviathan" attest to sumptuous interiors that would fit the lifestyle Kertész had been accustomed to as a star director in Europe, so he would expect nothing less on the high seas. Her reputation as a luxury liner is well-documented, but in 1926 she was both under-booked and a "dry ship" (alcohol was not permitted on the American-registered vessel during prohibition). [1] Nevertheless, she was a popular choice among those who could afford to lavish in the grand appointments.

The passengers on this particular crossing were treated to a spectacular evening sighting of a giant iceberg, as reported in the New York Times on June 8, 1926. No doubt a lot of talk and quite some stress accompanied the sighting. The Titanic had collided with just such a behemoth only fourteen years earlier in 1912. My own passage many years later was after iceberg season in October, but my stepdad Frank took pictures of some in late June.

On the last morning of the voyage, another wonder greeted the passengers of the SS Leviathan. What a sight it was arriving at New York – passing below the Statue of Liberty, sailing past Ellis Island where up until two years prior, immigrants took their first

steps on American soil. The luxury liner crossed the mouth of the
Hudson River, coasted past the Lower Manhattan skyscrapers –
buildings that were taller than any most of the newcomers had
seen before – and, after anchoring until she was cleared, slipped
into Pier 57 of the Chelsea group of landing docks.

*****

I need to say a word about my grandfather's name at this
point. In the May 1926 Warner Brothers contract that brought him
to Hollywood, he is named MICHAEL KERTESZ. Dropping the
accent is the first change towards his americanized name. After
he arrived in Hollywood in June, he is referred to as "Mr. Michael
(Kertesz) Curtiz" in a letter between the studio's California and
New York offices. His first telegram to my grandmother was signed
Kertes (*sic*.), but soon he asked her to address letters to him as
Michael Curtiz. In practice, he was Mike Curtiz very quickly, but
his legal name remained the Hungarian original without accents –
Mihaly Kertesz. It was only within the Petition for Naturalization
in 1936 – a full ten years after coming to America – that he applied
to have his name changed. The citizenship certificate dated March
12, 1937 is made out in the name of Michael Curtiz.

For my purposes here, I will be using CURTIZ from this
point on.

*****

Curtiz's arrival in America has presented a fair bit of frustra-
tion for me. The only article that seems to deal with this momentous occasion was written a full twenty-six years later, and subsequent mentions of his arrival tend to rely on that source. Whether
it was Curtiz's usual cavalier attitude toward truth or an honest
memory lapse, the connection between his arrival and the Fourth
of July does fit with his image. Here is the myth that Thornton
Delehanty's article created:

> At the approach to the Narrows, Curtiz was pleased to see
> signs of great activity in the surrounding waters, with lit-
> tle boats sagging under the weight of their passengers and
> everybody shouting and waving flags at the people lined up
> on the deck of the steamer.

"This," thought Curtiz, "is a bigger reception than I expected." ...

The boat finally hauled anchor and started up the bay, and
out of his porthole, Curtiz could see excursion boats with
bands playing and bits of bunting flying gaily aloft and
people crowding the rails fit to bust. But no knock [of newspaper reporters] came at the door, and finally Curtiz opened
it ... and went up on deck. As he stood at the rail, watching
them make the gangway fast, a fellow passenger happened
to remark about the inconvenience of arriving on a holiday.

"Holiday?" said Michael, "is this a holiday?"

The other man gave Michael a scornful look. "You wouldn't
know about that," he said. "It only happens to be the Fourth
of July."

"You mean all those bands that were playing, and all those
flags" –

Mike says he didn't finish that speech. The awful truth had
sunk in on him, but he has nothing but kindly feelings toward the Fourth of July today. [2]

Even though the journalist cleverly connects the director's arrival
date with *Yankee Doodle Dandy*, the patriotic film he made in 1942,
it simply can't be true that Curtiz arrived on July 4, 1926. He was
already in Hollywood on June 21.

The letter from the Warner Brothers West Coast offices to
Mr. Schneider in New York referred to earlier is also incorrect.
According to that letter, Curtiz came over on the *SS George
Washington* which arrived in New York June 3. Obviously someone
had made last minute changes in his travel plans.

The closest that anything written about Curtiz's arrival
comes to the truth is a note in the Warner Brothers legal file 2845,
which states that Curtiz "arrived in NY City on <u>Sunday, June 6,
1926</u> on the *Leviathan*, on a 6-month temporary [visa], which he
regularly renewed until March 1930."

I was not satisfied, however, until I could see the actual passenger list for the *Leviathan*'s voyage. That magic moment came
for me when I saw the entry on the screen of a microfiche reader
in the National Archives, New York, in 2008. The ship's Manifest

proves once and for all that the *Leviathan* arrived in New York on
<u>Monday, June 7</u>. Entry Number 27 on page 7 lists "Kertsz, Michael,
age 39, Male, Single, Film Director." His last address was given as
224 Friedrichstrasse, Berlin – the offices of Felner & Somlo. Even
though his last name is spelled wrong, that was definitely my
grandfather!

Online searches had not brought up this manifest, this voyage, because in the process of online archiving, Curtiz's arrival
records were linked to his 1931 naturalization – but that's another
story. When the attendant at the National Archives handed me
photocopies of the passenger list and I left the building on Varick
Street that day, I felt elated and justified in my search.

Ship passenger lists are a mainstay of genealogical research.
Although my goal was primarily to prove the date of my grandfather's arrival in America, there are other interesting details on
this document. An immigrant's name alone can cause problems,
and indeed Curtiz's "Family name" is misspelled KERTSZ. Errors
such as this often occurred because the person arriving gave the
immigration officer the information verbally. I was lucky to have
found this at all! The "Given name" MICHAEL corresponds to the
name he'd been using since arriving in Austria. His Nationality
is given as "Hungary" – his "Race or people" as Magyar – and
yet his name had already been westernized in Europe. If he
was using a Hungarian passport, his name should have read
KERTÉSZ, MANUEL MIHÁLY. There is no mention of a passport
or an Immigration Visa – Curtiz's line is blank on that subject. But
the three columns devoted to "Purpose of coming to the United
States" offer some clues.

Curtiz was entering the United States on the strength of the
contract he had signed with Warner Brothers, so his purpose of
coming was for work. On this Manifest of Alien Passengers, it
is noted that the "Length of time the alien intends to remain in
the United States" is *six months*. "Yes" is the answer to the query
"whether the alien intends to return to the country from whence
he came after engaging temporarily in laboring pursuits in the
United States," and this is further confirmed in a column that
lists *Germany* as the intended "Final destination / intended future
permanent residence." To the question whether or not Curtiz intended to become a citizen of the United States, the answer is "No."

These notations seem incongruous with the terms of Curtiz's
contract with Warner Brothers, which named a commitment of *one*

year at least. Column 19 of the Manifest, headed "Whether going to join a relative or friend, and if so, what relative or friend, and his name and complete address" appears to be a convenient loophole. Curtiz lists Warner Brothers in Hollywood as the "Friend" he is joining! This friend happened to be his employer.

Furthermore, this document was apparently used over the years as a way to keeping tabs on arrivals in the United States. Curtiz's record includes several entries labeled "Temporary admission extended." Some of the dates are illegible, but two are 12/7/29 and 4/1/32; the immigration department file number follows each entry. Interestingly, on this page with its list of thirty names, none of the other passenger records have such entries. For example, both a bishop and a teacher also indicate a six-month "stay" in America. But neither shows temporary admission being extended. Was the loophole used mainly by movie studios to bring new directors from Europe? And whose job was it to update the information over the years?

Some of the more personal questions asked on this Manifest are whether the alien is a polygamist (Curtiz says No), an anarchist (No), whether he or she can read and write (Yes) and in what languages (German and French). Do these questions reflect American ideals of individual rights and freedoms? Well, maybe not as we know them today, but the form does not ask for the person's religion.

******

But back to the docks of New York, June 6, 1926: The mention of flags and banners that were supposedly flying when Curtiz arrived continued to intrigue me. Why would he make up such a story for Thornton Delehanty and his 1942 article? Could June 7th have been another holiday? Flag Day that year was on Monday June 13th, the following week. I could find no sports victory to be celebrated, no civic occasion. What I did find, though, were stories about the *Leviathan*,  the giant ship that had sparked outbursts of ceremonious greetings as far back as its troopship days in 1917. As well, a look at some vintage posters of ocean liners gave me a better idea of the hubbub that often surrounded sailings and arrivals. Perhaps the best portrayal of what Curtiz might have seen is in this whimsical poster created by YesterdayCafe

Not quite bands playing, but the imagination is satisfied.[3] Once he had disembarked, Curtiz would have been lavishly greeted and ushered to the Warner Brothers Executive Offices at 1600 Broadway, perhaps in a limousine. Now that I've been to New York, I know that this address is high up on Broadway, past present-day Lincoln Centre, in the now ritzy neighbourhood west of Central Park.

Curtiz must have been was nervous. Although he'd been practicing his English on the ocean voyage, now was the time he would have to meet "the boss" face-to-face. If he was as studious as I believe he was, Curtiz probably knew some of the studio's history. The four brothers, Harry, Albert, Sam and Jack Warner originally from Poland, had dabbled in the entertainment business since 1903. By 1918, Sam and Jack Warner were producing films at their own studio on Sunset Boulevard in Hollywood while Harry and Albert took care of business from New York City. The company was officially incorporated in 1923.

New York to Hollywood

We know that Curtiz spent about eight days in New York in 1926. The letter to Mr. Schneider explains that Albert Warner apparently "detained" Curtiz there "awaiting the arrival of Mr. H. M. Warner from Chicago, so that they might go over some stories and other matters before he left New York for Hollywood." Besides these usual 'new man on the block' topics, the main item of conversation might have been what to do about his Hungarian name. The accent over the "e" had already been dropped in the written contract, but Kertész was now to become Curtiz. The letter's subject line reads "Re: Mr. Michael (Kertész) Curtiz."

As well, perhaps over lunch at Delmonico's, the men would certainly have discussed the Warner Brothers liaison with Vitaphone for the studio's upcoming feature film *Don Juan* starring John Barrymore. The new technology of the day was recorded music and sound effect tracks that could now be included in the standard silent movies. This would have interested Curtiz very much, as he had always embraced technological advances.

Although work-related subjects probably dominated Curtiz's mind, I'd like to imagine his first impressions of New York and

America in those first days. After the debriefing with the chief Warner men, Curtiz probably went to stay at a hotel near the company's offices, quite possibly the Ambassador on West 45th Street. A few years earlier this hotel had hosted the director Ernst Lubitsch on his way to Hollywood.

Let's imagine that Curtiz checked in around three o'clock in the afternoon, with instructions to rest up and get ready for a proper New York dinner and a night on the town. But he was restless. He unpacked some of his things and sent his best suit to be pressed, his shoes to be polished. Suddenly he was hungry, so he snacked on Hungarian salami that he found at the bottom of one of the suitcases – Ah, Mother! – and some hard bread crusts that he'd squirreled away from the ship's dining room. Old habits are hard to break.

He tried to lie down on the soft bed, but the sounds of traffic drew him to the open windows. He'd of course seen New York in films before, but the real thing struck him as if the city were a living being, the throbbing blood of progress pulsing through its streets. What a set he could create there on that corner ... With visions of his new career dancing in his head, he took a cold shower, shaved meticulously, and slicked back his hair. A knock on the door – ah. He dug in his pocket for a tip, and flipped a half-dollar to the young man who'd brought the pressed suit and shined shoes.

Soon another knock was heard, and a hotel clerk announced that the Warner Brothers car was waiting downstairs. With his charming smile perhaps a bit forced, Curtiz ventured out of his room and into the black sedan. The street scene was still new to him, but he tried not to look confused. He remembered with embarrassment the initial ride from the docks: utter astonishment had made him repeat expletives in Hungarian, totally forgetting himself.

In a few minutes, the car arrived at the Puncheon Club where he was treated to his first American dinner. In 1926, this exclusive private club was on West 49th Street: "It had a big iron gate, a peephole, and the best booze available on the black market." [4] This club would later become the famous Jack & Charlie's 21 Club on West 52nd Street.

Curtiz must have had some wild dreams after his first night on the town. The next few days were a blur of business meetings, lunches, and entertainment. He might have been treated to an Al

Jolson show at the Winter Gardens on Broadway and 48th, had some of his meals at the Lotus Club on 57th, and he might have worked out at the West Side YMCA on 56th. As he was new in town, new in America, he probably didn't venture out on his own as much as he did fourteen years later in 1940, when *New York Times* writer Theodore Strauss called Curtiz's time in the city "The Blitzkrieg of Michael Curtiz."

In that 1940 article, the "five-day excursion" to New York is linked to scouting some then current plays, and it tells of the other things Curtiz was interested in. Going by a list for the first day, he visited midnight emporiums, eavesdropped on police calls from the company car, checked out the markets, and viewed the Cloisters, the George Washington Bridge, the Stock Exchange, and Radio City Music Hall. And that was all before dinner and the evening's entertainment. He visited the 1940 World's Fair twice, went to several movies to watch audience reactions, etc. etc. [5] In 1940, he also visited his daughter Kitty who was living in New York then – but more about that later. In other words, he not only flew around New York, he also arrived and departed by air.

In 1926, however, he left by train. According to my calculations, it was on the afternoon of Tuesday, June 15 that Curtiz took a taxi to Grand Central Station. He stared at the great marbled hall and prepared to board the train. It's not clear but quite possible that Curtiz was accompanied by one of the studio executives on his overland journey. The trip was undertaken quite regularly between the financial and business offices in New York, headed by Harry Warner, and the studio in Hollywood, run by his brother Jack.

Just as some of my descriptions of Curtiz's first few days in New York is guesswork, so too is his trip across America. Comparing his experience with other directors who were brought over to America is useful. In 1922, Ernst Lubitsch arrived in much the same way: the Atlantic crossing, a time in New York, where he stayed at the Ambassador Hotel at 132 Ave. West & 45th Street, before "leaving for Hollywood on the Santa Fe Limited." [6] Lubitsch traveled with is own German assistant, and they "were met off the train at the old Santa Fé Railroad Depot in Los Angeles" by United Artists staff. Also in 1922, Willy Wyler was planning to take his career aspirations to Hollywood, and he persuaded his "Uncle" Carl Laemmle to give him work at Universal Studios. Laemmle loaned Wyler $160 for his train fare across the country, but this was not enough to "cover the cost on any of the first-class trains" such as the *Chief* nor, indeed, a sleeping berth. It took Wyler four days and five nights "sitting up" on less expensive alternative trains: the Western Express from New York to Chicago, and the *Scout* of the Atcheson, Topeka and Santa Fe line.[7]

In whatever way it was undertaken, the railway trip to Los Angeles was complicated. First one had to travel to Chicago, the rail head for the overland trains that crossed America on two main lines. The most direct and therefore the most likely route that Curtiz took in 1926 would have gone something like this.

The New York Central Railroad's express passenger train, the *20th Century Limited*, left Grand Central Station in New York at 6 p.m. Once it emerged from the station tunnels, the train traveled north along the Hudson River. Curtiz kept his eyes on the passing landscape as the light began to fade. The specially built locomotive speeded the train along at an average of 60 miles per hour. By the time the train crossed the bridge over the Hudson at Albany and turned west, the sun was dipping toward the horizon – sunset is around 9:00 p.m. at these latitudes during the longest days of the year.

The train carried on to Buffalo, New York, then along the south shore of Lake Erie. Except for the last leg of this route, the railroad follows water: thus the name Water Level Route. A major competitor, the Pennsylvania Railroad, traveled through the much more difficult terrain of the Appalachian Mountains, slowing down the trains considerably. Lake Erie would have shone brightly if it was a clear night and there was a moon, and maybe Curtiz got a few winks of sleep as the train sped along, made a quick stop at Toledo, Ohio, and then headed across Michigan toward the south end of Lake Michigan.

Sunrise comes early in June – around 6 a.m. – and Curtiz was one of the first in the dining car for breakfast. Soon, the train slowed as it neared Chicago's southern suburbs. He had studied the connection information, had rehearsed his English in case he had to ask for directions while in the Windy City for the day. Happily, the train for the West Coast arrived and left from the same station, LaSalle Street Station. His through ticket indicated a 9:00 a.m. arrival, with the next overland train departing at 6:30 p.m. He glanced at his watch and looked out the window to spot Chicago's famous skyscrapers shining in the morning sun. He had a short day to explore the city.

The train pulls into LaSalle in a straight line heading north, and the tracks end abruptly in the arrival hall. On a hot and humid June day a couple of years ago, I wandered through what was LaSalle and is now a METRA station for Chicago's busy commuter traffic. The unassuming façade of the ticketing area and small waiting hall that connects to the ultra-modern Financial Place complex belies the history of the site. However, one design feature, the huge semicircular windows, hearken back to the typical train station arrival hall of the early twentieth century. Through those windows, I spied the imposing copper roof of the Chicago Public Library two blocks east, with one of the wise old owls nodding gently towards me. They weren't there in 1926 when Curtiz came through, but I'd like to think that symbolically, the welcoming committee was watching.

I'd also like to imagine that someone associated with Warner Brothers – I'll call him Tom – was there to greet Curtiz at the station, to make sure his luggage was stored safely for transfer to the *California Limited*, to identify the platform for his departure, and to show him a good time in Chicago. Tom had a car waiting, but Curtiz insisted that he wanted to ride the "El" – the famous Chicago Elevated Metro, particularly around its new Central Loop.

"Ok," said Tom, "I'll have our driver meet us back here in a half hour."

They climbed the steps to the El at La Salle Street Station, and caught the first train to come along. Curtiz stared, gesticulated, and nodded as Tom pointed out the landmark buildings that could be seen from the elevated train. In a few moments, the train rounded the first curve, onto Wabash, and Curtiz could see out towards Lake Michigan through the streets. At Adams he caught a glimpse of the imposing façade of the Art Institute and asked, "Can we go there?" Tom looked at his watch. "Maybe an hour, after lunch" was his reply. At Clark Street Station they changed trains to ensure they wouldn't end up in the northern suburbs. Curtiz spotted the Chicago River and craned his neck to see the Wrigley Building complex and the Tribune Tower. Tom assured him that he'd get a closer look at those architectural marvels.

On the eastern track of the Loop, Curtiz saw the Post Office looming across the South Branch of the river, and his eyes lit up. "Great location for shooting," he mumbled without anticipating *Batman* and *The Dark Knight*. As they rounded the curve back to LaSalle Station, his director's eye took in the railway station building, and he was lost in thought again. He couldn't anticipate Alfred Hitchcock's 1959 classic *North by Northwest* or the 1973 movie *The Sting,* both of which used the station as a filming location.

Curtiz and Tom left the El and walked toward the waiting car. They drove out toward the lake, took a turn through Grant Park, and returned to cruise north along Michigan Avenue. The Magnificent Mile offered spectacle after spectacle, but when Curtiz spotted a Hungarian restaurant, that became the spot for lunch. It was a hot and humid afternoon, and thunderheads threatened from the west. The remaining time went quickly, and soon they had to return to the station. Curtiz expressed his thanks with a firm handshake, and boarded the *California Limited.* It was Wednesday, June 16.

******

The competition among railway companies was fierce in the days before motor car and air travel became the standard. There was a northern route across the Mid-West, over the Rocky Mountains west of Reno, Nevada, then down to San Francisco. This line was operated by Union Pacific. The more efficient southern route, operated by the Atchison, Topeka and Santa Fe Railway, was covered in record time by what was billed as the "finest train west of Chicago," the *California Limited.* This Grand Canyon Route dipped south-west from Chicago, through Kansas City, and continued on to La Junta in south-east Colorado. It crossed the lower mountain grades into California and then steamed through San Bernardino into Los Angeles.

The *California Limited* was a true "workhorse" of transcontinental rail travel, covered its 2,000 mile journey in three days (Thursday, Friday, Saturday) and offered all the amenities of first-class train travel. Curtiz was probably quite comfortable until the sheer measure of the journey hit home. Even though he had crisscrossed Europe numerous times, the distances in the New World cannot be compared.

With the schedule of the *California Limited* open on his breakfast table the next morning, Curtiz looked out onto the pleasant Kansas landscape. Then, hour after hour, the train steamed across the Mid-West, mostly flat country. It gives one a feeling of emptiness. And yet, he may also had a feeling of *déjà vu*: after nodding off for a while, he might have looked out at the flat, wide open fields and think he was back in the steppes of Hungary.

Another whole day and night passed, and with increasing anticipation, he shielded his eyes against the blazing Texas sun as the train passed through El Paso. The emptiness of the Arizona desert and the heat caused some discomfort, but by then he was too travel-weary to care. Finally, as the train crossed the last of the mountains and dipped toward Los Angeles, Curtiz, like many European directors and actors before him, was rewarded by the pleasant breeze coming off the Pacific Ocean.

In 1926, the main passenger terminal of the Santa Fe Line in Los Angeles was La Grande Station on Santa Fe Avenue at 2nd Street, on the west bank of the Los Angeles River. The Moorish-inspired architecture of the station, unique to Southern California, had piqued the interest of arriving passengers for over twenty years. Until it was damaged by an earthquake in 1933, the station was also used as a location for several films. Curtiz just stared as he stepped off the train there on Sunday, June 20.

As he gathered his belongings, he checked his wallet. The strange green money was all in a jumble, but he found some one-dollar bills to tip the steward who had looked after him on the train. The fare for the three-day train journey, according to the Warner Brothers letter of June 24, 1926 cost $152.00, and Curtiz had also received a cash advance of $250.00. The letter makes quite a song and dance about the details of Curtiz's travel expenses; the Warner Brothers were well-known for being sticklers about money. From the day Curtiz had signed the contract in Berlin, every dollar had to be accounted for, and conflicts over money were to become a common theme.

Curtiz spent the rest of his first day in Los Angeles settling into a small apartment that the studio had arranged for him. Someone from the studio showed him around a bit and took him out to dinner. They made it an early night, and on Monday morning, June 21, 1926, the newest Warner Brothers director took a trolley bus to the studios at 5842 Sunset Boulevard. [8]

Warner Brothers Studio

What kind of workplace did Curtiz walk into? By 1926, several studios had risen to the top of the American movie-making industry. Warner Brothers Inc. was a major business enterprise that not only made films but also showed them in its own chain of theatres and distributed them all over America and the world. Who were these Warner Brothers? And how did their background, their ideology and their management methods affect this new director from Europe?

Much information exists in books and on the Internet about the Warner Brothers, not all of it reliable. Harry, Jack, Albert and Sam Warner were four sons of Benjamin, a cobbler by trade, who changed his family name Wonskolaser to Warner when he arrived in America from Poland in the 1880s. He settled with his wife Pearl and their first children in Baltimore, Maryland. They were Jewish – most likely liberal – but spoke Yiddish in the home, and passed their culture's values onto their children

Hirsch (Harry) Warner was the eldest son, born 1881 in Poland. Abraham (Albert) and Samuel (Sam) were born already in America 1884 and 1887 respectively. The youngest brother, Jacob (Jack) was born in 1892 while the family lived in Montreal, Canada. According to one source, in all there were twelve children but only nine of them survived. [9]

Although Harry would eventually head the business end of Warner Brothers Studio, it was his sixteen year old brother Sam who planted the seed. That was in 1903 while the family was living in Youngstown, Ohio. Benjamin Warner and his son Harry were running a shoe repair business. Sam was more interested in scouting out the newest moving pictures. He was fascinated by the machinery that made this new form of entertainment possible. When he heard about a film for sale, it was the projector that came with the deal that interested Sam. He talked Harry and nineteen year old Albert into helping him to make the purchase, and the brothers Warner set off in a direction from which they never looked back.

Their first venture was to charge people admission to see the film *The Great Train Robbery* in a tent in their yard. Albert sold tickets and Sam ran the projector, and the profits were immediate. Over the next few years, they learned of ways to improve their business profits. They found more and better venues and offered their audiences an increasing number of films. From 1907 to 1910 the brothers also ran the Duquesne Film Exchange in Pittsburgh, Pennsylvania, purchasing films and renting them to other exhibitors. From exhibiting and distributing films, the next obvious step was to try and make their own movies.

As the American moving picture industry took shape, many others besides the four Warner brothers had gone through a similar process. Movie theatres sprang up in every town and city across the country, but the business of making and distributing films ultimately gravitated toward the East and the West Coast. As early as 1907, California came into the picture when William Selig shot a film in Santa Monica. By 1909, he had established a studio there, and in 1910, the Nestor Film Company became the first film studio located in the area north of Los Angeles known as Hollywood.

The Warner Brothers film business had a few years of ups and downs. Their first effort at making their own film, the western *Peril of the Plains*, shot in St. Louis, was not a success. When they "went broke" after trying to make films in an "early studio at Santa Paula," they decided to re-enter distribution. By 1916, Harry and Albert had set up business in New York while Sam and Jack were sent to California, Sam in San Francisco and Jack in Hollywood. [10]

Adolph Zuckor – the head of Universal – is generally credited as being the "force behind the studio system by integrating production, distribution and exhibition of films in the same hands – his." [11] What had been a trend became reality. According to Gabler, production had gradually shifted to Hollywood, and by 1918, it was well established as film capital: over 80 % of the world's movies were made there. Southern California was the ideal location for several reasons. The weather allowed outdoor filming year-round, the West Coast was not hampered by business practices in the East, and land was cheap and plentiful.

The Warner Brothers went back to producing films. Their success in 1917 with the war-time propaganda documentary My *Four Years in Germany* allowed them to purchase land and build their first studio. They hired Hal Wallis, a young publicity man to be producer, along with his sister Minna, to be a secretary. And in 1921, they got a lucky break in meeting Motley Flint, a banker who believed in them. The director of the Security Bank of Los Angeles, Flint began to make a series of loans to the Warners which assisted in their expansion over the next few years. [12]

Office space and production stages were added. In February 1923, a large library was announced, and in March, "a new interior stage was completed, with dressing rooms and scenery storage rooms alongside it." [13] A total of 64,000 square feet of space became available – six sets could be worked on at the same time. A new electrical plant provided the power. On April 4, 1923, Warner Brothers Inc. was officially established.

In those early years, the budding studio had tried its hand at documentary, comedy and dramas with which they were developing an ideology that reached back to their own family roots and experience. Their films

> not only reflected the brothers' parvenu background and suspicion of those who inherited wealth, they appealed strongly to the vast masses of the underprivileged at the outset of the 1920s, and had a strong, somewhat risqué contemporary flavor [14]

Much of the impetus for this ideology came from the patriarch of the family. Benjamin Warner's vision of great potential in America, combined with a strong Jewish faith, provided the ideals of racial and religious tolerance evident in many of the studio's early films. Benjamin's advice to his son Harry was straight-forward:

> Son, you're going to have to fight with the weapons you have at your command so that the children and their children may have a right to live and have a Faith, no matter what their Faith may be, in our great country, America. [15]

This strong ideology would eventually cause deep rifts among the brothers. But it also created a distinct position in American film compared to other emerging studios. Of the big three which included MGM and Universal, Warner Brothers films would be known for supporting the underdog and dealing openly with sensitive social and political issues.

Warner Brothers also took a lead in the technical advancements in the film industry. Sam had always been interested in the practical aspects of creating movies, and in the mid 1920's he was the one to push for the newest innovation – sound in film. In June 1925, the company announced its intent to make a series of sound films. [16] And the first story they would use was a play called *The Jazz Singer*, which opened on Broadway in September that year, just as Harry Warner and Motley Flint were scouting for their European director. The play ran for 303 performances, and on the last day, June 4, 1926 – two days before Curtiz arrived in New York – Warner Brothers bought the movie rights.

Jack (J.L.) Warner was a boy of eleven when Harry, Albert and Sam exhibited *The Great Train Robbery* in their Youngstown back yard tent in 1903. The youngest of the brothers turned out to be most suited for the entertainment industry, however, and twenty-three years later, he was head of the Hollywood studio into which Curtiz walked that Monday morning.

Curtiz had met and had serious business meetings with the older Harry Warner in New York. And it had been Harry, along with Motley Flint, who had first approached Curtiz in Paris where he was steeped in the European traditions of film production. Jack ran a totally different ship in Hollywood. Thus, it would be a challenge for Curtiz to re-establish himself professionally – and personally – in this new country, in this studio.

First Summer in Hollywood

Anyone who has lived in Central Europe can never forget the temperate climate, the gentle air comfortably humid, maybe a mild breeze, and a temperature span in which humans can manage quite well. Of course there are extremes and exceptions. In winter, that same humidity can make the freezing point feel like 20 below. But nowadays, winter in Europe also means skiing in the mountains or heading south to the beaches of Mallorca.

In 1926 things were different. Winter getaways were reserved for the well-to-do and in summer (before the age of air conditioning) inhabitants of large cities like Budapest and Vienna would try to escape the oppressive heat in July and August by seeking a vacation spot in the countryside. Those who could afford it may have had a *Schrebergarten*, a garden plot at the edge of the city reachable by public transit, of course. Other possibilities in Europe were and still are the summertime *Pension* at an inn or private residence in a small town.

Both my grandmothers had their favourite spots where they would typically stay for a month. Whole families would descend on these vacation spots; an older child or a working family member would stay in the city to look after the apartment. It's quite probable that the Kaminer/Kertész family had some similar arrangement for dealing with the summertime climate in Budapest, which is very similar to that of Vienna.

When Curtiz arrived in Hollywood it was late June, the beginning of the hot and dry summer. I can imagine him stepping down from the air-conditioned train. Perhaps a Warner Brothers Studio representative stood on the platform with a sign in bold letters – CURTIZ. In the confusion of the moment, he forgot to take off his big black overcoat. Even if the car that took him to his apartment had air conditioning, he might have felt quite uncomfortable.

Arriving in Hollywood in the heat of a California summer was not the only shock to greet Curtiz. He had already been practicing his English, but now he was faced with this new language on a daily basis. At the age of thirty-nine, it's difficult. The patterns of one's first language are most pervasive in speech. That's why adult immigrants rarely lose their accent.

Although there are only a few clips of Curtiz's voice available, the errors he made in phrasing his English are notorious. His written German and his published written English (edited?) were both better than his spoken English. His so-called mistakes using English came to be called Curtizisms. The jury is still out, however, on whether or not he – and other immigrant directors like him – didn't actually use faulty phrasing on purpose, to get a reaction from the people around him.

In reality he always felt inadequate about his English. As late as 1940, he still made glaring errors whenever he wrote a letter by hand, as in this one to his daughter Kitty.

> I hope you can read my letter. I'm terible in English. I shuld
> go to a private school between picturs. But I supose I need
> little rest and have no ambition to go in school – But I shuld.[17]

When Kitty was ready to come to America in 1928 at age thirteen, he had written to her in German, which was – then – much better than his English would ever be. He told her it would be "very necessary" to have good English skills on the long voyage. On the ship it isn't so difficult, he tells her, especially on a German ship. But she would "sit 5 days on the train from New York to Los Angeles" where only English was spoken.

Over the years he repeats the same advice to Fränzi, and in a letter to my father when he was just a boy, Curtiz writes, "I want you to keep on studying English because I have in mind to bring you over here." [18] Michael Vondrak did, in fact, take private lessons for English in Vienna during his teens.

Both Kitty and my father came to America when they had actually had an opportunity to learn some English before they arrived. When I came to Canada at age nine, I'd had no formal instruction. My mother could speak only a smidgeon of the new language, and she had recited some common sayings: "Early to bed and early to rise makes a man healthy, wealthy and wise." Or she'd sing the song of Little Robin Redbreast. In 1957 there was no ESL (English as a Second Language) program in my first Canadian school, so I had to get along as best I could. I was lucky to have a boy in my Grade Three class who could speak German. I was told to sit beside him.

But there are other ways to augment formal learning. One of the most vivid memories of my first years in Canada is listening to the radio. The Marconi that we brought from Austria was beautiful, with a polished wood exterior and gold-colored fabric covering the speakers on each side of the dials. My stepdad hooked it up to a large battery because we had no electricity on the farm. I'd stand near the set with a scribbler, pencil poised, waiting for the hit songs, and I'd start writing down the lyrics of songs by Jimmy Rogers, Ricky Nelson, Johnny Cash. Even the titles intrigued me: "Honeycomb," "Kisses Sweeter than Wine," "Don't Take Your Guns to Town." I could easily follow the ballads, and after hearing the songs over and over again, the lines and verses took shape in my scribbler.

If Curtiz were listening like that in 1926, he might have heard the Paul Whiteman orchestra accompanying vocalist Franklin Bauer singing "Valencia, A Song of Spain"

> Valencia, in my dreams it always seems I hear you softly call to me,
> Valencia, where the orange trees forever scent the breeze beside the sea...

That song went on to feature in the Broadway production "The Great Temptation." Closely related to the film work he was about to embark upon, Curtiz would have heard Al Jolson sing "When the Red-Red Robin Comes Bob-Bob-Bobbing Along," another hit of 1926. Who doesn't know the lyrics to "Bye Bye Blackbird"? Many songs of enduring popularity made their debut in 1926. One of my favorites is "Tonight You Belong To Me." The old recordings they play on CKUA's "Play it Again" program sound tinny compared to later versions, but the words endure.

My grandfather, having been athletic from an early age, was probably more interested in sports, however. With the opening of the "Grand Olympic Auditorium" in August 1925, boxing became one of the most popular sporting events in the Los Angeles area. On any Tuesday night, many members of the Hollywood crowd attended matches in the huge venue. On Friday nights, one could also watch prizefighting at the Hollywood (American) Legion Stadium. John Meredyth Lucas remembers going there as a young

lad with his new stepfather. [19] Partaking in the fights would have
been a way for Curtiz to immerse himself in American language
and culture.

Immigrants often try to assimilate, but they also tend to find
their homeland community again. For those who came on their
own, like my stepdad Frank, the search for community begins
on the ship where stories and plans are traded. I have a picture
of my stepdad with some new possible comrades, but I can only
imagine what they spoke about. "Where are you headed?" they
would ask each other in the universal language of these migrants.
And in broken English, my stepdad would have answered, "I go
to Winnipeg. I hear work is there to have." For my stepdad it was
not Winnipeg, but Edmonton, where he finally found his German-
speaking community. There are many German-speaking people in
Northern Alberta, its members hailing from all the various parts
of Germany, Austria and elsewhere, each with their own cultural
background and dialect. Through his work in house construction,
Frank made friends with people from Northern Germany. Soon
they started talking about his fondest dream, owning land. That
is how he got to know Carsten and Liselotte Jensen, who were already farming north-west of Edmonton. With Carsten's help, my
stepdad found the farm we lived on near Perryvale. The Jensens
had four children, and their oldest daughter Ursula became my
best friend. Whenever we got together with the Jensens in the
years to come, we spoke German, ate German foods, listened to
German music, and watched videos of German movies.

Curtiz's early experience in Hollywood was probably less
casual. He had arrived under contract to Warner Brothers. He had
a specific destination and a job to do when he got there. However,
the opportunity to meet other Hungarians also came through his
work. Some, like Alfred Zukor who had begun at Famous Players
in 1912 and William Fox who had started Fox Film Corporation
in 1915, were solidly established. George Cukor was a director at
RKO and MGM. Curtiz's old friend Alexander Korda was based in
England at the time, but later also came to America to direct for
United Artists. The actors Bela Lugosi and Peter Lorre were also
in Hollywood.

Some Hungarians would have been accustomed to dining at
Babin's Kosher Restaurant on South Spring Street where, earlier
in the 1920s, the menu featured authentic Hungarian cuisine. In
Southern California, there was no Little Hungary as in New York,

but the more than seventeen hundred Hungarians did manage to create their own community. [20] Curtiz's first Hungarian meal after dealing with English/American foods on the passage over must have been a real treat. When my mother and I finally reached Edmonton, my stepdad had made Vienna Schnitzel and potato salad in celebration of our arrival – it felt like home.

Even if Curtiz had to get his Hungarian goulash and dumplings at a restaurant, he would have been happy. And he could finally speak Hungarian again! As time went by he was probably invited to some of their homes as well. A few years later, Curtiz would be able to return the favor: he brought over a Hungarian cook and had his breakfast room decorated in the Hungarian style. He served Hungarian food at parties for his compatriots, business acquaintances and friends.

And isn't that what most of us do? My mother's friends still have their houses decorated with German mementos, dishes, ornaments. And when they go back to Europe, immigrants always bring more from the old country back to America to make it feel more like home.

Curtiz Re-establishes Himself Professionally

Stuart Jerome, a Hollywood screenwriter who worked for a number of years in the Mail Department at Warner Brothers Studio, gives an unabashed account of the attitude toward the European imported talent.

> We lumped all foreigners together under the generic term "f...ing Hungarians," although factually only Curtiz bore that ancestry. If we seemed radically prejudiced, we did have good cause. Early on, we were made aware of their directorial harshness. Perhaps it stemmed from their European beginnings, where in the early days Herr Director was all-important. Despite the fact that in our factory they had only a limited amount of leeway as far as script changes, casting and cutting were concerned, they did exert a total authority over everybody on their sets, much in the manner of Feudal lords despotically ruling over their little fiefdoms. [21]

Curtiz had learned his autocratic manner in Europe, where it was expected. He was not prepared with the way producers took control of his work. The studio system had taken hold in Hollywood and there was less and less free-wheeling and dealing among the producers, actors, writers and directors.

When they met in Europe, Curtiz and Harry Warner had discussed plans for filming another epic like the one he had directed for Sascha Films in Austria. As in *Sodom and Gomorrah,* Curtiz would use a biblical story to present a metaphoric tale punishment for the sins of mankind – a parallel from antiquity in modern times. Now, in Hollywood, he was told that *Noah's Ark* – with the great flood once again used rightly or wrongly as the Biblical example of God's wrath – would not be his first American film.

To add to his discomfort, his business and personal obligations in Europe haunted him. His contractual obligations in Germany were in the hands of Warner Brothers' lawyers. Although he probably kept in touch with his family in Budapest, he wrote no letters to my grandmother until February 1927, Theresia Dalla Bonna received no support at all until at least 1928, and Thilde Foster was supporting Curtiz's son on her own.

He was also worried to be in America only on a six-month visa. The industry itself was under scrutiny regarding imported workers, as is evident from this excerpt of a letter written July 26, 1926 to Mr. Jack Warner by Will Hays, the then President of the Motion Picture Producers & Distributors of America, Inc.

> During the past few weeks there have been so many requests for extension of stays in this country that Mr. Husband, the Second Assistant Secretary of labor in Charge of Immigration cases, approached us for a discussion of the situation and to make it clear the attitude of the Department in the matter.
>
> It appears that a great many people, especially Germans, have come to this country on a visitor's passport for six months. After they are in the country for a few months, they secure positions with motion picture companies, and then make application for extension of stays in this country. During the past ten days we have had eight of these cases.
>
> The Department takes the attitude that our companies have a perfect right to go abroad and make contracts with foreign stars and directors. When these stars or directors come to this country, they should state on their arrival that they are coming to fulfill a motion picture contract. The Government

will then be glad to give them the necessary extensions when their time is up on their original entry....

If an extension is needed, they then must make an application on the proper forms and file it at the port of entry not less than fifteen days nor more than thirty days before the expiration of their stay. [22]

Having signed the contract with Warner Brothers before entering the United States helped Curtiz to some extent. According to a letter signed P.A. Case, US Immigration and addressed to R.L. Schrock at Warner Brothers, the original visa for Michael "Kertész" was valid from June 6 to December 6, 1926. After the proper exchange of letters and forms, the visa was extended for one year to December 7, 1927. [23]

But Curtiz was not satisfied with extensions. In August 1927, well before the visa deadline, he wrote to Harry Warner that "this ever expiring permit business causes me constant worry." Curtiz is asking for his boss's intervention to speed up the citizenship process; nevertheless, the extensions continued until 1931, when, on his return from a trip to Europe, he declared his intention to obtain American citizenship.

*****

Of course the studio was eager to have Curtiz earn his contract salary, so while *Noah's Ark* would have to wait, Jack Warner did keep him busy. He assigned Curtiz to direct *The Third Degree*, a melodrama that involves questionable police interrogation practices. Not knowing anything about these American institutions, Curtiz immersed himself, even spending a weekend as a "guest" of Los Angeles sheriff Eugene Biscailuz, in jail. [24] Such earnest research became a well-documented aspect of my grandfather's work habits.

Despite the difficulty of the material he was working with, Curtiz was used to taking risks. James Robertson in *The Casablanca Man* suggests that the circus shots in this film (the leading lady was a circus performer) "include two of the most exciting moments in silent film history – a motorcycle accident during a Wall of Death act and a 40-ft human dive into a tiny pool of water filmed from a camera at the transparent pool bottom." [25] It's interesting to speculate if his adept portrayal of that circus performance was indeed rooted in Curtiz's personal experience as a young man, and we will see later that his interest in circus also reaches also into his creative side and may have a role in a romantic relationship.

While audience and critical reaction to the film was mixed, Jack Warner recognized Curtiz's ability. Not only was he fully accepted at Warner Brothers, his salary was increased and he was given three more films to direct in 1927. They were shorter, low-budget films, and as expected, *A Million Bid, The Desired Woman* and *Good Time Charley* were not box office hits, but Curtiz gave them his best effort. He was, after all, working in a new environment, with a new language, for a new audience. In a letter he wrote to my grandmother, he reflected on this time of transition:

> I strove and worked very hard but for 1½ years it just didn't succeed – But now that I can speak English well, and have gotten used to the American mentality, things are going better and I have good success with my last film. [26]

As Robertson points out, Curtiz also needed this time to become familiar with the way things were done at Warner Brothers, get to know the people he would work with, and test the limits of his own influence with the studio bosses. [27]

Thus, just short of two years after arriving in America, the forty-one year old Curtiz was still a somewhat nervous immigrant and employee. He was still living in a small apartment, still taking the trolley bus to work, still wearing his black trench coat. [28] But the warm California sun helped to put a large grin on his face. He could begin to believe the words, "I've made it!"

Toward Hollywood Success and Bess Meredyth

Although Curtiz brought with him the status he had gained in Europe's motion picture industry, it was Bess Meredyth who introduced him to Hollywood film society. She may not have been able to change him into a true California American, but she did get rid of his overcoat. It has been mainly through the memoirs of John Meredyth-Lucas (1919 – 2002), Bess's son from her first marriage to Wilfred Lucas, that I've been able to capture some aspects of my grandfather's private life in America. Once Bess became part of Curtiz's life, his days as an isolated new immigrant were over.

Most immigrants come to their new homeland with their own familiar clothes on their backs, and so it was with Curtiz. Even thirty years later, my stepdad Frank wore his long Lederhosen for the voyage (*Knickerbocker* come to below the knee). In Austria, these pants were not only fashionable, but they were also very practical. The leather is nearly indestructible; it keeps out the wind and protects against heat and cold. But in a couple of years, that vestige of Frank's Austrian life had disappeared under direct or indirect pressure. My own garb as a child was less disturbing to my new acquaintances, except perhaps for my woolen stockings – a necessity in humid-cold Vienna winters. My mother, a seam-stress, made most of my clothes and it took me some years before I became ashamed of them. She also made many of her own clothes. One of her favourites was a light-brown tweed skirt and suit jacket which I will never forget, especially when she wore it, along with rubber boots, to milk our first cow on the farm.

Curtiz in 1926 no doubt had a much more sophisticated wardrobe: tailored suits in the English style, shirts made of Mako-silk (Egyptian Mako cotton so fine it feels like silk), fashionable pullover vests, and a grey city-hat with a white band. [29] He might have brought several outfits in the current sport-style, including a knicker-suit with its "plus-four" knickers that fell four inches below the knee. One item of clothing that was a must in Europe's rainy winters and which would have served him well on the decks of the ocean liner – even in late spring, was his black ankle-length overcoat. He might have bought it in London, since English clothes were all the rage in Europe in 1926.

Like my stepdad's Lederhosen, Curtiz's overcoat was all-around practical, keeping him warm and dry; he may even have thought it could insulate against the heat. Regardless, it had to go. John Meredyth Lucas remembers that his mother always tried to hide the coat before going out with him and if that didn't work, she had the chauffeur turn on the heat in the limousine. "The coat eventually vanished," he writes. [30] Curtiz adopted the light-colored and lighter-weight American-silhouette suit in the college style, clothing typical in 1920's California.

By the time Bess was influencing Curtiz's wardrobe choices, they'd met again and rekindled an attraction they felt in 1925 when she was in Italy assisting MGM Studio with the script for *Ben Hur: A Tale of Christ* and he was scouting around Europe for work. Now that he was in Hollywood, Bess also became involved with Curtiz's work. She wrote the titles or "scenarios" for his first American film *The Third Degree* (1926) and she worked on the script for *Noah's Ark* in 1927. They married in December, 1929. In the already-mentioned 1931 article for Hungarian film magazine Mohezit she is quoted:

"I wrote his first American films. We became good friends." And she flatters the reporter by graciously adding, "I am very, very happy that I listened to [my husband] and followed him to Europe. Budapest is so different and beautiful... ." [31]

****

She was born Helen Elizabeth MacGlashan in Buffalo, New York, on February 12, 1890. On her father's side, the background was Scotch Presbyterian, but her mother descended from French and German roots. Bess's parents were rebels. The father Andrew (Andy) Fuller MacGlashan of Buffalo, New York, rebelled against his minister father by becoming and remaining a tradesman. The mother Julia Ginther rebelled against her family's Roman Catholic religion in marrying Andy.

The young couple first had a son William Frederick MacGlashan in 1876, and a daughter Viola MacGlashan in 1878. Helen Elizabeth (Bess) came along a full twelve years later in 1890. Growing up more or less alone, Bess was introduced to the world of entertainment at an early age. She spent a lot of time at the local vaudeville where her father was manager. Through her sister Viola's interest in music (she was a member of the Agnes Woodward Whistling Chorus) and by way of her brother's connections to higher society through marriage, Bess received formal musical training and almost embarked on a career as a concert pianist. But she also had a passion for the literary arts. With the encouragement of a teacher, Bess wrote and eventually published her first stories in a Buffalo newspaper for $1.00 per story.

As a teenager, Bess was also somewhat rebellious. She liked being part of the football crowd, and secretly married a young boy without her parents' permission. The union was promptly annulled. Playing the piano for silent movies in the local theatres was her ticket to New York and showbusiness. She did some stage work and touring, but finally got into film as that industry took hold. Barely into her twenties, Bess signed with Biograph Company to play as an extra in D.W. Griffith films and a stock player for the studio on the East Coast.

Her first credit as a writer came in 1910 when Biograph made her story "The Southerner" into the short film *The Modern Prodigal* also directed by Griffith. A remake in 1931 by MGM simplified the title to *The Prodigal*. There are two stories about how Bess came to live in California around 1913: one is that she deserted the piano concert tour on which she was active, and the other is that she sought the mild climate due to suspected tuberculosis. [32]

At twenty-four, Bess met her first husband, actor Wilfred Lucas, on the set of *The Desert Sting*. Wilfred, fifteen years her senior, was a Canadian of Empire Loyalist background, originally from New York. He had been a professional theatre actor before breaking into film, and he already had two sons from a previous marriage. In Philadelphia three years later, Wilfred and Bess were married, and in 1919 they had a son, John Meredyth Lucas. Before their boy was a year old, Bess and Wilfred traveled to and worked in Australia for several years before returning to Hollywood.

That return was, however, the beginning of problems for the couple. As Wilfred's star began sinking, Bess's only climbed higher. Bess had already written some one hundred and forty scenarios for silent film. She was among a number of successful women screenwriters such as Frances Marion, June Mathis, Anita Loos and Carey Wilson, and she became friends with Louella Parsons, Louise Ettinger and other powerful women of the Hollywood in-crowd. According to Cari Beauchamp, "almost one quarter of the screenwriters in Hollywood were women. Half of all the films copyrighted between 1911 and 1925 were written by women." [33]

The article "Beginning a Scenario" written by Bess herself is about the art and craft of screen writing, how it evolved from a time when scenarists strayed as much as possible from an original story, to an attitude of trying to stay true to the source material. Bess also explains the concept of "continuity writing," the mapping out of sequences to hold together the action, sequences that are then "split up" into scenes for filming. [34]

In 1925, after Bess came back from working for MGM on *Ben Hur* in Italy and her marriage to Wilfred Lucas was over, she branched out professionally. Under a separate contract with Warner Brothers, she wrote scenarios for John Barrymore's hits *Don Juan*, *The Sea Beast* and *When a Man Loves*, and many of the last silent films produced at the studio. In his memoirs, her son suggests that it was during this time – after her divorce from Wilfred Lucas – that his mother met "this new director" from Europe, Michael Curtiz. [35]

According to her son, at first "it was not an exclusive attachment." [36] But it's likely that, besides working on his scripts, Bess also helped Curtiz with conversational English. Their budding relationship came at an exciting time in the film industry.

Sound was in and Silent would soon be out. While the technology was still being developed, Curtiz directed *Tenderloin*, one of three films Warner Brothers produced in part-silent, part-talkie format. Despite some rough spots, the film made a good profit for the studio and bolstered Curtiz's status among the directors.

The Film he Came to Make

Finally came *Noah's Ark*. Although it had been on the back burner, the project was revived in 1927 with Daryl Zanuck supervising the million-dollar film. It would be in "preparation and making for more than eighteen-months." [37] Bess Meredyth was involved as well; she had been put to work on the script early in the film's production, and she was seeing Curtiz privately on a regular basis. In Bess, Curtiz had found a natural companion professionally. They were both committed to their work, and as she explained to Edmond E. Behr of the *L.A. Examiner*, the scenarist's role is closely tied to the work of directing a film:

> A scenarist must describe every action of every character, no matter how unimportant, in every foot of film from start to finish of a picture. ... Of course, the director may change, omit or add, as he sees fit, but the entire framework is there for him to work on when he gets the completed script.

Much has been written about the elaborate production of this film, but the mystery surrounding the story line was succinctly explained by Curtiz himself. Like his Austrian hit *Sodom and Gomorrah*, this film parallels modern sequences with Biblical teachings, says Curtiz:

> Human nature of 1928 is animated by the same passionate motives and desires which are exemplified in sacred writ.... For instance, I have no neighbors who own oxen. I would not be covetous of them in any present-day circumstances. But motor cars, ah, that's different. [38]

Noah's Ark is mainly a silent film, but in a few scenes the dialogue was recorded. The sound sequences are surprisingly effective, although John Meredyth Lucas recalls that "Mike fought a running btattle with [sound] mixers." [39] Jerome Strauss of the Los Angeles Examiner asked Curtiz about the "art and business of the motion picture." Curtiz replied modestly, "I am afraid I know nothing about business," but he readily shared his theory about "the art" of motion pictures:

> I consider them a blending of five [arts] – music, painting, literature, architecture, and sculpture. Thus the motion picture is not a true creative art, but a creation of the five. Therefore, I fear that even the best pictures will be only temporary – that is, in comparison of such artistic achievements as the Iliad, the Parthenon, or the works of Michelangelo.

When asked to elaborate, he continued,

> Read Flaubert's "Madame Bovary," written some sixty years ago. Then look at a good picture, made, say sixteen years ago [1912]. Can you enjoy the picture as you do the book? The appeal of the book is changeless. But in the picture the antiquated technique will stick out, like the ribs of a starving horse. [40]

Because film is dependent on technology, Curtiz suggests it cannot achieve the artistic permanency of the traditional arts. When I watch those movies from the 1920s I have to agree as far as antiquated technique is concerned. However, I disagree with my grandfather on this point. I believe that the art of film can also transcend technology; that is, effective presentation of multiple art forms is undeniably evident in the best pictures of any era.

Regarding *Noah's Ark*, I'm sure Curtiz did the best he could. And yet, when I watched the 2010 reconstructed version of I found the parallels with *Sodom and Gomorrah* strangely out of synch. In my opinion, the Biblical and modern stories do not fit as well in the American film. In *Sodom and Gomorrah* the dual characters of Mary Conway / Sarah played by Curtiz's then-wife Lucy Doraine are established so much more plausibly as strong female and main characters. In the modern section she is the heartless seeker of fortune, and in the Biblical section she is Lot's wife and a personage of power and influence. The female lead in *Noah's Ark*, played by Dolores Costello seems, in comparison, to be a minor female character. In the modern story she is Mary, and in the Biblical sections she is Miriam, the intended bride of Japheth in Noah's family.

In the American film, the male dual character Travis / Japheth played by George O'Brien has an overall more important part. It is Travis who carries the plot in a modern war drama, and it is Japheth who saves the day by warding off the King of

Akkad's soldiers just as the Ark is about to float away on the flood waters. The character of Noah himself is introduced in the modern part as an impromptu preacher. In the Biblical section, he just does not come across as the leader of his large family and their mission.

Poster for Noah's Ark [44]

Could it be that these differences had something to do with who wrote the screenplay? *Sodom and Gomorrah* was written by Ladislaus Vajda, a fellow-Hungarian, and Curtiz himself. Darryl Zanuck, the producer of *Noah's Ark*, is credited with writing the script and making all the decisions about how the film would be produced. Curtiz is credited with causing death and injury to extras during the scene where the flood is destroying the sinful city.

Shooting of Noah's Ark was complete in June 1928, and while the massive output of film celluloid went to editing, Curtiz was assigned four more films in quick succession: *The Glad Rag Doll, Madonna of Avenue A, Hearts in Exile,* and *The Gamblers.* In July, Bess suffered serious facial injuries in a car accident and was "confined to hospital for some time." [42] Her son remembers her in the hospital, "her face swathed in bandages" that muffled her voice. She had been on her way "to pick up Mike when their car was broadsided by a speeding hit-and-run driver." She would carry the scar on her lip for the rest of her life. [43]

The couple would finally see the results of his work on *Noah's Ark* in the fall of 1928 just before it premiered at Grauman's Theatre on October 22.

The premiere was an elaborate affair followed by more media attention. Curtiz explains some of the challenges he faced filming the biblical scenes.

> To many of us, the folk of Noah's time are shadowy and unreal. Translating the same characters with the same complexes and relationships to our own period gives them a credibility that may be lost behind the veil of antiquity. [45]

The film was a big success for Warner Brothers and for Curtiz, even though the financial gain in America was modest compared to profits reaped from subsequent international distribution. [46] Over the following two years the film was released in Germany, Denmark, Finland, Austria, Turkey, Estonia and Portugal. Along with the necessary translations for subtitles in those countries, its distribution abroad was a huge undertaking. Curtiz was back in the international film scene for the first time after leaving Europe.

Overall, the contemporary critical consensus was that *Noah's Ark* was not a best picture. After comparing it with *Sodom and Gomorrah*, I can see why. Not because the music is bad, not because the lighting and camera angles are bad, not even because the sets lack the grandeur of those in *Sodom and Gomorrah*. It is not a best picture, in my opinion, because the manner in which the plot is constructed falls down.

The initial performance of *Noah's Ark* at the box office could have sunk Curtiz's Hollywood directing career, but Zanuck's sheer determination for his own personal success, along with a temporary economic crest, created the necessary smoke screen. As well, even while the film was under production, the media showed interest. It was the first time in Curtiz's American career that he was showered with attention.

On a personal note, my grandmother Fränzi kept a clipping from the film's first showing in the Adria-Kino in Vienna. The review calls the film a triumph of technology, the comparison between the World War I story and Biblical scenes "splendid." There is nothing but praise for the director, the actors, and the cinematography. I can well imagine the pride with which Fränzi read these words, and I wonder how many times she went to see the film. She had kept a programme and she told me that whenever she watched a film of his, she could see him, feel him, behind the scenes.

Thus, before the end of 1928, Curtiz definitely breathed easier. His passport was returned to him and he successfully petitioned for a renewal of his visa in December, just before he turned forty-two years of age. His relationship with Bess Meredyth was blossoming. The future looked bright.

Who is This New Director?

Curtiz's new contract with Warner Brothers early in 1929 raised his salary to $1400 per month, with a further raise to $1600 in 1930. The June 1929 official biography prepared by the studio was another seal of approval. I've mentioned this document several times: its cavalier attitude toward accuracy, unsubstantiated claims about Curtiz's family, education, war experience, and his early career in Europe. The four-page document "from Hal Wallis" is basically a new construct of the man, his background, and his abilities. It's easy to see, however, that these so-called facts were created for studio publicity, for the media, even for Curtiz's co-workers and acquaintances, perhaps even for Curtiz himself. Did he begin to believe them?

Under the circumstances, constructing a personal history may have been a bit like constructing scenes in a film. Audience reaction is of primary importance, so the film maker leaves out, adds, embellishes or plays down certain details. The Warner Brothers 1929 biography of Curtiz does just that. It shows the man in a limbo between reality and fiction.

This document not only sketches a convenient and convincing picture of how Curtiz came to film, it also names film companies, actors and directors to add credence. A few early films are listed. It mentions Harry Warner's discovery of him and the contract that Curtiz was "very happy to accept." His early output in Hollywood is noted. There are no personal details except for the final paragraph which addresses his language issue but closes on a patriotic note.

> Coming to America with but the most superficial knowledge of English, Curtiz gained considerable attention from the industry for his unique misuse of American vernacular. Undaunted by this handicap, he attacked the study of the language at the same time he was working intently on his pictures and is now almost as conversant as a native. He has taken out his first citizenship papers. [47]

The publicity machine ground away, but it was a double-edged situation. He'd been in America for three years on a visitor's visa that was extended periodically and his "first citizenship papers" were really just a Declaration of Intention. I'm not prepared to guess at a deeper meaning of his words to my grandmother Fränzi in July, 1929. She had pressed him about coming to America with their son, but Curtiz made it clear that he had "no right to bring someone here because [he is] not an American citizen." [48]

After an imposed two-week 'vacation' without pay in the summer 1929, Curtiz continued to work at breakneck speed. And he was now seriously courting Bess Meredyth. When the subject of marriage came up, he had to clear up a lingering doubt: would his being Jewish jeopardize her accepting him? John Meredyth-Lucas recounts the marriage "proposal" this way:

> Mike had a small apartment about a mile from the Crescent Heights house. Mother would occasionally stay there or he would stay at our place. After a while of this, Mother said, "It would probably be simpler if we were married."
>
> "Bessky," he said, nodding sadly, "I like very much we should be marry, but – " He looked away.
>
> "But?" Mother asked.
>
> His voice was very low. "I am Jew," he told her.
>
> "I know," Mother said. "I have no idea what I am."
>
> Mike looked incredulous. "Is not matter?"
>
> So they got a judge who was a friend of Mother's. [49]

Historically, we remember the latter part of 1929 for another reason – the stock market crash. Not only Curtiz, but the whole of the American way of life had been reaching for the stars for more than a decade. Unlike Curtiz's career and personal life, though, the market and with it the economy came crashing down on October 29, ushering in the Great Depression. The Wall Street events had an immediate effect on the film industry. Fewer films would be started until the damage could be assessed.

Nevertheless, personal plans were made. Bess prepared for their wedding and Curtiz prepared a honeymoon home for his bride. He had purchased a stretch of property in Laguna Beach, south of Los Angeles, and built "one of the most artistic cottages in this interesting colony." [50] The couple obtained a marriage license under the names Helen Lucas and Mahala Kurtez (sic.) and on December 7, Michael Curtiz and Bess Meredyth stood for a civil ceremony in Superior Court of Los Angeles. It was Judge Dudley Valentine who performed the ceremony in his chambers, witnessed only by another judge and a Court clerk. [51] The reception took place in Number 101, the Roosevelt Hotel on Hollywood Boulevard. [52]

This hotel suite became their prime residence for some time, and they are included in the 1930 census prepared in April of that year. <u>Curtiz</u>, Michael and <u>Curtiz</u>, Bess Meredyth are each listed on that census record as "Lodger" to distinguish them from "Guest" which shows they were residents.

Before the year was out, Curtiz had to deal once again with his right to stay in America. He received an official notice that extended his visitor's visa another three months to the end of March, 1930. He was ordered to pay a $500 bond or leave the country. However, now that he was married to an American citizen, his position was a little more secure. I can only imagine the birthday party that Bess threw for her new husband when he turned forth-three on Christmas Day, 1929.

PART V

THE PAST NOT FAR BEHIND

As Bess Meredyth settled into the notion of being Mrs. Michael Curtiz, she may not have realized that his past was not too far behind. She already knew about Lucy Doraine, his first wife and their daughter Kitty, and she would find out about Michael Forster when that boy's mother Thilde pursued Curtiz in the American courts in 1933. The summons was served at their Laguna Beach house. However, only by accident – if at all – would she ever know about Theresia Dalla Bonna and Fränzi Wondrak, and the children they had borne Curtiz in Vienna.

From the other side, knowledge of Curtiz's marriage to Bess would have come through the media. I know only of my grandmother's reaction. For her entire life – for she told me this several times – she was convinced her beloved Miska married Bess "for convenience" and that he continued to love her, Fränzi. This belief kept alive her own dream and made it part of my father's experience.

As the Roaring 20's made way for the Great Depression in America and the looming Nazi threat in Europe, all of Curtiz's children were still innocent of the world around them. Lucy Doraine had established herself in the German film industry, but the other three mothers were living in the long shadow of Curtiz's exit from Europe, their lives by turns tragic and heroic. The status-filled life of a major film director had given these women some sense of superiority and expectations of a better life for themselves and their children. On the other hand, the insecurity of their position – financial, social, even political – would have caused daily stress and worry.

The children for their part suffered as well. For one, they were growing up without a father. I can relate to that because I too was fatherless until I was six. I will never forget how devastated I was when, on entering Kindergarten, I suddenly realized that I was different from most of the other children. On the way home, I asked Fränzi Omi, "Why don't I have a Papa?" The reason I had no Papa then – a generation later – was also because of Michael Curtiz.

Lucy Doraine and Kitty 1926 - 1931

Lucy Doraine's marriage to Curtiz had ended in 1923, a year after they completed the film *Sodom and Gomorrah* together in Vienna. In the aftermath of the personal and legal matters of this separation and divorce, their daughter Kitty, seven years old at the time, was bounced around Europe. In 1926, when Michael Curtiz left Europe, Kitty was just ten years old, living in Berlin with her mother and the girl's governess, Fräulein Rosa. Eventually, however, Kitty was back in Vienna. I believe that Curtiz corresponded with Kitty in those years, although the letters I've had the privilege of seeing begin only a few years later.

Lucy continued to work as an actress, and she also produced several films in Germany. But like everyone else she in the industry, she wanted to work in America. Finally in 1927, she obtained a contract with First National Pictures. She left Kitty in the care of Fräulein Rosa and made her way to Hollywood. Her first role was that of a minor character, Ninette, in the silent film *Adoration* released December 2, 1928. It's hard to know whether their paths crossed, since the two of them worked for different studios, and Curtiz was already involved with Bess Meredyth. But Hollywood was a small town then.

Over the next three years, Lucy kept trying to establish herself in Hollywood. An early sound film, *Christina* produced by Fox Film Corporation, saw her as the character Madame Bosman. The film was released December 15, 1929, two weeks before Curtiz married Bess.

These early promises of at least some success might have prompted Lucy to make plans to have Kitty join her in Hollywood. At this point Curtiz was definitely involved, and he was looking forward to having Kitty nearby again. As the fourteen year-old girl and her governess were preparing for the voyage to America, a letter came from her father. He writes in German, that he's happy she finally received the visa – "it was high time" they'd gotten the documents. He encloses $150 and says that he would send more money for both her and "Fr. Roza." Her father's letter might have made it easier for Kitty to leave her beloved Vienna. "I hope to see you soon again, a thousand kisses from your Papa," he signs off on this undated letter.

Kitty's trip to America followed the typical immigrant route. First, she and Fräulein Rosa took the train to Bremerhaven where on April 16, 1930 they embarked on the ship Europa to New York. [1] I love passenger lists for all the unexpected information one can find. For instance, this one confirms Kitty's citizenship as Hungarian, and it gives Fräulein Rosa's full name: Rosalia Bublan. More intriguing is that the destination noted for Kitty's "Gouvernante" is Vienna, while Kitty's is Hollywood, CA. Did that mean Fräulein Rosa would not be staying in America?

After the ocean voyage, there would be the rail trip of several days to California where Kitty would begin a whole new life. Just like it was for me, Kitty's life revolved around school where English became her everyday language. She made new friends and became a California girl. Her young life was, however, much different from mine in that Kitty did not enjoy a relatively stable family life. She lived with an actress mother and – at least for a while – with Fräulein Rosa. She did not come home from school to a baby sister like I did. Her father was remarried but John Meredyth Lucas would never be her brother. In his book about life with Curtiz, John does not mention that he ever met her. Although Kitty now lived in the same city as her divorced parents, she would have been in emotional turmoil.

It's no wonder that Kitty grew up to yearn for the childhood comfort that Vienna had instilled in her psyche. I believe that child immigrants do not yet feel homesickness the way adults do. But as we grow up, we begin to associate things and even people with that familiar first home. If we do go back as teenagers and adults, the childhood memories flood over us. Sometimes these feelings can become very powerful; they can even interfere with our new lives and relationships. The pull from our first home is never far behind and some of us even go back to stay. Kitty lived out her last twenty-five years in Austria, something she probably did not foresee when she first stepped off the train into the California sun.

Thilde Forster and Michael 1926 – 1931

The Vienna resident registry indicates that in 1926, the small Förster family consisting of the widow Helena Förster, her daughter Thilde and five-year old Michael, left their apartment at Dapontegasse 2/2, Vienna III, "destination Italy." There is no clear evidence of her immediate plans for work, but the filmography of Thilde Förster as screenwriter shows that her first film, *Venus im Frack (Venus in Tails)*, was released in Germany April 13, 1927. [2] It had taken her less than four years to realize her dream to be a screen writer. She nurtured connections in Germany, acquired an apartment in Berlin, and wrote two more stories that were turned into films: *So küsst eine Wienerin (This is How a Viennese Kisses)* and *Ein besserer Herr (A Better Gentleman)*. [3] For a time in 1928, her brother Ludwig and son Michael lived with her in Berlin. But she must also have traveled to Italy, for she is credited for writing the screenplay for the film *Corazones sin rumbo (Hearts Without Aim)* produced there in 1928. [4]

Riding on this wave of success, Thilde could begin to expect a better life for herself and her son Michael. One of her acquaintances in the German film industry was director Arnold Fanck, famous for his mountain films and his militaristic treatment of actors. Fanck's son was attending an exclusive private boarding school, the Freie Schul-Gemeinde at Wickersdorf, Thuringia, about half-way between Berlin and Frankfurt. It was perhaps through this connection that Thilde enrolled her son at the school. About this time, she sold a story to MGM and obtained a contract to work on the scenario for *A Woman Commands* starring Pola Negri. Hollywood was calling.

Michael Forster (the *Umlaut* has long been dropped) remembers arriving at Wickersdorf in the winter of 1931 after he had turned ten. Snow covered the fields and woods surrounding the small town. His mother soon left for America while the boy would spend the next two years learning much about life and himself. Things were changing rapidly in Germany, the Nazi movement becoming a prominent aspect of life even at the remote boarding school. Michael could feel "there was something wrong" when it came to Jewish boys and teachers. Segregation and persecution were beginning. In a strange twist of fate, he did not know that he was Jewish, his mother having kept that a secret. On one of the resident registry entries from Vienna, she had given their religion as Catholic. Here was a lady with much foresight.

As soon as she arrived in Los Angeles, Thilde consulted lawyer Max Lewis to validate the maintenance order against Curtiz that she had obtained in Vienna in 1923. An agreement was drawn up and signed on July 11, 1931 It is not clear, however, if the terms of payment were honoured for long, because less than two years later, she was back in court.

Theresia Dalla Bonna and Sonja 1926 – 1931

In April 1926, the Vienna Youth Court determined that Michael Kertész was working and living in Berlin. A note was sent to the District Court Hietzing to the effect that the father of the child Sonja Dalla Bonna should be pursued in the German capital for non-payment of support. But the lack of response or further documents suggests that he slipped through the cracks and left for America without dealing with this obligation. It would take two more years until the courts caught up with him in Hollywood.

Sonja had her third birthday in August, 1926. Three – that lovely age when a little girl is really becoming part of the human family. She talks and asks simple questions: "What's that, Mama?" She can draw somewhat recognizable shapes, try to catch a ball, and eat with a fork. She plays seriously with whatever is available, enjoys music, and loves to go with her Omi for a walk in the park, where she wants to spend hours at the playground. Her mother Theresia tried to make ends meet by working in a milliner's shop; she had a knack for fancy sewing, and hats were a staple item in the wardrobe of Viennese women of all classes and ages.

There's a picture of Sonja when she's about four. With both chubby little hands, she is holding up the hem of a light-colored knee-length satin dress and making a kind of curtsey with feet clad in dark, ankle-high shoes. A shy little smile lights up her sweet face surrounded by blonde curls.

A photo of her mother Theresia from about the same time tells a different story. The young woman's face shows sadness, especially around the eyes. Her smile is not quite convincing.

In contrast, Leopoldine, Theresia's mother and little Sonja's Omi, portrays a strong-willed middle-aged woman, thin and rather severe-looking. Sonja's grandfather Felix had been out of the picture for a number of years, so this little family of three females lived a quiet life in the apartment on Mondscheingasse.

Theresia Dalla Bonna, 1925

Sonja Dalla Bonna, 1927

Leopoldina Dalla Bonna

There is no evidence that Curtiz paid child support for the first two years he was in America. During that time, Theresia received emergency relief funds from the City of Vienna to the tune of 20 Schillings (about $3) a month. [5] To the credit of the Austrian court system, efforts to get support from Curtiz continued and sometime in 1928 he was tracked down in Hollywood. By that time the outstanding support payments had risen to 2,350 Schilling ($335 US). For several months he sent $50 or $100 payments, the Court opened a special bank account, and Theresia received her 120 Schilling ($17) per month. It may seem a small amount, but the Court held to the position that these payments were meant only and strictly for the support of the child. In 1931 when the case manager submitted a petition to have the payments raised on the strength of Curtiz's substantial salary as a director in Hollywood, the Court refused the request.

> … The claim that the requirements of an eight-year old child cannot be covered by 120 Schillings a month would have to be substantiated. The allocation of a monthly alimony of 240 Schillings for an eight-year old child would be extremely rare for conditions in Austria. It is unlikely that a judge could be found who would grant such an allocation. [6]

The petition had voiced concern about the meagre amount remaining in the account, but the court struck down this argument with a dismissive comment: "with the vigilance of the Case Management, the child's father is certain to resume payments before the money runs out."

What sounds like blind trust is actually based on a distressing legal precedent. At that time in Austria, an illegitimate child and its mother could not actually *force* maintenance payments, in or outside of the country. They could not garnishee Curtiz's wages. In other words, the ability for the mother of an illegitimate child to get money from the child's father was not supported by the law. All they could do was to *encourage* Curtiz to fulfill his duty. Thus, a further letter dated April 16, 1931 sent to Curtiz at the Warner Studio, ended with the request, "You are requested to transfer funds promptly."

If the legalities of the fight for maintenance weren't enough of a continuing headache for Theresia, you can add to that the bureaucratic vagaries of a system such as the youth courts and social services everywhere, anytime. Reading through these files, I note that Theresia had signed over Power of Attorney to a court official in April, and tried to reverse that decision, unsuccessfully, in June. Once you give up control, you've lost it. Some time later, a new guardian was appointed, resulting in changes as to where the money is to be paid, and by whom it is handled.

Little Sonja may have been oblivious to these goings-on, but at six, seven and eight-years old, even a child begins to understand the problems of the adults around her. No doubt she heard her mother lament her situation, wishing that things were different, expecting that things would be different, if only, if only…. When Sonja grew up, she told her own children that Curtiz had always wanted to bring her and her mother to America.

Fränzi Wondrak and Michael 1926 – 1931

Fränzi Wondrak, my grandmother, was twenty years old in 1926 when Curtiz left Europe. After she had given birth to their son Michael Emmanuel Wondrak in April, 1925, she remained in Bolzano, Italy and found work there as a seamstress. The baby had been placed with the Family Mauracher in the town Kastelruth which lies in a high mountain valley where the Dolomite peaks crowd the eastern horizon.

Fränzi had decided to stay close to her baby, and she tried to visit him often. To do so, she had to take the train north along the main line that goes over the Brenner Pass into Austria. At Ponte Gardena, she would disembark and ride the Post Bus up the mountain. It broke her heart to see how attached the boy was becoming to his wet-nurse. Despite the apparent advantages of fresh air, plenty of food, a family environment, little Michael developed a mild case of rickets which left him with slightly bowed legs. It's a common result of the lack of fresh vegetables. The Maurachers, on their part, were grateful for the small allowance that Fränzi sent or brought them, whether or not the money was from Curtiz.

In the little pile of letters that I have inherited, there seems to be a gap of about ten months from the last letter and money transfer before he left Europe in the spring of 1926 until February 1927. In all these papers, the missing letters are hardly noticeable, but in real life – in Fränzi's life at that crucial time – ten months is a long time indeed. If she didn't hear from Curtiz for all this time, the money he had sent earlier would run out quickly.

There had been a telegram to Abbazia dated August 15, 1926 but then nothing until the letter from postmarked February 21, 1927 on Warner Brothers stationery. It is addressed to Fränzi at 75 Schopenhauer Gasse, Vienna. Had Curtiz lost or misplaced the address in Bolzano, or had she temporarily returned to Vienna? I know only that sometime that year, Fränzi took her son down the mountain, out of Italy and brought him to Abbazia to live with her sister Anni and brother-in-law Franz Palka.

The letters from America during this time are few and far between. In May 1927, Curtiz mentions that he had been in Mexico for six weeks on a film assignment, and that he intends to come to Europe on holidays that year. That hope and promise would not materialize for another four years, however. During this time, he wrote only a handful of letters, and the money he did send was obviously never enough for her needs. A number of the letters are written in longhand, which makes them special treasures. I include one from 1929 here to show the passion with which he writes when not dictating to a typist. My translation reveals the roller-coaster of emotions.

> My Dear Franzi,
>
> I am very sorry that you are always and always worried and waiting for an answer – waiting for my letters – You are judging the long gap very badly. You must understand that while I am busy with a film I have no time for my private correspondence or business, my private things. I also do not write to my mother who is always worried too – she writes the same thing in every letter, just like you: why no answer?
>
> So you need to understand the long gap between letters is no change in my feelings, just the work.
>
> Dear Franzi, I enclose a photo for Michael and cash money of $30 for you!
>
> You mentioned America, which I think would be <u>wonderful</u> for Michael but I don't know how you could get permission to immigrate. I am not an American citizen so I have no right to arrange this for anyone.
>
> Maybe if you go to the American Consulate and give a petition – say that you have an Aunt over here maybe you can get permission after 2 years. Try this and I will send you the money for the passage.
>
> I hope to see you and Michael in December.
>
> Many dear Greetings, Michael

Of course little Michael was oblivious to all the adult plans and problems swirling around him. The boy – my father – told me that he spoke mostly German with a smattering of Italian during those first years, but when he turned five in April 1930, he began working with private tutor whom he remembers fondly as Guri. He loved this young woman who prepared him for Kindergarten and school where he would have to be fluent in Italian. The few times that Fränzi brought him to Vienna, she introduced him as a child she was only looking after.

During 1930, Curtiz wrote only twice and sent a hurried telegram at Christmas. He thanked Fränzi for a photo of little Michael,
and he responded to her mention of legal issues - this time regarding the child's legal status as he comes of school-age. "You should
go to a lawyer, maybe the Child Authority" he writes, "and ask
what papers one must send to Vienna (Michael should have my
name legally) so that when he goes to school he doesn't have to be
ashamed." [7]

Fränzi was again living in Abbazia with her sister Anni and
brother-in-law Franz Palka in the Villa Niri. Little Michael became
aware of the world around him. He spoke fluent Italian but only
broken German. Late in his life, he told me about his first serious
illness:

> When I was five or six, I had an appendix burst. It all started
> with a high fever and a swollen tummy. After a few days
> of bearing the discomfort and pain, my mother and uncle
> finally took me to the doctor in a car – by then it was critical.
> Another half hour and it would have been over... The doctor
> Lehel was very nice. Later he took his life when Mussolini
> came in – to avoid going to concentration camp. That was the
> first big shock in my life. The hospital was so primitive, there
> were no elevators. A big black man carried me to and from
> the operation room. [8]

The receipt from Dr. Alessandro Lehel for 1,450 lire is dated April
28, 1931, the day before Michael's sixth birthday. In May, Curtiz
sent $150, and his letter contains specific instructions to pay the
doctor. This letter also solidifies the apparent intentions for Curtiz
to adopt my father: "I received a letter from the lawyer and I en-
close my answer to him." The letter to Wienninger & Wagner begins on a positive note:

> Regarding your letter of 17 April, I am happy to know that
> the adoption for Michael Vondrak to my name, as well as
> obtaining Austrian citizenship [for the boy] will not present
> great difficulties. [9]

But Curtiz wants to know what this will all cost before he agrees
to the process. Over the next months, there are several letters
with which he sends money and assures Fränzi of his support.
He also announces the long-awaited trip to Europe: "I am coming to Europe – to Budapest on 15 July, and also to Vienna and I

will take care of everything personally." [10] On July 15, she received the further letter on stationery from the *Aquitania* and mailed in Cherbourg: "I will be in Budapest at my mother's on the 16th or 17th..."

Immediately she traveled to Vienna with little Michael. It was an exciting time for Fränzi. She had money and great hopes that her dreams for her child would finally come true. Curtiz came to Vienna twice that summer, for the portrait taken at the Residenz Atelier of him and his son has July, 1931 written on the back. My father is wearing a sailor suit with short pants as he sits on a cloth-covered prop beside Curtiz. Their smiles look a little forced.

Then, on August 5, Fränzi received a telegram at the apartment on Schopenhauerstrasse: "I am in Vienna for one day. Please wait for me tomorrow, Thursday, at 8 o'clock in the morning, Café Opera. Kertész." Café Opera is located in the state opera building itself, just across the street from another famous café, the Sacher.

I will imagine that Fränzi was there fifteen minutes early, waiting for Curtiz nervously. Then he breezed in and he placed two orders of *Wiener Frühstück* (Vienna breakfast) that consists of Kaiser rolls, butter and jam, and coffee, but Fränzi could not touch the food. He promised to take care of the legal business, and afterwards they would take little Michael to the Prater amusement Park. The legal business did not happen, but the promised outing did. This photo taken at the Prater is a family treasure.

Michael Curtiz, Michael Wondrak, Fränzi Wondrak, 1931

A series of letters between July 28 and September 17, from the lawyer Dr. Adolph Mathias to Fränzi, reveals the anticlimax of the entire summer. An Agreement for Adoption had been drafted, but there were problems obtaining Curtiz's birth records and/or a passport number. By September, he was long gone back in America. Fränzi and her son had also returned to Italy where little Michael began his Grade One.

The Kaminer/Kertész Family in Budapest

I am very curious how much Bess Meredyth knew in the summer of 1931 about all of this letter-writing, money-sending and actual meeting between her new husband and Fränzi Wondrak and the child she'd had with him. She would have seen the Warner Brothers layoff notice for eight weeks starting June 15 and addressed to Curtiz at their home, 715 North Alpine Drive, Beverly Hills. A second notice postponed the "vacation" by a month, but by mid-July they were finally on their way. Once in Budapest, she was caught up with his family and former colleagues.

From the time Curtiz left for America in 1926 he had kept in close touch with his family in Budapest, and being with his them all, especially his mother, was a priority. In 1931, Aranka Kaminer was sixty-eight years old, already a widow for eight years. Further research would be needed to determine the exact whereabouts of all the siblings and what they did for a living. But I believe they were not too far away and certainly all in Europe, all married and most with children. In 1931, they ranged in age from forty-nine (Etel) to twenty-eight (Gabor the youngest and the only one still single). Aranka already had ten grandchildren.

Life in Hungary had been politically and economically chaotic ever since the end of World War I and things would only get worse in the years to come. I am certain that Curtiz did as much as he could to make it tolerable for his Budapest family.

The prodigal son was also received as a celebrity by the entire Budapest film industry. Curtiz and Bess were wined and dined by the film elite and interviewed by the press. Incredibly, I found a tattered copy of the Film Magazine *Szinhazislet* among my grandmother Fränzi's memorabilia. She had saved this testament to her Miska's success from that summer 1931 while experiencing her own highs and lows. She used to tell me that she had understood and accepted the fact that Miska had married Bess Meredyth.

The headline of the feature article in this magazine is a question: "More Beautiful Than Hollywood?" Bess Meredyth begins by explaining that she had been to Europe before:

> Four years ago was the first time I came to Europe.... Ben Hur was filmed in Rome, and that's where I met my husband. I wrote his first American films. We became good friends. I am very, very happy that I listened to him and followed him to Europe. Budapest is so different and beautiful... [11]

In another part of the magazine, there are pictures of Curtiz and some of his colleagues from the early days at the film studios and the Hungarian Theatre. The article gushes on:

> All the greeting and hugging and kissing and the emotional outbursts have no end. They are standing by the gate, and they don't want to let each others' hands go. Here we are together again as in the good old days. When are you going to come home for good?

Curtiz doesn't mince words in answering:

> I thought about coming home for a year, but in Hungary they don't pay much for directors. I love my mother and siblings very much and want to give them a better life. One day I am going to have enough money to produce my own films...

Within ten years, he would succeed in helping many of his family members to come to America, and eventually, he did have his own Hollywood production company.

For me, the most surprising image that came along with the articles in this 1931 Hungarian magazine is a reproduction of a formal portrait of Kitty, captioned "daughter of Kertész Mihály and Lucy Doraine." The photograph, credited to Photo Alberts, Hollywood, shows the teenage girl with long dark hair, wearing a dark dress with a white collar. It must have been taken when she first came to Hollywood the year before, and had probably been sent to Curtiz's Budapest family by her proud father. On what's left of the magazine page, there is an illegible inscription penned in Hungarian, but there are also defacing scribbles over Kitty's smiling oval face.... Who would have done such a thing?

*****

*Curtiz with his mother Aranka, brothers Dezsö (David)
and Oszkár (Gabor) and a nephew. (Notice the picture of Bess on the wall beside Gabor)*

From the Hungarian magazine Szinhazislet, 1931

The Curtizes' return to America is recorded on the passenger list for the ship *Europa*. It departed from Bremen but picked up passengers in Southampton and, finally, Cherbourg where the couple embarked. The ship arrived in New York August 24, 1931. The passenger list details include Curtiz's correct age – 44 as of December 1930 – and the pertinent information about Bess. As I discovered at the National Archives in New York, it was this arrival, and not the 1926 date, that finally set in motion the steps for Curtiz to become an American citizen, but he would have to wait another five years for the process to be complete.

The years between 1926 and 1931 had been eventful to say the least, not only for Curtiz, but also for his family – his families – in Europe and now in America. Professionally, he had established himself in Hollywood, with eighteen completed films for Warner Brothers under his belt. He had married again, married well – whether for convenience or not. His ex-wife Lucy and their daughter Kitty were also in Hollywood.

Regarding his Vienna children and their mothers, Curtiz had experienced much turmoil legally and – I do believe – emotionally. Thilde Forster showed up in Hollywood and promptly filed for renewed support for their son Michael. Theresia Dalla Bonna and their daughter Sonja were stuck in Vienna, but the Youth Court did its best to get Curtiz to honour his obligations. My grandmother Fränzi had – from my perspective – been the least public but perhaps the most successful in keeping Curtiz's attention. Even though things did not work out, I do not believe his promises toward adopting their son, my father, were simply a ruse. At this juncture in his life, Curtiz's children were fully in his line of vision, not to be ignored.

American Citizenship

In August 1931, Curtiz was prepared to enter the United States as a permanent resident intent on becoming an American citizen. While in Budapest that summer, he had arranged for declarations of character and good health that enabled him to get a Quota Immigration Visa and Identification Card issued by the American Consular Service in that city. It would expire December 8, 1931, so he had to proceed without delay. By the end of October, he had filed his Declaration of Intention to become an American citizen, but then matters began to stall. He would wait another six years until this dream came true.

Naturalization is "the process by which U.S. citizenship is granted to a foreign citizen or national after he or she fulfills the requirements established by Congress in the Immigration and Nationality Act (INA)." [12] This process was firmly established by the 1906 amendments to the old Immigration Act of 1802. [13] The Bureau of Immigration and Naturalization, part of the Justice Department, oversaw the following steps.

First, you had to be "lawfully admitted to the United States of America for permanent residence." Curtiz's Certificate of Arrival dated October 3, 1931 documents his arrival on the *Europa* in New York on August 24, 1931 with that description – check.

Next, you had to file a Declaration of Intention to become an American citizen. Curtiz filled out his on October 19, 1931 and filed it at the District Court of the United States at Los Angeles – check. When I read this declaration carefully, I noticed some irregularities. The date of marriage to Bess is out by a year – 12/18/28 instead of December 7, 1929. A more obvious error is in regard to children: only Katheryna (Kitty) is included and even her birth date is out by a year. This error would surface two years later when, in August 1933, a letter signed "An Hungarian spectator" states that "Als (*sic*) a matter of fact he has four children. One legitimate and three illegitimate children by three different women in Europe." Details including the name Tilda Forster (*sic*) are given; a search of Budapest and Vienna court records is suggested. The Bureau did follow up, and the result was an affidavit sworn by Curtiz that neatly sidesteps the question of illegitimate children by stating that he had been married only twice, and that besides Kitty, he has "no other children by either of said marriages." [14] This would serve to explain away Thilde Forster's claim as being an attempt to extort money from him. The affidavit still contains errors, but nobody appears to have investigated any further. Ultimately, the anonymous letter did not prevent Curtiz's naturalization.

The next step was to file a Petition for Naturalization which could be done within two but no later than seven years after filing the Declaration of Intention. Curtiz did not file this Petition until December 4, 1936, more than six years after the Declaration of Intention. Why did he wait so long?

The 1924 Immigration Act and the business of Quota and Non-Quota Immigration Visas may have been a factor. Curtiz's 1931 Quota Visa was subject to the strict limitations of the Act and it is possible that by the time his intention to apply for American citizenship was processed, the annual quota for immigrants from Hungary had been reached. He was in no danger, however, because he had established domicile: he was married to an American, and he was employed in the United States.

The opportunity to move things along came in 1934 with Curtiz's next visit to Europe. When the layoff notice from Warner Brothers came to North Roxbury Drive, the house where he and Bess lived that spring, the couple began to make plans. Bess would go to England to be on location fort the filming of *The Iron Duke*, a historical drama about the Duke of Wellington. Bess had written the screen play based on a story by H.M. Harwood. Filming was taking place at Gainsborough Pictures studios in London and Surrey, England. A perfect way to spend the summer!

After accompanying Bess to England, Curtiz's prime goal was to visit his family in Budapest. While there, he applied for and obtained a Non-Quota Immigration Visa from the American Foreign Service office. As a foreign national, he still needed a visa to re-enter the United States and that visa indicates he is "returning to unrelinquished domicile to the United States from a temporary visit." He and Bess arrived in New York aboard the *SS. Rex* on August 15, 1934.

The fact that he now had a Non-Quota Immigration Visa meant that Curtiz was no longer limited to the maximum number of Hungarian nationals that could apply for American citizenship in any one year. A big part of the pressure was off. Regarding the accuracy of data on this visa, it is one of the very few documents where his birth date is given – correct according to the birth record I saw in Budapest – as December 25, 1886. The section on "minor" children is left altogether blank, however. Of course Kitty was already eighteen, no longer considered a minor. And the others simply didn't exist!

When Curtiz finally filed his Petition for Naturalization December 4, 1936, it required supporting affidavits of two witnesses who could state that the applicant has resided in the United States for at least five years and is "possessed of good moral character." Incredibly, even there are still some errors. This time the date of his marriage to Bess is given as 1930 – a year late – and once again Kitty is named as his only child.

Two momentous steps are also taken in this Petition: Curtiz had to "renounce absolutely and forever all allegiance and fidelity to any foreign prince, potentate, state or sovereignty, and particularly the Present Government of Hungary." No matter how much an immigrant wants to become part of his or her new country and culture, there is always a twinge of regret in making such a statement about one's fatherland. I know about this from my own family. We became Canadian citizens in 1966 with great pride. However, when my stepdad Frank returned to Austria in his fifties, he sorely regretted having given up his first citizenship. He could not obtain dual citizenship after the fact.

Curtiz's Petition for Naturalization also included a provision for formal name change, and he duly filled in that portion of the document. He had used the name Michael Curtiz unofficially since his arrival in Hollywood in 1926. Now, more than ten years later, it would become legal. Many years earlier at seventeen, Curtiz had changed his last name voluntarily from Kaminer to Kertész. He had Germanized Mihály to Michael when he came to Austria in 1919. Lastly, he had signed himself Michael Curtiz on his contract with Warner Brothers when he came to America in 1926. Now, finally, his legal name matched the one that is still recognizable.

It seems like such a simple thing, but a name is intimately tied to one's personal identity. Were all these name changes for convenience just as it happened thousands of times with millions of immigrants? Doesn't changing one's name change the person in some fundamental way? In his business correspondence Curtiz was either Michael or Mike, and the English short form was what he used to sign letters to his daughter Kitty. But he kept signing himself Miska in his letters to my grandmother Fränzi. Was he more himself with her?

My own name is an example: Ilona is Hungarian for Helen, but I learned this only after I heard that my husband's Aunt Helen's name had been changed when she immigrated as a girl back in the 1930's. At that time it was common for an immigrant to Anglicize his or her name, but by the time I came to Canada in 1956, the practice was fading. For some reason I'm happy that my name was not changed – I feel more grounded, especially when people learn to pronounce it the way I first knew myself.

As a final step in the process of naturalization, American legislation in the 1930's provided for an investigation by the Bureau of Immigration and a subsequent hearing before a judge. After my grandfather got the green light from the Bureau, he began to prepare for the big day. His stepson offers this humorous account:

He hired a teacher who would come to the house at night, sometimes go with him to the studio, working with him on the set between takes. He learned American history, the theory of government, the list of presidents and would ask us to test him at the dinner table...

\When the citizenship test came, it was done before a judge... [who] turned out to be a great fan of motion pictures... The citizenship test was somewhat less than cursory. Mike was very disappointed. "Goddamn," he said, "Why hell, all this time I break my head to be American and he ask me only goddamn actors?" [15]

Regardless, the judge issued an order of admission to citizenship, Curtiz swore his oath of allegiance to the U.S. Constitution, and Citizenship Certificate No. 4,261,907 was issued as of March 12, 1937 in the name of Michael Curtiz. The passport-style picture on the certificate portrays a tanned but tired-looking fifty year old man. He had waited a long time for this day.

*****

Becoming an American citizen had long been a personal goal for Curtiz, but in his correspondence with my grandmother Fränzi, he expressed some underlying doubts. Up until 1937, Curtiz was still travelling with his Hungarian passport. As Europe plunged into political uncertainty, this could be a disadvantage, even a danger to him. He worried that "should war break out, I might be forced into military service." [16] When Fränzi pressured Curtiz to arrange for herself and little Michael to visit him in the U.S., he replied, "you could not get a visa ... only American citizens can sponsor children, wives or parents." [17] This last statement affected not only Fränzi and my father; it also affected Curtiz's ability to bring over members of his own family. Once he had his citizenship, he moved quickly to get them out of Hungary and he increased his efforts to bring Fränzi and their son over to America.

PART VI

WORK, LIFE, LIBERTY

During the long wait from arriving in as a permanent resident in 1931 to finally becoming an American citizen in 1937, Curtiz made work his primary objective. The renewal contract he signed with Warner Brothers in April 1931 before the trip to Europe ensured that he would have work for another year, with the option of four years' further extensions and salary increases set out clearly.

But the work had its challenges. While he directing the film *The Woman from Monte Carlo* in the fall of 1931, he became embroiled in a dispute, or as the press put it "lack of accord" between Curtiz and the leading lady Lil Dagover over which the star was so upset that she fainted, and the day's filming was suspended. [1] The studio also caused headaches. As the Great Depression deepened, pressure to reduce salaries culminated in a letter of December 1, 1931 in which Curtiz reluctantly agreed to a pay cut from $1600 to $1400 per week. He continued to churn out the films: with *Alias the Doctor, The Strange Love of Molly Loudvin,* and *Dr. X,* the Warner Brothers contribution to "the horror bandwagon." [2] Not all his films were well received by American audiences and as a result, did not do so well at the box office. More pressure from the studio.

In directing the 1932 film, *The Cabin in the Cotton,* Curtiz worked for the first time with Bette Davis, another actress that would give him both great trouble and great success. Despite his apparent rough treatment of her in the making of this film, I am convinced that he had great respect for Davis. He made a total of six films with her, the last one being *The Private Lives of Elizabeth and Essex* (1939). There is a production still of Curtiz, kneeling in front of Davis as Queen Elizabeth I. He is, of course, setting a scene, but it does look like he's begging rather than ordering, and it fits!

The studio's practice of summer closures became firmly entrenched; almost every year the studio would announce a closure of six to eight weeks. This meant no salary for up to two months, a hardship that Curtiz complained about in his letters to Fränzi. When he worked, he worked hard. In his November 1932 letter to my grandmother, he mentions working on *20,000 Years in Sing-Sing* "until midnight" for weeks. When there was no work, it was difficult to keep up with his many financial obligations. This was a recurring theme in his letters, but I think Fränzi did not fully understand the actual scope of his obligations and the pace of his work.

On March 10, 1933, Curtiz experienced his first "significant" California earthquake, but more than the Long Beach landscape was shaken up. The Great Depression had taken its toll in the movie industry. Salary cuts had already been announced by many motion picture studios, and in April, there was talk of consolidating film distribution facilities in an effort to gain "large economies" in tough times. [3] Upheavals also involved the Screen Writers Guild, which struck a committee to review working rules; Bess Meredyth sat on that committee.

The struggles may have helped Bess, though. By November she was working again after what is described as a "long, long siege of illness." [4] She joined Twentieth Century Pictures to "scenarize" – that is, to adapt a version of *Les Miserables* for the screen. The film, starring Frederic March, was quite a success. It was nominated for four Academy awards in 1936, including best picture. Bess was back. And even though the marriage between herself and Curtiz was increasingly rocky, their relationship as far as work was concerned remained amiable. Perhaps they were better business than personal partners.

Through sheer determination, Curtiz weathered the economic storm and continued to be busy at Warner Brothers Over the next three years, he directed fifteen more films of varying genres and box office successes until the happy accident of *Captain Blood*. Much has been written about Curtiz's relationship with Errol Flynn – whom he supposedly called Flint – but from all the background material, stills, and watching *Captain Blood* itself, I get the sense that Curtiz was finally settling into his work in America, finally enjoying himself.

In earlier years, he had expressed an uncertainty about his work and even about remaining in America. "The situation in Hollywood is very sad," he writes to Fränzi in July, 1932. "I haven't decided yet whether I'll continue to work here or return to Europe." The same sentiment is repeated in October: "I don't have any idea yet if I will stay in America for the next year. I can get my contract renewed anytime, but I would really rather be in Europe already."

It's realistic to say that 1932 was the ultimate low point in job satisfaction for Curtiz. He was working at breakneck speed, churning out the films as fast as they were assigned. "There are many demands on me" and "I am very busy right now" seem to be the constant refrain in his letters to Fränzi. In early 1933, there appears to be a shift in his thinking, however. While he admits that conditions in Hollywood are not the best, he now thinks "it's still better to work HERE where no one has to deal with political unrest." [5]

The Great Depression had affected people's outlook on life, and that included their appetite for entertainment. They sought relief from the tougher times, and the film studios, including Warner Brothers, had to rethink their offerings. From their habit of producing realistic films on social issues which had brought them success in the 1920s, they moved to making films with lighter subjects – at least on the surface – and faster action. Curtiz obliged, and thereby found the opportunity to excel at what he did best: getting his actors and crew to create fast action.

Over the next two years, and certainly by the time he directed *Captain Blood* in 1935, Curtiz seemed to have a more positive attitude toward working in Hollywood. No doubt he'd also gotten more used to how things are run at the studio. James Robertson, in detailed coverage, suggests that Curtiz may have had a role in casting decisions for *Captain Blood*, and that in this, his longest film since *Noah's Ark*, "he was determined to stamp his personality all over it." [6] As often was and would continue to be the case, the battle behind the scenes was between Curtiz and Hal Wallis. Curtiz wanted more time and resources to do things his way; Wallis wanted to hold the line on costs and production time. Curtiz usually won the day.

Curtiz's creativity is demonstrated when, during shooting in a cove near Laguna Beach, the roar of the waves threatened to drown out the actors' voices. After some trial and error, he came up with a solution when he realized that the breakers came eight seconds apart, "as evenly spaced as the marching beat of well-trained soldiers." He quickly rearranged the script to provide pauses in the dialogue to allow for the crashing waves. "During those periods he instructed the players to do bits of soundless action," then as a wave crested, he shouted "Action!" Dialogue ensued; a reply was snapped. Curtiz was very happy with the result. The sequence gained "a swifter tempo, and the dull, booming echo of the waves provided a vital touch of realism." [7] I viewed this segment of the film carefully, and I have to agree. Whatever concessions Curtiz had requested, Hallis would have had to concede they were worth it.

Captain Blood was released in December 1935 and was nominated for best film at the 1936 Academy Awards. Although it didn't win the Oscar, the film became a profit maker for Warner Brothers and Curtiz's biggest economic success since coming to America. As we know, this first of a series of swashbucklers is still popular today. It regularly appears on TV, and it has been released in Video, DVD, and in Errol Flynn box sets.

As she had done before, Fränzi kept a brochure published in Vienna when the film was released there in 1936. Even though Curtiz didn't write to her in detail about his films, she probably wrote to him whenever she'd seen one, either dubbed in German or with German subtitles. I can imagine her going to see this film with eleven year-old Michael. The boy would have loved the action scenes: the sword fight on the beach and especially the final ship-board battle between the English and French. For Fränzi, the scenes with Errol Flynn and Olivia de Havilland would have tugged at her heart strings. She could feel her Miska behind the scenes, directing the action. She might have imagined that he was thinking of her when he brought the two stars together in close-ups.

I am conscious of Curtiz's presence also when I watch this film, but my interest lies mainly in the composition of scenes and individual shots. The final product is, of course, much different from the often hodgepodge way that shooting takes place, and George Amy's editing magic must be acknowledged. However, deciding on how the actors and crew do their job is the director's responsibility. And when I concentrate on Curtiz's work with Olivia de Havilland on the character of Arabella Bishop, I can really appreciate his ability and vision.

In the story, Arabella is a young, privileged English lady, the niece of the cruel plantation owner near Port Royal, Jamaica. On a lark, she buys Dr. Peter Blood to be her slave but doesn't quite know what to do with him. The gravity of the circumstances seems to escape her until the moment he speaks to her, before he is led away. As Errol walks away, Curtiz has the cameraman zoom in on Olivia. Her head is held high; back-light illuminates the wide brim of her satin hat and outlines her flawless features: forehead, nose, full lips, and chin. This crisp image is set apart from a blurred background of soft grey. The composition is completed by some darker bands to bring out the tip of the hat and her white shoulders. The effects in black and white are stunning.

More than technical excellence, however, the shot reveals Arabella's emotions and thereby showcases De Havilland's talent. Pride is mitigated by a yearning look, the dawning of love is written on her face. The mixture of pride and uncertainty gives her a melancholy expression that is both moving and exciting. James Robertson comments, "Olivia de Havilland's beauty was emphasized in several close-ups, and she was given opportunities for character development." Robertson's overall assessment is that "it was unquestionably Curtiz's direction that made stars out of both the young leads." [8]

De Havilland also worked with Curtiz on his two next major hits, *The Charge of the Light Brigade,* released October 1936 and nominated at the 1937 Academy awards for best picture, and an all-time favourite *The Adventures of Robin Hood,* released May 1938 and nominated for best picture that year. Although neither film took the prize, Robin Hood did get Oscars for music, sets and editing. James Robertson keeps his comments on the acting brief: "Flynn and De Havilland have some of their best love scenes together, showing Curtiz's unerring instinct for balance between hectic pace and character development." [9] In looking closely at De Havilland's performance, I agree and find the scene at the open window of her chamber most striking. It is introduced from an impossible angle and done as a "glass shot" for which Curtiz had to get special permission.[10] De Havilland and Flynn became a crowd-pleasing film couple that worked together again in Curtiz's large-scale Westerns, *Dodge City* (1939), *Virginia City* (1940) and *Santa Fe Trail* (1940). Soon after, however, De Havilland left Warner Brothers and Hollywood and eventually settled in Paris.

I am still amazed how it happened that I actually had a visit with her there in 2006. I was planning to visit my son Robert in Paris while he was there as a graduate student. I had written to

DeHavilland – as I had to other actors who had worked with my grandfather – and despite being busy with plans for the Hollywood Tribute to her later that year, she did answer and did arrange for me and Rob to come for a cup of tea. DeHavilland was most gracious in sharing what she thought of Curtiz. In the early days, she said, Curtiz was a hard taskmaster. He always wore the riding pants and ran his set in a military fashion like all the European directors she had come across. He had kept his authoritarian tone even though working in Hollywood in 1935 was not like working in Europe a decade earlier.

De Havilland noted that Curtiz was a master of the technology: he knew the camera, light and shadow, and composition. His use of close-ups, like the one of Ingrid Bergman at the end of *Casablanca*, a close up "that big – that's the director" she emphasized. Almost twenty years after she had first worked with "Sergeant" Curtiz on the swashbucklers and westerns, De Havilland had another opportunity to get to know an older, more mature Curtiz. When he was preparing to direct *The Proud Rebel* (1958) for Samuel Goldwyn and Buena Vista (Disney), Curtiz wanted De Havilland in the main female role. She remembered the long distance phone call during which he charmed her to put her life in Paris on hold and come to Hollywood.

Her worries about what it would be like to work with him again were proven wrong. In particular, she was impressed with the gentle way he treated David, Alan Ladd's son. And she elaborated on two scenes that demonstrated "the best directing" she'd ever gotten. One example is the scene with the oil lamp. After reading a bed-time story to the boy, her character – his mother – is to turn out the lamp and leave the room. De Havilland had been instructed by the set people on how to turn down the wick. So when Curtiz told her to blow it out instead, she objected. He insisted, and she went along with it. Only later, when she saw the result did she realize how much more effective was the immediate darkness. The incident was criticised in Time magazine as being dangerous, she said, but in this case, he was right.

The other scene involves a shift in character from drab farm-wife to dressed-up woman and back again. As she recalled the details, De Havilland still sounded as surprised as she had felt that day: Curtiz's exact instructions had created quite involuntary emotional changes in her. These examples, in her words, are "pure directing, very good directing." [11]

*****

Unlike De Havilland, who had fought and left the studio system, Curtiz remained under its iron hand. At the end of his 1934 summer trip to Europe, for example, Curtiz had to ask for permission to extend his time in England by one and a half weeks. The irregularity was allowed, but on his return, the Assistant Secretary noted a change in his current contract. The next deadline was to be extended by exactly one and a half weeks. Curtiz signed his approval and acceptance. [12]

I include this detail of studio bureaucracy to make the point that after eight years, Curtiz was still working under a yearly contract. The extension options were never a shoo-in. Warner Brothers was a very powerful machine indeed. From one year to the next, he could not be sure of his earnings and whether or not he would be laid off during the summer. By extension, even though it appears he intended to go back to Europe regularly, he could not plan for the trips until the last minute.

Nevertheless, the pace of Curtiz's career at Warner Brothers during the 1930's continued unabated. In his letters to my grandmother, he is always busy, busy, busy! In January 1936, for example, he writes that not only was he preparing for his next film, but he was called in to complete directing five films for other directors. He takes it in stride, however: "I have to work hard, but when you commit to a film career in Hollywood you cannot allow yourself to slack off." [13] The results of his commitment eventually came to fruition.

Behind the scenes, however, Curtiz continued to be involved with his personal affairs. Developments in Europe were threatening his family in Hungary. Closer to what was now home, his marriage with Bess continued on a rocky road, and his daughter Kitty's life was beginning to take shape. The stories of his Vienna children become increasingly complex and each tale moves along in its own direction. Life made sure that work alone was not enough for my grandfather.

The Budapest Family 1932 – 1939

After the honeymoon trip of 1931, Curtiz continued to be in close contact with his family in Hungary. I do not have the same treasure of letters that I have from Curtiz to my grandmother Fränzi, but I think it's safe to assume that his correspondence with his family was at least as frequent. He did notmake it back for another visit until 1934, however.

During this time, Curtiz helped to support his Budapest family financially, eventually purchasing the house at Number 32 Szövetség utcá in which they had lived since about 1903. Curtiz's father Ignatz had acquired the property before he died there in 1923 and it seems that gradually, as the Kaminer children grew up, married and had their own children, the family took over the whole house.

From being privately owned, the property became state property during the Communist years after World War I, and the family – now tenants – had to pay rent. The rent was low, but rent all the same. When Communism was ousted, the property could once more become privately owned, by someone else. By this time, most of the Kaminer/Kertész family were gone. Individual apartments came to be condominiums and the tenants were invited to buy their little part of the house.

Only one member of the Kaminer family experienced all of these changes first hand. Zsuzsa, the only daughter of Lajos and his Gentile wife Rosza, was born there, grew up there with her parents until her father was taken by the Nazis in 1945, continued to live there until her mother died, and beyond. She paid the rent during the Communist years, but could not afford to buy the apartment. Her mother's family came to the rescue, and Zsuzsa was able live out her life in the house on Szövetség utcá. The agreement was that when she passed away the family would sell the condo. This came to pass in 2010. [14]

✳✳✳✳✳

In 1934, after he saw Bess settled in England for her work with *The Iron Duke*, he traveled to Budapest to visit and make plans with his family. At this point, the objective of helping family emigrate to America was still primarily economic. Although Hitler had risen to power in Germany in 1933, the direction taken by him and the Nazi party was still largely rumour, especially as far away as Hungary. The family of Michael Curtiz focused on his success in the American film industry and saw it as a way to increase everyone's fortunes. No doubt he left them with high hopes and promises.

With the Non-Quota Immigration Visa under his arm, Curtiz left Hungary, spent about two weeks with Bess in England, and

Photos, Ilona Ryder, 2014

entered America as a "Returning alien." I've already traced my grandfather's road to becoming an American Citizen; he reached that goal three years later, in 1937. By that time, the Nazi threat was much more real in Europe, and getting his family out of Budapest became a priority.

Except for his nephew Loránd Manhart who had left years before, the first of Curtiz's immediate family to leave Hungary were his mother Aranka and his two brothers Deszö and Gabor. Aranka had obtained a Non-Quota Immigration Visa, but her two sons had only Passport Visas, which allowed them to make the voyage from Europe but they could not remain in the U.S.A. The threesome left Europe from Cherbourgh on the SS *Queen Mary* and arrived in New York April 20, 1939.

The story of Curtiz's brothers, as they made their way to Tijuana, Mexico to await their quota number to come up, is one that was repeated thousands of times for desperate immigrants from Europe. In the case of Deszö and Gabor, they most likely accompanied their mother by train from New York to Los Angeles, and then made the short trip down to Tijuana.

Aranka herself – my great grandmother – was by then a frail seventy seven year-old woman for whom the journey might have been quite a blur. But she summoned all her strength to greet her first-born son Manó when he met her at the station in Los Angeles. Curtiz had a grand welcome for his mother at Canoga Ranch, just north of Hollywood.

At least a part of the family was united, briefly. After the celebrations, and after Deszö (David) and Gabor left for Tijuana, his first concern was his mother's health. Within one month, Curtiz took Aranka to see Dr. J. B. McDonald for heart problems. Soon after, he installed her in comfortable living quarters at 4035 Sixie Canyon Avenue, Van Nuys.

On November 2, 1939 Aranka filled out a Declaration of Intention to apply for American Citizenship. For me, this Declaration is a treasure because it reveals the whereabouts of her seven children and allows me to create a snapshot of Curtiz's family:

- Regina – Curtiz's oldest sister nicknamed Denda was now fifty; she ha d been married to Armin Deregnyöi for thirty years. They lived in **Budapest** with their twenty year old daughter Katalin.
- Deszö had turned forty-five and was now in **Tijuana**

Welcoming Aranka Kaminer, 1939 (L to R: David, Mike,
Aranka, Bess's mother, Lorveretö, unknown, Bess)

- Lajos at forty-three, had been married to Rózsa (born Molnar) for fifteen years; they also lived in **Budapest** with their eight-year old daughter Zsuzsa.
- Margaret (Margit) at age forty lived in **Nagyvarad, Rumania** with husband Jenö Manhart; their twenty-two year old son Loránd had previously left for the USA.
- Kornellia (Nella) was thirty-seven, married, either to her first or second husband Jenö Rosenberg or Arnold Engel and living in **Budapest**; there were no children.
- The youngest brother, Oszkár (Gabor), turned thirty-four that October, the only one still single, now in **Tijuana**

Of Curtiz's six living siblings and their families, three were still in Europe, still in danger. Their safety would still occupy him as he tried to keep his work and his own personal life on an even keel.

Bess and John Meredyth Lucas 1932 – 1939

After their trip to Budapest in 1931, both Bess and her husband were busy working. The next eight years were relatively easy for him, but Bess had to struggle. In the transition to sound film, she expanded her skills as silent-screen scenarist to include working up her own stories (*Chasing Rainbows*, 1930), dialogue continuity (*Gay Madrid*, 1930), writing full scripts (*The Iron Duke*, 1934) and even working up theatre plays (*The Mighty Barnum*, 1934).

In 1935 they sold the house on Roxbury and bought the Canoga Ranch in the San Fernando Valley. The original property had the main house "surrounded by 110 acres, 90 acres of it in citrus". [15] While the Curtizes owned it, it grew to 265 acres, with a horse stable and other improvements. John Meredyth Lucas recounts scenes of life around the ranch: 'Mike' working on scripts, a tight-knit Hungarian community of actors, writers, and directors coming and going. A good example was the reunion dinner with Ince Sandor where the theatre manager cooked Hungarian food for the family. [16]

This appears to have been a "period of increasing domestic tranquility" but by September 1936 they were separated and Bess moved to Long Beach, where she filed for divorce on the grounds of mental cruelty. [17] Her comments to the media are conciliatory:

> You see, it is very difficult for two people whose careers make such great demands upon them to make a success of matrimony, which is a full-time job in itself. So Mr. Curtiz and myself, without further animosity, 'agreed to disagree' [18]

Even though an interlocutory decree of divorce was granted, within six months the couple was seen together again and there were rumours of reconciliation. [19] In the family photos of 1939 when Curtiz welcomed his mother and brothers to the charmed life of a successful Hollywood film couple, Bess Meredyth and even her mother were present.

Bess seems also to have been involved with Curtiz's personal finances regarding his daughter Kitty. He was still supporting the twenty-four-year old, and Bess had asked for a legal opinion. Whether or not Roland Swaffield's answer satisfied Bess's displeasure, he attempts to treat the matter in a businesslike way and takes it out of her hands.

> As both Mr. Curtiz and Miss Curtiz are aware, the former is under absolutely no obligation to continue to support her …. Miss Curtiz must understand that the allowance that has been made to her, and any allowance which may hereafter be made for her, has been and will be purely gratuitous and made at Mr. Curtiz's pleasure. [20]

The monthly allowance was $150 but there had been additional payments – some in secret – that continued to cause frustration and discord between Bess and Curtiz.

Despite their differences, the Curtizes weathered the separation and reconciliation during this time largely because of Bess's son John Meredyth Lucas. Although Curtiz didn't formally adopt him, he treated John as his own son. He recognized John's talent for writing and got him into the business as soon as he could. Then John's biological father Wilfred Lucas died in 1940, leaving the young man emotionally vulnerable. The war in Europe promised to pull him out of the doldrums, but when John was drafted in 1941, he was diagnosed with asthma and discharged on medical grounds. [21]

In his memoir, Meredyth Lucas tries to come to an understanding of how the dynamics of Bess and Curtiz's marriage and their careers panned out in the long run.

> Whether Mike's extra-marital actions caused her to withdraw from her work or whether it was just the way in a very cruel and competitive business works, she hid her grief in illness. You keep yourself on top or you're on the slide to oblivion. But for whatever reason, Mother's career trailed off as Mike's ascended. [22]

Kitty and her Mother Lucy Doraine, 1932 – 1939

Lucy Doraine's coming to America did little for her career, and after 1931, her American filmography is practically empty. Sometime in 1932, Doraine took up with Jorgen Dietz, a German-born chemical engineer, who had broken up with his Danish wife Solveig. According to Dietz, the popular star Douglas Fairbanks Jr. had caused the split. However, an investigation spurred by the Fairbanks legal team uncovered some shady dealings that Doraine and Dietz had cooked up in an attempt to raise money for their own wedding. The wedding did take place March 1933, and the couple continued their attack on Fairbanks Jr. with another lawsuit in October of that year. By February of 1934, Dietz and Doraine were themselves separated, and by July, she had filed for divorce. [23]

I can only imagine how all of this affected Kitty, her daughter by Curtiz. While Kitty was in her teens, she still lived with her mother, but she also had regular contact with her father. In letters to his daughter, Curtiz says he hasn't seen Lucy Doraine for years. [24] Regardless, the teenager must have been confused about her parents.

Kitty attended Hollywood High. How she made out in this celebrity environment after having grown up in Vienna and with Fräulein Rosa is a story all its own. She had a restless heart. In 1935 after she graduated, the nineteen-year old Kitty returned to Budapest, but she was back in Hollywood within a year.

Among my grandmother Fränzi's memorabilia, I found an article that Kitty, signing herself Katharina Kertèsz, wrote about her father for a German magazine. In "The Field Marshall of Film" Kitty gives us her understanding of Curtiz's approach to actors within the context of *Captain Blood*. It had been the first time she'd had the "opportunity to observe [her] father during an entire film" – first, because some scenes were shot on Laguna Beach near Curtiz's beach house where she may have been visiting, and second, because he also invited his twenty year old daughter to the sound stage at the studio, a rare event indeed.

In this exposé, Kitty describes Curtiz's lengthy preparations and stresses his need to know the very essence of his cast, so that during shooting there would be no "unpleasant surprises. – In short, he knows his Army down to the last man." Above all, Kitty says, Curtiz valued the genuine; he "preferred simple and natural people." [25] Was Errol Flynn one of these natural people? According to Kitty, the adventurous young man had come from England to start up a sports academy in Hollywood and it was through his wife Lili Damita whom Curtiz apparently knew intimately in earlier days that the two men became acquainted. Curtiz insisted and got his way in having Flynn assigned to the film that made him an instant star, says Kitty.

When I was involved in final settlement of the Kitty Curtiz estate after her death at ninety in 2006, a set of letters from her father to her were provided to me by her long-standing friend Helga. Although there may have been earlier letters, the first one in the file folder I was given is dated March 4, 1937. Kitty was already twenty-one years old, and her handwritten notes in the margin indicate that she meant to quote from this letter in her autobiography. That work remains unpublished, so I cannot refer to the many details that I would like to have shared here, but I'm thankful to have permission to use these letters.

Reading the letters, I can see similarities in the ways Curtiz hands out advice to his daughter and to my grandmother Fränzi. The subject matter is different, of course, but his approach is equally specific and engaged. On the topic of money, he is generous but clear about limitations. When faced with complaints or sadness, he encourages strength and determination. His faith in doing the best one can – his philosophy of life – always comes through as positive. At the same time, there are differences. The most striking is that with his daughter, he signs himself as "Mike" and not the more intimate "Papa" as I might have expected. And yet there is no mistaking the fatherly voice in his letters to Kitty.

A grave event occurred in the summer of 1939. Kitty attempted to commit suicide in a hotel room on Sunset Boulevard where she was apparently living. The incident, though reported in the media, was played down largely due to the influence of Curtiz. The records at Warner Brothers Archives include an unpublished piece for the *Los Angeles Examiner*, a news story that Curtiz kept out of the papers. Instead, newspaper clippings describe the incident with vagueness and melodramatic detail:

> Under circumstances thinly veiled with her remark that she was wanted by no one, Katherine Curtiz, 24-year-old daughter of Michael Curtiz, prominent film director, attempted suicide yesterday. [26]

> … "I tried to kill myself, but the blood – the blood, it flowed so red. I was alone, so alone. It seems I am always alone." [27]

Family and friends protect each other. When, upon Kitty's death an Austrian reporter asked me about the real reasons for her 1939 suicide attempt, I did not divulge any further details. If her autobiography is ever published, the rest of Kitty's story will come out.

Thilde Forster and her son Michael 1932 – 1939

Thilde Forster was already in Hollywood at the end of February, 1933 when she heard the news about the fire in the Reichstag in Berlin. In the next few days, Adolf Hitler the newly elected Chancellor ordered a purge of Communist government members and established his Nazi party (National Socialist German Workers' Party) as the majority power. In full awareness of the consequences for Jewish people living in Germany, Thilde immediately contacted her brother Ludwig in Berlin, who phoned the young Michael Forster at the Wickersdorf boarding school. He said, "Pack your things, we are leaving. Der Reichstag brennt." [28]

Michael and his Uncle Ludwig ended up in the small village of Hirschberg am See in Sudetenland, the German-speaking part of Czechoslovakia. They managed to survive for several months with no money, but eventually they had to move on. They were forced to walk the fifty kilometers to Leipzig to seek help from the Jewish Community, and this is when Uncle Ludwig finally revealed to Michael that he was Jewish, that his parents were both Jewish. The secret came as a shock to the twelve-year old boy.

The two travelers were in a precarious situation: on the one hand, they could be persecuted as Jews by the Nazis but on the other hand, as Jewish refugees they could get help from organizations that were being set up all around Central Europe. Eventually Ludwig and the son of Michael Curtiz made it back to Vienna, where they became part of the Jewish refugee community. In the fall, the young Michael was enrolled in the Jewish high school, Chaies Gymnasium, where he quickly fit in as the newest Jewish kid on the block. The entire Jewish community was trying to come to grips with their position in a Nazi dominated world and everyone was trying to get out of Europe. Thilde, already in America, was in a good position to make sure her son would be able to leave as soon as possible.

While events were unfolding in Europe, Thilde was also fighting for her child a half a world away. On February 1, 1933, she filed a suit in Los Angeles Superior Court for an increase in the maintenance "allegedly paid" by Michael Curtiz according to the 1923 Austrian Court Order. The court battle would go on for some time, bringing brief media attention to the fairly new Warner Brothers director, a situation that the studio bosses did not like. In fact, they sent out a news release in which they identified her as a dancer, their way of branding her as a gold-digger for trying to pursue Curtiz.

Thilde's lawyer managed to get Warner Brothers to retract that statement. However, an internal memo from a person identified only as "hhm" indicates that yes, Miss Forster would be "designated as a writer in any future stories. The joke was on [her lawyer], not knowing there won't be any more". [29] It's clear that the studio's intention was to quash any further bad publicity for Curtiz.

When Thilde's court case against Curtiz was over, the newspaper did publish the outcome, but the result was disappointing for the young mother. Curtiz's legal team had objected on the grounds that the child in question was not actually in the United States, and the Court upheld that argument. It was back to square one for Thilde. The lesson she learned from this was that she had to bring her boy to America, and as things stood in Europe, doing so was of utmost importance. First, she had Ludwig apply for Michael's permanent residency, which had to be made outside of the United States, and then she arranged for his passage.

In February 1934, the boy and his uncle left Vienna, spent some time in Paris, and finally arrived at the port of Le Havre, France. There, Michael was put on the passenger-freighter ship *Wyoming* which would take him through the Panama Canal and up to Los Angeles. Uncle Ludwig stayed behind. Thilde had arranged for her son's immigration to America, but she could not do the same for her brother.

As soon as young Michael is settled in Los Angeles with his mother, she filed another law suit against Curtiz. It is a new attempt to fully establish Curtiz's paternity and responsibility for maintenance now that the boy was an American resident. Curtiz's lawyers filed a counter-suit in which they attempted to get Thilde to repay earlier support payments because she had allegedly "expended on herself [the money] that was meant for the boy's support." [30] The persistent mother eventually got her way, however, and Curtiz continued to pay.

Curtiz was becoming a star director at Warner Brothers, earning a huge salary and generally living the high life that came with success. His secretary Desider Pek took care of his personal business, including his financial obligations. When a single mother like Thilde became bothersome, Pek would keep her off his back. Pek was probably the person who bought gifts, such as the silver ball point pen that Michael Forster received "from his father" when he graduated from Hollywood High School.

About his father personally, Michael Forster still has more questions than answers. He got to know him only briefly even though they lived in the same town, Hollywood. It was only in 1946, when Michael was twenty-five and a mathematics graduate at University in California at Los Angeles (UCLA), with a short wartime career in the American Army behind him, that he actually met his father. Thilde had proudly made the arrangements for her war hero son to meet his father. It was a difficult time for Curtiz at Warner Brothers, and Michael Forster's memories of those meetings reveal some of the strain.

I met him several times when I returned from the war in 1946, and we had many talks. I would watch him shoot a scene from one of his movies, and then we would have lunch...

On one of these visits, I was still in my Army uniform and I could see that my father was proud of me. He was obviously nervous, more nervous than I. On another occasion, he was working on a movie called "Jim Thorpe," a biography of the famous Indian athlete. My father pronounced it Jim Torpee ...

I think he wanted to help me with a movie career, but at the same time he was afraid of breaking some unwritten Hollywood rule about nepotism. His own career was then in decline... While I was attracted to the glamour of the movies, I could see that it would take an awful lot of fawning and hanging about to get a foot in the door. I decided to do it my way and to forget about the movies. [31]

His way turned out well for Michael Forster, no doubt in part because he had inherited a strong will from his mother.

Theresia Dalla Bonna and her daughter Sonja, 1932 - 1939

Because there appears to have been no direct contact between Theresia Dalla Bonna and Curtiz over the years, and the family has no stories that were passed down by Sonja, Curtiz's middle Vienna child, I rely on the guardianship files for clues about this period of time.

In 1931, the District Court responsible for Sonja's welfare sent a letter that included a personal appeal from the girl's guardian to Curtiz through the Austrian Konsul in Chicago. In response, Curtiz sent $50 (about 3500 Schilling) to the authority in Vienna and indicated that he hoped to pay all outstanding amounts by the end of the year. And then Curtiz did something unexpected. He raised the monthly payment from 120 to 200 Schilling. Perhaps the appeal affected his sense of duty toward the girl, but whatever the reason, Theresia would have sighed with relief when she found out about it.

She did not actually receive the higher amount. For a rew months, she is handed 150 Schilling per month, apparently a de-

Sonja and Theresia, June 1939

cision of the formal Guardian to keep the bank account balance from slipping too low. Prudence and thriftiness is a virtue. From time to time there would be extra expenses – all documented, all individually requested for approval. If they weren't careful, the money would run out. Indeed by July 1932, there were barely 75 Schilling (just over $10) in the account. Obviously Curtiz's payments did not keep up.

Then the Guardianship situation changed. The court-appointed Guardian had to leave his job due to health issues, and Theresia herself took over legal guardianship. All monies still had to flow through the court authority, however. When, at the beginning of 1933, she admitted that she got $40 from Curtiz directly, she was promptly reprimanded. In February 1933, Theresia (now spelling her name Therese, but I will continue with Theresia) tried another approach. Unrepresented by legal counsel – she could not afford to pay a lawyer – she petitioned the court to pursue Curtiz to fulfill his obligations toward Sonja. The two-page document outlines her dire circumstances: Curtiz's payments are sporadic at best, and Theresia is unable to find work. She requests an accounting of the arrears, that Curtiz be "warned" through the Austrian Consulate in Chicago, and that he should also pay the court's costs instead of having them taken out of the support for the child.

In her petition, Theresia indicates that Curtiz should live up to his promise to "care for his daughter's upbringing, befitting her station." When and how such promise was made is not in evidence. In the letter where Curtiz raised the monthly support, he had wished Sonja to be enrolled in a boarding school. Theresia had done that but there were insufficient funds after only five months.

Nevertheless, Theresia succeeded in the fight for her child. At least for a time, Curtiz paid regularly, and by the end of 1933 the balance in the account for Sonja's support is approximately 3000 Schillings. Monthly cheques of $50 continued in 1934, and Theresia also obtained employment in a café. Sonja finally got her piano. The special request for 880 Schillings for the piano, plus 36 Schillings for the bench and moving costs, was granted. French lessons were added to the girl's extra-curricular activities, so that in 1935, when she was about to turn twelve, Sonja was living a fairly well-rounded young girl's life, a life befitting her position as a film director's daughter. Her own children remember Sonja telling them that, because she had aspirations to be a pianist, her mother and grandmother did not ask her to do housework.

Sonja even had a summer holiday in Italy that year. Theresia had to jump through hoops to get the 400 Schilling fee for the girl to stay at the holiday resort for forty days. Not only did she have to show that the money was available in the bank account, she also had to prove that neither she nor her parents – the girl's grandparents – could pay the amount from their own resources. It all turned out well, and the future appeared bright for Curtiz's second Vienna child.

And then things became more complicated. Over the next few years, Sonja developed health problems, as did her mother Theresia. Curtiz's payments became sporadic again, and as Austria descended into the maelstrom of Nazi takeover and then war, the mother and daughter could no longer rely on his support. In 1938 Sonja was well enough again to attend secretarial college, but her mother's health deteriorated. There were no payments from Curtiz at all in 1939.

Despite this downward spiral in their fortunes, Sonja had her Confirmation in June, 1939. The picture of her taken for the occasion shows a tall, serious but handsome looking young woman – strikingly like Curtiz.

Fränzi Wondrak and her son Michael, 1932 – 1939

In 1933, on the advice of Curtiz, Fränzi brought her boy back to Vienna for good. She told me that, rather than tell people the truth, she passed him off as a child in her care. She moved back into the apartment on Schopenhauerstrasse with her mother Anna Wondrak and placed Michael in a boarding school nearby to add to the illusion that he was not her child.

Because his first language was Italian, Michael was set back one year in his schooling. Instead of going into Grade 3 in the fall of 1933, he was placed in Grade 2. This reminds me so much of my own experience coming to Canada as a nine-year old. The upheaval of immigration made me miss a half year of school altogether, and the change in language saw me enrolled in Grade 3 instead of Grade 4 after Christmas. For my father, an aspect of normality returned to his life, at least in terms of his schooling, but his feelings were in turmoil.

> I hated Vienna that first year. Even though I went to school in my family's neighbourhood, I lived not at home but in boarding school. To a six-year old that feels like he is unwanted.

> When I did visit [my mother], she was often too busy chatting with her mother to pay any attention to me. [32]

Adults often don't see how their actions affect children, even if they have their best interests at heart. Fränzi had her own difficulties with the situation, and her loyalties continued to be tested.

One disturbing event occurred in the summer of 1934 during Curtiz's visit to Budapest. He sent for Fränzi and their son Michael, now nine years old, to come to Budapest from Vienna. My grandmother told me how she was introduced to little Michael's aunts, and how Curtiz suggested that she leave the boy with one of them to simplify the process of his adopting the boy and taking him to America. I can imagine her emotional state: here was a chance for her son to begin a new life with his father, but without her! The mother instinct did the rest; she flew back to Vienna as fast as the train would take her, with her son safely by her side.

Soon after, Michael contracted scarlet fever. Curtiz was again fully engaged. In his letters he tried to calm Fränzi by telling her that scarlet fever is not so dangerous nowadays with medical advances. He also suggested they take a vacation to let some fresh country air help his son to recover.

So it was that Fränzi and the boy went to Annaberg for the first time. In this quaint mountain village not too far from Vienna, the Bauer family took boarders into their seventeenth-century farm-style home. At 976 m. elevation and surrounded by forests, Annaberg was the perfect place for Michael to recuperate. The Bauers' son Josef was close in age and the boys spent a lot of time playing and exploring. Michael soon regained his strength. It was the first of what became an annual summer vacation and lasting friendships, through the tragic wartime death of young Josef Bauer, through the years of Fränzi's shattered dreams, all the way into the next generation. Vacationing in Annaberg became a ritual for me as a little girl before I came to Canada. And now, whenever I am in Austria, I always make a pilgrimage to Annaberg.

Back in 1934, trouble was brewing with the rise of Hitler and the Nazis. In his September letter Curtiz voiced his concern about Fränzi and Michael's safety and advised her to take their son to live in Italy. For some reason she did not do this, remaining instead in Vienna so the boy could continue his schooling.

In April 1935, Fränzi was reminded that, although her correspondence with Curtiz was quite regular and seemed open and

Michael Wondrak in Budapest, 1934

honest, he had not come through on the major step of adopting their son as his own. The brief letter from her lawyer suggests that Curtiz is said to be in Vienna, that he had been there previously but not dealt with the matter. He asks Fränzi for news as soon as possible, but nothing more seems to have come of the entire plan.
33

That summer, she sent young Michael to Bolzano to stay for a while with the Maurachers who had taken care of him in infancy. Also during this time, Fränzi wanted to make more of a life for herself and her child, and she must have written to Curtiz about it because he agreed that she should look for a small apartment of her own. If the rent for a "room and a kitchen" is reasonable, he'd send her "a little more money every month." [34] It's quite clear that Curtiz's regular monthly payments of $65 at this time had provided for Fränzi living with her mother in the Schopenhauerstrasse apartment as well as the boy's boarding school fees. I should mention that even in years where there were few letters from Curtiz, his payments were regular. Not only did Fränzi keep all his letters, she also kept several stacks of receipt stubs.

Fränzi's wish to having her own place would indeed require more money, and there is no talk of her taking any work. Perhaps Curtiz's cautionary tone discouraged her, or she simply couldn't find a suitable place, but it appears that nothing came of the idea. It was never mentioned again.

With so many plans going awry, it's no wonder that Michael became somewhat withdrawn. "As soon as I could," he told me,

> I managed to get a bicycle and spent my free time riding to Pötzleinsdorf, a suburb that borders on the Vienna Woods. Both were to be my sanctuary for many years to come, but early on, I rode only as far as the old town centre and the cemetery. In this calm and quiet place, I spent many hours, reading and thinking. [35]

For a time he lived with his uncle and aunt, the Palkas, now permanently back from Abbazia. They had a larger apartment just three blocks away, but Fränzi continued to live in the same apartment long after her mother died and until shortly before her own death in 1991.

In fact, more than twenty years after Fränzi passed away, her name "Wondrak" still appeared on the outside the apartment house Schopenhauerstrasse No. 75. I let it go when I first saw it in 2013, but when I walked past again the next year I took courage and rang the buzzer. A woman's voice answered and actually let me into the house but not into the apartment on the second floor parterre. Through the peephole, I saw a single eye and I told it that I had spent a large part of my early childhood in that apartment, had run up and down the stairs and hallways. A man's gruff voice somewhere in the room behind the eye said something in a foreign language, and our conversation was over. On the way out I noticed a different name on the mailbox. As the big doors to the street slammed shut behind me with a familiar echo in the entrance hall,

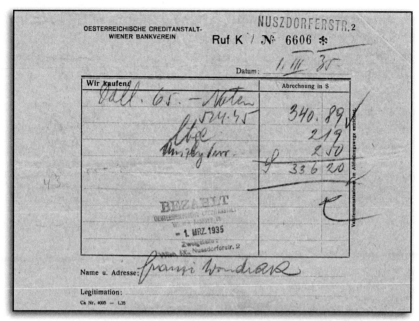

One of 47 receipts between June 1934 and March 1939.
Amounts range from $50 to $90.

I wondered what prevented these people from changing the tag
on the street side.

*****

In 1935 Curtiz promised Fränzi that he would come to
Europe in 1936 if there was no war. War did not happen then, but
he could not come in 1936 because the studio remained open over
the summer. However, Curtiz did do something special for her.
He set up and sent her a life insurance policy for US$3000 so that
she would be "protected in case something unforeseen happens.
We have to be ready for anything." [36] He also advised her to stay
in Austria for the summer because of the political developments
in Italy. Clearly he was concerned about her and little Michael's
safety. With that year's Christmas letter, Curtiz sent a glossy PR
photo of himself with the studio bosses, signing it to "Franzi and
Bubi! Greetings and Kisses from Miska, Hollywood, 9 December,
1936." Another treasure that my father kindly gave to me; it now
hangs on my wall.

The promises continued. In 1937 Curtiz was proud to say he
had obtained American citizenship and a new American passport. However, he could not travel to Europe again that summer.

By November, he mentioned a possibility that he might come to Europe if he were assigned to make a film in London. That doesn't appear to have happened, however. Again, he planned to come the following year.

During 1938, the political situation in Europe deteriorated and once again, Curtiz did not travel. He wrote to Fränzi that he had "VERY MANY OBLIGATIONS TO SATISFY," that he was supporting his entire Hungarian family, and that perhaps in a year or two, he could send her money for passage to America.

With everything else that was going on, it is to his credit that as late as 1939, Curtiz was still trying to get Fränzi and their son to America. He even wired an extra US$150 in February, but time was not on his side. As the situation escalated to Anschluss – the Nazi takeover of Austria – and toward war, he was still asking pointed questions and making suggestions.

> I need to know, dear Fränzi, … whether you are recorded as having been married and whether Bubi shows up as my son. … [In the Affidavit] I'd prefer to name you as my cousin and Bubi as my nephew… Once you are here, these things will not matter… [37]

> Because Czechoslovakia already belongs to Germany, Bubi will also need a German passport. In any case, ask there at the proper authorities what kinds of documents you will need and if you are allowed to emigrate. As reasons for emigrating, you should say that you want to send Bubi to school in America… [38]

> I advise you NOT to come over with a visitor's visa since you can stay only 6 months… There is a possibility that Bubi could come here as a student, with you accompanying him, and you could both stay until he finishes his studies. But it would still be best if you could come to America as immigrants… [39]

He goes on in this last letter to speculate about the pros and cons of using a German passport compared to a Czechoslovakian passport, and he comments on the Italian emigration quota. He promises to send the necessary Affidavit so that "you will not be a burden to the United States government." Unfortunately, war did break out and Curtiz's efforts to bring my grandmother and father to the U.S. ground to a halt.

*****

The six years of World War II changed everything. Correspondence and money transfer were interrupted, although Curtiz like so many others found ingenious ways to support loved ones left behind in Europe. Like so many others, he suffered loss: his brother Lajos and his sister Kornellia became victims of the Holocaust. Curtiz's half-Jewish children in Vienna – Sonja Dalla Bonna and my father Michael Vondrak – were subjected to discrimination, but they survived. And as if the chaos of the war in Europe wasn't enough, Curtiz's work in Hollywood hit highs and lows he'd never before experienced.

PART VII

WILD YEARS AHEAD: 1940 - 1952

Over the next dozen or so years, the contact that Curtiz had with his children centered mostly on his first-born daughter and his last Vienna child, my father. Kitty went through much personal turmoil and moved several times between New York, Hollywood, Washington DC and back to California. After World War II was over, my father Michael Vondrak was set up to emigrate to America, with disastrous outcomes. The other two, Michael Forster and Sonja Dalla Bonna, were relatively out of range. In his relationship with Bess, the rocky road continued although they remained married. Regarding his Budapest family, Curtiz endured the ups and downs of rescue and loss that the war in Europe brought to so many. And if that wasn't enough, his career – ever his rock – was catapulted through great changes.

Curtiz's star at Warner Brothers was still rising at the end of the 1930's. There had been the westerns *Dodge City* (1939), *Virginia City* (1940), *Santa Fe Trail* (1940) with Flynn and DeHavilland, the screen couple he had made popular in *Robin Hood*. He also worked with Flynn and Bette Davis to make the Tudor drama *The Private Lives of Elizabeth and Essex* (1939). I love the studio still of Curtiz kneeling in front of the haughty-looking Queen, showing her exactly how to respond to Essex.

Reviews of the film were less than flattering. James Robertson, in *The Casablanca Man,* also concentrates on the difficulties surrounding the actors and the screenplay rather than the director's handling of the material. Still, the film did get five Oscar nominations.

I personally do not agree with most of the criticism, and I believe Curtiz did the best he could with what he was given to work with. His characteristic camera angles and effects – the clever use of shadows – do help. Davis is as great a dramatist as in any of her films, but Flynn is not given the opportunity to show the physical prowess for which he is known. I also think Curtiz tried hard to make the love between the two believable, but it was a tall order!

The script is based on a play by American Maxwell Anderson (1888-1959), but the Tudor story about Queen Elizabeth I and the Earl of Essex (Roberto Devereaux) has been and remains a long-standing favourite in the theatre arts. I had the great pleasure of seeing the opera *Roberto Devereaux* (1837) by Gaetano Donizetti in Vienna, and you can bet I paid attention. Both Donizetti and Anderson's treatments offer us a slice of Elizabethan life in an entertaining way. Each version of the story plays loosely with historical facts, being more concerned – two and three hundred years after the fact – with showing the audience the culture and politics of those respective time periods.

At the risk of comparing apples and oranges, I believe the plot of the opera is more realistic than that of the screenplay. In the opera, the relationship between Elizabeth and Essex is less private and thus more in line with how people in their station, in those times, probably did act. As well, the love between Essex and Sara, one of the royal attendants, creates a more solid base for the Queen's anger. In the opera, the Queen is fooled by love itself while in the film, the political intrigues of life at Court bring her to the fatal decision. However, while the personal motives are stronger in the opera, the film better clarifies the charge of treason; the Queen's verdict is justified in the law. I wonder if Curtiz had seen Donizetti's opera by Donizetti or any other version of the story, but this will have to remain one of those tantalizing unanswered questions.

The more enjoyable projects for Curtiz were probably directing James Cagney in *Angels with Dirty Faces* (1938) and working with Claude Rains in *Four Daughters* (1938). The latter set in motion a series of three sequels, two directed by Curtiz: *Daughters Courageous* (1939) and *Four Wives* (1939). Action films during this period included *The Sea Hawk* (1940) and his contribution to military themes with *Dive Bomber* (1939) and *Captains of the Clouds* (1942).

In keeping with developing international events, *Yankee Doodle Dandy* (1942) was a musical epic of intense patriotic proportions. Through James Cagney's Oscar for best actor, Curtiz reaped the status that pushed his career at Warner Brothers to even greater heights, culminating in his own long-awaited Oscar for best director a year later with the continuing cult favourite, *Casablanca*.

The single most disruptive element for Curtiz in the thirteen years between 1940 and 1953 when he left Warner Brothers was, of course, World War II. As it did with countless people around the world, the war in Europe affected the way he lived and thought. This fundamental change cannot be overstated. It affected his work, his personal relationships and perhaps in the most long-lasting ways, his children and his Budapest family.

Portents of what was to come were already felt in the mid 1930's. Disbelief and political failures allowed the Nazi machine to begin its work. But things came to a head when Hitler invaded Poland in September, 1939. Escalation of military action and declarations of war followed, and soon everything fell apart.

1940 - 1943

Before America was fully involved in World War II, Curtiz tried to keep control of his personal responsibilities as he had been doing. After Kitty's attempted suicide in 1939, his daughter returned to New York, and he kept in touch with her there. Some of his letters are hand-written and others are dictated to Desider Pek, his personal secretary, for which he apologized. He admits that he is "terrible in English" and the sample below clearly demonstrates those shortcomings. [2]

But as I've seen in his letters to my grandmother Fränzi, it was the same with German. Curtiz wrote to Kitty about money, about his work, and about her health and happiness. Officially he was supporting her with $120 per month paid in two instalments, but he also sent her extra money when he felt she may need it. For example, in November, 1940, after she'd had an accident and needed medical attention, he sent money and fatherly advice: "don't hesitate to go to a Hospital, and tell them to send me the bill." [3]

On occasion Curtiz traveled to New York, usually to do research for the studio. And he would visit Kitty, if only briefly, whenever he could. These trips also offer a rare glimpse into the

Dear Kitty! I finished my last
picture. So I have little time
to answer your last letter. And
not a typewriter for my dictatory!
I'm terrible sorry but I will
not come to New York till December
I wish I could but will start my
pictures in 1 October — so you must
have patient till then.
I dont know whatt was the reason
that you moved away from your
old home — but I hope you find
a good place, where you can relax
affter theschool, the home where
you lived was nice little place
and I hope you will select the
rigth one. You better notifiod
Swafield Kath he shuld send
the check to your New Adress!
Otherwine she will Obiby!

IMPORTANT
LETTER   ①

I recived again 15 ₤ in this letter
the last I send 10 days ago to your
old adress - hope yo get it.
What have you heard from Lucy -
She never send me a letter or
not even a Card - I wonder how She
is feeling ?
I hope you feel allright and
will Continue be in god spirit
and hope that's time will Come
and you will not be allwaine
alone, and lonsom longig for
kindnes and home.

thinck on me allwaine
as your best friend, and
dont forget I stand back on
you in Everything

          must love and god
          Belt your
                Mike - ③

I wonder that you have forgotten
your Idea, to open a store - to
establish your future - I'm worried
the Time flys, and you muss have
something wish Occupy youre mind
- I hope you can read my letter
I'm terible in English - I should
go to a private school between pictures
But I suppose I need littee rest
and have no ambition to go in
shhool - But I should.
I'm starting my picture "the Sea Wolf"
in two week - plenty preparation and
work - I wish I could wisit you againe
But I promise affter finished - I'm sure
to wisit you againe. forgive my English
I'm made - but generely I dictade
letters to my secratary!
I hoppe miss Beth touis is better
poor girl she go true polenty truble.
Give her my love and god wishes.

②

wider American media's ideas about Michael Curtiz. Articles with headlines such as "Everybody Called 'Bum' by Mike Curtiz," "The Blitzkrieg of Michael Curtiz" and "Director Mutilates English On Purpose..." present a few outlandish tid-bits. [4] Because he "concentrates all his energies on the picture, [Curtiz] becomes so preoccupied that he is very absent-minded." One journalist, Elizabeth Copeland, links an accident during filming of *Four Wives* to his apparent lack of a "sense of direction" that causes him to "frequently get[] lost around town, though he's been [in America] for twelve years." [5] Cursing when he gets angry, being annoyed at time wasted, and disdainful of mystery stories are other fillers.

Theodore Strauss's article is more positive but echoes Curtiz's preoccupations and prejudices.

> During a recent five-day excursion to this metropolis ... he launched a one-man tourist Blitzkrieg upon all points of interest within a twenty-mile radius. ... As a director, Mr. Curtiz finds the New York film-going public an exasperating problem. He finds 20 percent comparatively sophisticated and 'most difficult to please' but 80 percent – "the average man in the street, 'easy to laugh, easy to cry'.

The article in the *Brooklyn Daily Eagle* focuses on the so-called "Curtizisms" – lapses in his use of English idiom – but in a positive way. Familiar phrases such as "bring on the empty horses" (*Charge of the Light Brigade*) and commands such as "stand around in bundles" and "bark the dog from left to right" are quoted, not in light of failure but rather as being on purpose. This writer suggests that Curtiz is creating a trademark for himself in a business that "at times, can be pretty grim. It needs the gayety aroused by Curtiz' assault on syntax."

Articles such as these served to perpetuate myths and misinformation about Curtiz: "It is said... that he works for inhuman periods at a stretch ... and that he plays polo like a desperate man." He refers to technicians as 'Wednesday bums' and 'ten cent bums'." "His father was an architect. His mother was a concert singer in Vienna." But all of these tidbits differ from the usual news about celebrities' news in one obvious way: there isn't much juicy gossip, which is not to say Curtiz's life was devoid of personal juicy bits.

That autumn 1940, he did write to Kitty again about finishing *Santa Fe Trail* and beginning a new film. Just as in his correspondence with my grandmother, Curtiz often used his work as an excuse. This time, because of *The Sea Wolf*, he couldn't come to New York until December, and in November that promise fell through because "the picture I'm doing is the toughest assignment I've ever had, and I really have no time to write."

Financial arrangements regarding Kitty continued through the lawyer Roland Swaffield, who was not always privy to her movements, however. When she returned to California at the beginning of 1941, he "was surprised" and added the veiled threat that he was "not able to make any commitments relative to further allowance." [6] Kitty was always still in the picture, and the topic was almost always about money. Curtiz also did see her from time to time, and I'd like to believe the following rare photo of Curtiz and his daughter was taken in front of his own garden.

Besides Curtiz himself writing to Kitty, his secretary Desider Pek became a confidant and middleman, sending her "secret checks" to add to the formal allowance, advising her on how to write letters to Swaffield, and revealing her father's personal struggles. After Curtiz's brothers arrived from Tijuana in November, 1940, Pek writes to Kitty:

> ... Now the real worries begin, how and where to place them. The worries, of course, are shouldered by Dad who has more responsibilities than any other man I know. ... But please keep it under your hat as though I wouldn't have said anything. [7]

In another letter to Kitty, Pek tells her about a possible split between Curtiz and Bess Meredyth. According to Pek, the pair had been fighting constantly; secretly he hopes that the current separation will "end up in a divorce." At this point, Bess was living at 4900 Oakdale Ave., Canoga Park, and not with her husband. Pek also tells Kitty that "financially Dad is almost wiped out," although "it won't affect your monthly allowance." This letter includes "another one of those 'private' checks." [8] At this point, Kitty was still single, trying to find happiness in her work and studies.

*****

Michael Forster was not yet nineteen when World War II broke out in Europe. He had graduated from Hollywood High School in 1938 and opted for Los Angeles City College for his first two years of post-secondary. At City College, Forster remembers

Michael Curtis and his daughter Kitty

still having "tremendous conflicts about being Jewish." [9] but overall he was a typical young man and successful in his studies without having to apply himself. In the summer of 1941 before he attended UCLA, Forster was lucky to get work at Yosemite National
Park, where he gained some practical experience.

In his own words, Forster's two years at UCLA "were un-
eventful." As the war escalated, he was anxious to get involved
with one of the reserve officer groups, which would lead to an
officer's "commission upon graduation and a fancy cadet officer's
uniform to swagger around in while still in school." [10] But it was
not to be.

Thilde Forster had brought up her son well, making sure
he had everything he needed. It helped to have financial support
from Curtiz who otherwise stayed out of their lives. She also protected young Michael as long as she could from what was going
on in the world. Instinctively she had made a decision not to apply
for his American citizenship for fear he would be drafted. Her son,
however, had a different view. He wanted to be part of the "new
class of sahibs, pilots, naval officers, all sorts of immensely glam-
orous people." Years later, he of course learned to appreciate her
wisdom, but then, as soon as he graduated with a BA in math-

ematics in 1943, he "volunteered to be drafted. That was the only way I could get into the war...," he says. [11] As he writes about this time in his life, Forster admits that he didn't think about reality:

> I felt inferior, shabby, unwanted, compared to my glorious classmates, some of whom had by now reached the ranks of Major and even Lt. Colonel.

> Others of my classmates were already dead – killed in the war. And my classmates from long ago, the Aryan supermen from Wickersdorf, and the Jewish victims from the Chaies Gymnasium – many, many of them were also dead by the summer of 1943. But I did not think of that. I only wanted to be part of the war. [12]

So he waited for his draft notice. He worked as an extra at various Hollywood film studios where war movies were being ground out "by the dozen, but with so many young men in the service, there was a shortage of extras who could be used to play soldiers." [13] No one knew that he was the son of Michael Curtiz, and he wasn't about to tell anyone.

*****

Curtiz had not sent any payments for his daughter Sonja Dalla Bonna during 1939. By March 1940, the account balance stood at nil and was closed. Theresia mustered her strength to write this last statement to the Court in April, 1940, but it was Sonja who wrote the note excusing her mother's absence at the hearing due to illness.

> I am aware that the child's father has not paid support since August 1939; I have tried unsuccessfully by letter to get him to resume payment. I do not file a petition because of this [failure]. I am also aware that the Wardship account is exhausted. The minor will be finished with her schooling at the end of June and will then take up employment immediately. There is therefore nothing further to be done in this case. [14]

Theresia Dalla Bonna died May 26, 1940 at the age of thirty-three. Her fight was over. Within the space of a few months, Sonja became independent from the Court system. She had been attending secretarial school. In August she turned seventeen, and by September she was working as a stenographer in a liqueur-making company.

But the Nazi threat was all around her in Vienna. Her daughter Christina, who lived in Calgary, Alberta until her death in 2012, told me that Sonja was followed around and was restricted to her neighbourhood. She had been identified as an undesirable because they knew her father was Jewish. She had to carry papers at all times. Apparently there was no further contact between Curtiz and his daughter until Sonja wrote to him many years later, after she was married to Jack Hill, a British officer she met in Vienna, after she'd had the first two of their four children, and after they had moved to Canada. Unfortunately all correspondence was lost in a hurricane when the family lived in Belize.

*****

Despite war already raging in Europe, and despite Austria already being part of the Third Reich, Curtiz was still planning to bring my father Michael Vondrak and my grandmother Fränzi to America. His May 4, 1940 letter, however, shows that much had changed:

> I was happy to receive your dear letter of April 8 and also Bubi's English letter. I am surprised, however, that you haven't received news from me since August 1939. I wrote to you every six weeks, but in the war, letters will often "disappear." ...

> Enclosed I am sending you an affidavit so that you can get your passports and your American visas. Also enclosed is a document in which Warner Studios confirms that I am in a financial position to support you both here. ...

> Regarding the 200 Deutsch Mark that you still haven't received through Berlin, I can't make any inquiries until I know in which month you should have received the money. Write me about that ...

The ongoing "uncertain postal situation" mentioned in his next letter shows evidence of personal mail being opened. *Geöffnet* by *Oberkommando der Wehrmacht* (High Command of the Armed Forces) is stamped on the envelope.

Between May 1939 and September 1941, there are seven letters from Deutsche Bank in Berlin addressed to Fränzi Wondrak.
They bear the unmistakeable mark of the powers in charge. In July
1939, the bank signs off with *Heil Hitler!* a grim reminder that the
dictator's influence had replaced the earlier closing *Mit deutschen
Gruss* (with German greetings). These seven letters, another one
from the Hamburg America Line, and two further letters from the
Commerzbank attest to Curtiz's efforts to continue support payments for his son, my father.

In all these letters, monthly payments in varying amounts
were announced, sometimes with the warning that the money
was to be used strictly for support of the child. For my grandmother in war-torn Austria, the payments far outstripped those
needs. Through Fränzi, Curtiz helped the rest of the family to
buy food, coal and other necessities that many had to go without. After September 1941, there were no further bank transfers
until September 1946, when payments resumed through the
Creditanstalt-Bankverein in a liberated Vienna.

While we think about what the world and the adults were up
to, we can forget the effect that such times had on the young. My
father Michael Wondrak, a fifteen year-old boy in Vienna at the
end of 1941, wrote a letter to his dad to wish him a Happy Birthday,
Merry Christmas and a Happy New Year. The reason I have the
letter is that it was never delivered. Fränzi took it to the neighbourhood post office where the clerk stamped it December 6, 1941. But
by the time the letter reached the central Post Office for overseas,
several days had passed and the world stage had changed to a new
scene. The stamp on the returned letter says *Zurück – Postverkehr
eingestellt* (Returned, Postal Services discontinued).

My father's experience is a good example of being caught in
the middle of world events. Like thousands of Viennese he had
gone to see the Führer on March 15, 1938. He shared this and other
memories with me verbally:

> Hitler's march into Vienna was a major event – everyone
> was there: thousands lined the Ring Strasse on both sides for
> the parade. I climbed up and stood on top of the temporary
> metal toilet booths set up for the show so that I could see
> better.

Yes, that was a show, but the sinister side of the Anschluss would
soon be felt by everyone. Since he was sixteen, Michael had been

involved with *Wanderfögel* (the Wandering Birds), a youth group with a charismatic section leader. Their group did not join the Hitler Youth when the push came for that to happen. For his resistance, their leader was arrested and prosecuted. Michael remembered his losses vividly.

> There was an adventure company that would launch gliders from a Vienna Woods height where there was a distinct drop. I worked with this adventure company, helping them to catapult the flimsy craft off the bare top of the mountain. Daring young men would fly these gliders, thereby learning the basics of controlling the gliders in the air currents. It took six or eight young men to pull the glider back on a rubber band rigging and then release it. To get to the job, I took a train up 15 or 20 minutes. After doing this for a year or so, I had earned the right to learn to fly. But by that time, Hitler had marched into Vienna and only Hitler Youth were allowed to fly or even work there. I had to quit... Mother told me this... would be dangerous for me to be there.
>
> So I missed my chance on something I'd looked forward to and I thought was rightfully mine. But of course it was lucky too: For the Hitler Youth these glider flying lessons were the beginning of the road to becoming Luftwaffe pilots. Many of them probably never came back alive...

Michael's experience at school took a similar turn. He had enrolled in the *Technisches Gewerbe Museum (TGM)* – the Technical College in Vienna's 19th District, and he was good at math and science. But even before he was forced to leave the school, he felt he was harassed by at least some of the professors.

The truth is that his mother Fränzi was in great fear that the fact her son was half-Jewish would be discovered through formal channels. Perhaps because she voluntarily admitted this at the school, the Headmaster was able to protect Michael for a while. But on November 18, 1938 the German investigation into his background was documented. From Michael's birth certificate the father's name (even though it is only a handwritten note on the back) was traced to the Israelite Cultural Community of Budapest. The Hungarian excerpts from birth documentation were translated into German, proving my father as half-Jewish. He had to leave the college.

Fränzi herself, an able-bodied thirty-six year-old woman, had been called up to work for the Red Cross. She fulfilled her official tour of duty under the Order for Emergency Duty from August 1942 to the end of 1943 in Graz, a city some 190 kilometers south of Vienna. During that time, young Michael lived with his aunt and uncle, Anni and Franz Palka, but without his schooling and his mother to encourage him, he was left without purpose. These early clashes with the new order threw Michael into confusion and depression. Through the war years, he barely escaped physical danger, and the psychological scars remained his whole life.

To his credit, Curtiz kept in touch with Fränzi and Michael as long as possible. The money he sent helped to support the whole family. And the hope he presented – that Michael would eventually come to America – helped to keep her dream alive. But in June 1941, Curtiz had written to Fränzi, "you'll have to wait there until the war is over." He advised her to "hold on to the affidavits I sent you…. Tickets for your ocean crossing I will send when I am sure you can get a visa." [15]

*****

In Hollywood, the show went on, with plots increasingly on the subject of war. In the spring of 1941, Curtiz and a select Warner Brothers crew went to San Diego to do some filming for *Dive Bomber*, a drama about the medical problems of flying high speed planes. Errol Flynn was there too, "hobnobbing with society" but otherwise apparently well-behaved. Curtiz had to bow to the navy's rules about filming – how much and when, but he did manage to have them produce some otherwise banned "picturesque" black smoke billowing out of the funnels of an aircraft carrier. Except that at first, the smoke went in the wrong direction: "I want that the smoke should go toward the left, not the right." The carrier's course was changed and all was well. [16]

Tuesday, December 11, 1941 was a historical day for the United States. Four days prior, Japan had attacked Pearl Harbor, destroying ships and aircraft, killing over 2000 personnel and wounding over 1200 more. The country was in shock. Californians were paralyzed by fear. President Roosevelt declared war on Japan.

But the very next day, filming continued at Warner Brothers studio in Hollywood as per schedule. The cast and crew for *Yankee Doodle Dandy* had just begun to gather when the radio broadcast the news that the United States had now also declared war on Germany. Earlier in the day, Italy and then Germany had declared war on the US under the Tripartite Agreement they had with Japan, and President Roosevelt was responding in kind.

There is a wonderful recording by Rosemary DeCamp that recounts her memories of Curtiz at this very crucial moment. DeCamp, who was playing Nellie Cohan, the mother of George the "Dandy," was on the set of *Yankee Doodle Dandy* when the radio announcement came through. In the audio reading of her book, *Tales from Hollywood*, DeCamp's voice echoes the emotion of the time as she relates how Curtiz listened along with the cast. After the national anthem had played, she tells how

> Mike bowed, and with his inimitable accent said, "Now boys and girls, we have work to do. We have bad news, but we have a wonderful story to tell the world so let us put away sad things and begin."

The scene keeps haunting me as an example of my grandfather's attitude: human compassion in the face of necessary action. In fact, DeCamp corroborates my feelings when she describes Curtiz: "He was very sentimental about home, mother, birth, and sometimes death."

The fervor of patriotism remained high throughout the production, and the film was released on Memorial Day, 1942. The same energy that was there at its beginning carried *Yankee Doodle Dandy* through to numerous Academy Awards, including Best Actor in a Leading Role for James Cagney. As well, there were Oscars for Best Music, Best Scoring of a Musical Picture, and Best Sound Recording. Five other nominations, including Best Picture and Curtiz as Best Director, rounded out its rise to glory. Fifty years later, the film was recognized by the US National Film Registry as being "culturally, historically, or aesthetically significant."

*****

Casablanca, the film that finally won Curtiz an Oscar for best director at the 1943, is the one that really gets a reaction from anyone when I say, "My grandfather directed that movie." The film's rough start in the summer of 1942 is well-documented in numerous books and articles. It was created under some of the strangest circumstances, beginning with the casting and continuing with the script, written in bits and pieces by the Epstein brothers. In his book *As Time Goes By* (1979), Howard Koch refers to that rocky road:

> For the leads, [Jack] Warner had in mind George Raft and Hedy Lamarr. However, Raft turned down the role.... At this point the casting took a ninety-degree turn – Dennis Morgan for Rick, Ann Sheridan for Ilsa, and – believe it or not – Ronald Reagan for Laszlo.... For whatever reason, the casting wheel took another spin and this time stopped at the lucky number... [17]

Harlan Lebo's comprehensive *Casablanca: Behind the Scenes* (1992) delves into the subject of casting differently: it was Hal Wallis, the producer, who made the decisions. By early February 1942, he "had a star assigned to the project" – Humphrey Bogart. Ann Sheridan had been considered for the role of leading lady, but Wallis had second thoughts. According to Lebo, he approached David O. Selznick to "loan out Ingrid Bergman, his top female star," who in Wallis's opinion "was the only actress with the luminous quality, the warmth and tenderness necessary for the role." [18]

By this time, Wallis had also assigned Curtiz, "his favourite director – then and now" to the project. From these sources – Koch and Lebo – one would dismiss any idea that Curtiz had anything to say about the casting in this or any other movie he made for Warner Brothers. However, we must remember that Curtiz and Wallis had more than an employer-employee relationship.

On this subject of casting, my own research gives me an unexpected peek at the inner workings of the Hollywood studio and the film industry. Several letters from the talent agent Paul Kohner, on file at the German Archive of Cinematography, suggest that Curtiz was indeed involved. In March 1942, Kohner responded to a conversation between the two men by sending him a "list of clients" and writing, "For your picture "CASA BLANCA" I particularly want to recommend to you..." And he lists several actors, unknown to us, of course, because they weren't chosen. In another letter, Kohner thanks Curtiz for having met and arranged screen tests for a couple of them. [19] Paul Kohner was the 1938 founder of a talent agency that still exists today. His efforts to introduce possible actors and other assistants to Curtiz during the beginning stages of Casablanca suggest that Curtiz and Wallis would have collaborated on choosing the players.

The rest of the story, as they say, is history. So many books and articles have been written about *Casablanca* that I won't even attempt to select material to repeat here. Suffice it to say that I share the admiration of the millions who have seen this entertaining movie, and I appreciate all the critiques and analyses that add to my understanding of it.

There are, however, two lesser-known details that I will add. The first has to do with the timing of the film's release and its nomination for Academy awards, and the second is an update on the Oscar's whereabouts.

Filming of *Casablanca* as it concerned the director was completed in August 1942. By the time all the post-production editing was done, the film music composed by Max Steiner added and the approval of preview audiences obtained, it was November. The premiere took place November 26, 1942 at the Hollywood Theatre in New York, followed by showings in select theatres only. With it being so close to Christmas and the USA embroiled in World War II, the official general release was delayed until January 23, 1943. Under the rules at that time, this made the film ineligible for consideration for the 1943 Academy Awards.

Commercially, *Casablanca* did very well during 1943, but the January release date meant that a whole year's output would be its competition for the next Academy Awards. Enter Paul Kohner, the already-mentioned agent and personal acquaintance of Curtiz. In December 1943, he wrote to Curtiz and enclosed the text of a telegram he had sent to Steve Trilling at Warner Brothers.

> DEAR STEVE. AFTER CAREFULLY LOOKING OVER THE LIST OF PROSPECTIVE ACADEMY AWARD WINNERS, I FEEL CERTAIN YOUR PICTURE "CASABLANCA" SHOULD WIN THE AWARD HANDS DOWN. HOWEVER AS TIME GOES BY QUICKLY PARTICULARLY IN OUR TOWN, THOSE WHO VOTE ON THE AWARDS ARE APT TO PARTIALLY FORGET OR OVERLOOK A PICTURE RELEASED AS EARLY IN SEASON AS "CASABLANCA". TO REFRESH THEIR MEMORY I BELIEVE IT WOULD BE MOST ADVISABLE TO MAKE AN EFFORT TO SECURE ANOTHER RUN OF THE PICTURE IN HOLLYWOOD DURING THE NEXT FEW WEEKS.... [20]

Curtiz thanked Kohner for his suggestion with the modest comment, "and if some people do consider my picture worthy of an

'Oscar', it'll be your merit, because your idea brought it to their attention. ... I talked to Trilling who said the studio will release it again." [21]

Harlan Lebo's otherwise excellent book on *Casablanca* fails to include this interesting detail, saying only that "When the Academy Award nominations for 1943 were announced on February 7, 1944, *Casablanca* was clearly the picture to beat." [22]

Receiving the Oscar for Best Director surprised Curtiz, and the often-cited Curtizism "Always a bridesmaid, never a mother" was meant to explain why after three previous nominations, he had no speech ready. For me, the whole subject has a more personal connection. At the height of doing my research I had met his daughter Kitty and I felt she, if anybody, should have this prize. For this reason – and also out of curiosity – I tried to find out what happened to it. Back in 1944, the Academy of Motion Picture Arts did not have a regulation about keeping track of the coveted statuettes' whereabouts. So when I visited their offices in 2002, they couldn't help me.

As it happened, Curtiz's Oscar had remained with the family of Bess Meredyth until it was offered up at Christie's New York auction in 2003. A November 19 online news article noted that it was "sold for $231,500 to magician David Copperfield, who bid by phone." A few weeks later, another article that mentioned the sale of the Oscar added this: "Copperfield's disappearing Oscar trick won't make Academy happy." I appealed to Mr. Copperfield on behalf of Kitty, who I thought should at least know where her father's treasure ended up, but I did not receive an answer to the request I sent through Copperfield's website, the only way I could try to get in touch with him.

✳✳✳✳✳

But back to 1942. The film *This is the Army*, planned and filmed between October 1942 and June 1943, was another Warner Brothers contribution to the war effort. The story follows two generations of talented singers and dancers who became soldiers, only to be sidelined from combat – at least for a while – to perform benefit shows to raise money for the U.S. war effort. The film tells the story of Irving Berlin's 1941 musical revue written for the stage, but the ambitious screen presentation includes parallel stories from both world wars. This was right up Curtiz's alley, I thought, as I watched the film and remembered his epics *Sodom and Gomorrah* and *Noah's Ark*. I tried to see the film from the viewpoint of a contemporary audience, probably with little success.

I recognized Ronald Reagan, of course, who in the World War II portion plays the son of the organizer of the World War I show. Curtiz worked with other well-established actors in this production, including Rosemary DeCamp, Joan Leslie and Dolores Costello. Irving Berlin, who also wrote the music, makes a personal appearance to sing his song "Oh! How I Hate to Get Up in the Morning." [24].

In watching this movie, I felt that certain scenes – the exit of the soldiers in the World War I part, Kate Smith's legendary performance of "God Bless America," and the extravagant tribute to the navy and the finale in the World War II part – go well beyond "largely routine" directorial work as James Robertson calls it. [25] For me, these scenes, along with the love story that runs through the World War II part, garner a lot of tense emotion. A deeper message comes through with the character Jerry Jones (George Murphy) refusing to marry Eileen (Joan Leslie) thereby putting his responsibility to the nation before personal goals.

Finally, Curtiz's adeptness with the genre of musical is particularly strong in the number "What the Well-dressed Man in Harlem Will Wear," featuring African American soldiers and a cameo appearance by the world heavyweight boxing champion, Sergeant Joe Louis. And this brings up an important personal trait: Curtiz had no prejudices against "the Negro" as Black or African Americans were called then.

An article in the *L.A. Tribune* a couple of years later illustrates the point. To answer the journalistic question, "How does the European mind function when it considers the American Negro in films?" the reporter Phil Carter asked Curtiz, who had the necessary background: he was of European heritage and he was one of Warner Brothers' top directors.

> Mr. Curtiz' answer to the stock question, "What do you think of the Negro?" brought an answer so forthright, I felt embarrassed for having asked it.
>
> "To me," he said, "the Negro is like anyone else. When I came to America, I was told a difference was made. However, in this business you cannot attach any importance to the color of a man's skin. The thing that counts is whether or not he's a good actor." [26]

Curtiz had good reason to be pleased with this film. It presented a good mix of nostalgia, patriotism and panache. As James Robertson reminds us, This is the Army made even more money than Casablanca, but as the studio's contribution to the war effort, Warner Brothers took in only the costs of making the film. Even the main actors relinquished their salaries, and the soldiers were, of course, on military pay. [27]

1943 - 1945

The last two years of World War II continued to permeate every aspect of life for all of Curtiz's families in Europe, but in Hollywood it was business as usual. Curtiz's work as the top director at Warner Brothers continued unabated. Of the movies that Curtiz directed in this period, I am most familiar with *Mildred Pierce*, a great example of the *film noir* genre, in production from December, 1944 to May, 1945. Joan Crawford won an Oscar for Best Actress, which was a boost to what is sometimes called her second career. In his biography about Crawford, Bob Thomas recounts how she had not come to the Academy Awards because she wasn't feeling well, but that Curtiz delivered her prize.

> Michael Curtiz came into the room with the Oscar he had accepted for Joan, and the room went white with flashbulbs. He and Joan greeted each other like old lovers, not the fierce antagonists they had been when he directed her in *Mildred Pierce*. [28]

Apparently his directing style was still abrasive! The film is based on the 1941 novel of the same name by James M. Cain, the plot having been cleverly manipulated into a successful screenplay by Jerry Wald, writer and producer at Warner Brothers. Its lasting interest for twenty-first century audiences, however, is that it is the story of a woman who turns her life around to become successful in business. Although Mildred becomes mired in the problems surrounding her rebellious daughter Veda, which eventually lead to the very dark and violent ending, the character of the hard working businesswoman has no doubt been a role model for liberated women over the decades since the film's release.

One thing that has intrigued me about the making of *Mildred Pierce* is the location for both the opening scene and the murder near the end. Apparently it was Curtiz's own beach house in Malibu. Although I have not found definite proof of ownership, a recent real estate record of the property address suggests the 0.4227 acre parcel and home is worth a cool 10.9 million dollars! [29]

*****

In his personal life, Curtiz was no stranger to strong, liberated women. Nor was he unfamiliar with difficult daughters as his own Kitty had taught him. At the beginning of 1943, Kitty was still unsettled in her life. She was back in New York, taking a secretarial course that Curtiz was paying for in secret.

Desider Pek wrote her a long letter outlining her father's precarious financial situation that was at least in part due to the new Current Tax Payment Act (June, 1943), which for the first time called for withholding of taxes at the source of payment. Specifically, the federally imposed ceiling of $25,000 "income" blurred the lines between salary and wages, and threw everyone into confusion. Pek suggests that once this law was in force, Curtiz's income would be compromised.

> ... after making some lawful deductions, [it] will be cut to $25,000.-- a year. This is pretty big money for you or I, but considering the tremendous obligations Dad has to live up to, the 25,000.-- will shrink to almost nothing, because of Bess and the mounting expenses of the upkeep of his ranch. Dad can deduct the publicity, ranch-help, charity, secretarial wages, but he cannot deduct your allowance and your tuition fee, because you're over 18.

> ... but he'll take an advance on his salary, so that he can pay you the allowance and tuition fee. ...

> I needn't ask you to economize, because I KNOW that you're watching now every penny you're spending, but I wanted to tell you everything so that you know the situation we're facing. ... [30]

If Kitty, now twenty-seven, found such information threatening, one could sympathize. Things worked out fine, however. Not only did Kitty continue with her course, but she also met the man who would be her first as well as her third husband, Karl Eberson. He was a "boy from Vienna" with whom she felt she had a lot in common. Eberson, five years her senior, was in the process of becoming an American citizen, and in 1943 he had already enlisted in the American army. [31]

In May, Pek wrote to her again, and his initial emphasis on the joys of home-making was tinged with more of the same dire financial outlook.

> Dad fully approves of your plans to get married, and you have my blessings, too. ... You've been a homeless gal for practically all your life, and it's time that you move into a place that you can call your own....

> If Dad would have enough money, he'd buy you a little home. But – under the circumstances – he can't do it. ... Here's what he can and will do: he'll give you some money for the furniture, dishes etc. Go around a little window-shopping... For the time being, buy only the necessary pieces ... try to buy your furniture at auctions... [32]

Such advice and the promise of Curtiz's assistance could be Pek's sense of protective love for the young woman, and it's unclear what actual contributions or gifts she actually did receive.

The intrigue continued even after Kitty and Karl were married in the summer of 1944. Curtiz has been in contact with his daughter, even if somewhat secretively. In writing to her in October, he suggests that she write to Bess, send her a picture, but "don't mention anything about finances ... that I sent you money for furnitures (sic.) and that you had been receiving those $15.-, etc. etc." He also mentions Lucy, Kitty's real mother, who occasionally called him and asked about Kitty. He even includes her address. [33]

Kitty must have followed her father's advice. A few months later, Bess wrote a friendly letter of congratulation on the marriage. In a second letter, more than a year later, Bess wrote to her stepdaughter in a real woman-to-woman way, with family news and motherly worries about Karl's role as an American soldier:

> I do hope that your "Karl" doesn't have to go out of the country during this next chapter of War. I think the West Coast looks upon this Japanese phase more seriously than they do in New York. ... There was practically no celebration here on VE Day. Everyone felt grateful and relieved, but realized what was still ahead of us. [34]

VE (Victory in Europe) Day was May 8, 1945 but the war in the Pacific continued into August. Karl was eventually released from the military in November, 1946. Bess Meredyth's next letter to Mrs. Karl Eberson also sheds some light on Curtiz's concerns about his own siblings and family back in Budapest.

> Mike is really terribly upset about the fate of his family in Europe. As you doubtless know, Margaret and her daughter (Margaret is Mike's sister) was in Stalag III – a concentration camp near Berlin. He has heard nothing further about them nor of any of the rest of the family. [35]

I'm wondering if there isn't an error in naming the camp in which Margaret was held. Stalag III, also known as Stalag Luft III, was used mainly for military prisoners of war, officers for the most part. More likely, Bess meant Stalag 311, the famous Bergen-Belsen concentration camp located west of and much nearer to Berlin than Stalag III. Another clue is that in July 1944, the SS established within the camp at Bergen-Belsen a "Hungarian Camp" for more than 1600 Hungarian Jews who were slated to be released to Switzerland on payment of cash, or exchange for goods.

Margaret (Margit) Kaminer, born 29 May, 1897, had been married to Jenö Manhart – ten years her senior – since February, 1916. They had two children, Loránd and Katalin. The full story of this couple is yet to be uncovered, but on the family chart I have from Anikó, Margaret's granddaughter, Jenö's year of death is given as 1944, age fifty-seven - most likely a victim of the Holocaust. Margaret Manhart eventually did make it to America and lived to the ripe old age of ninety-eight.

✳✳✳✳✳

Curtiz's worries about his siblings and their partners remaining in Europe were not unfounded, although whatever he learned about their fate would have come to him much later. In fact, besides Jenö Manhart, the husband of Margaret (Margit), Curtiz's his brother Lajos Kaminer, his sister Kornellia Engel and a niece Gabriella Kertész (daughter of Antal) are also listed with that same 1944 year of death on Anikó's family chart which, as these things go, is an ongoing work in progress.

About Antal's family I have discovered nothing. About Kornellia I know only from her mother Aranka's affidavit filled out in November 1939 upon entering America that she was living in Budapest, presumably with second husband Arnold Engel.

On that same document, Margaret (Margit) is noted as living in Bucharest, but I have not traced her movements during the war. Her son Loránd shows up on a 1940 list of American immigrant arrivals "Held for Special Inquiry," on subsequent American military listings, and he lived his life out in California as "Uncle Paci" to my cousin Anikó. Margaret's daughter Katalin may have been with her throughout the war, was married and had her two daughters Anikó and Ági in Hungary before they all came to America in the early 1950's.

Lajos's story has revealed itself with the help of his wife Rózsa's niece who I was fortunate to meet in Budapest. Eva Nagy's family had helped Lajos's daughter Zsuzsu Kaminer in connection with the house on Szövetség utcá where she lived since she was a girl. When Aranka, David and Gabor left for America in 1938, Lajos, a gentle man and a jeweler by trade, decided to stay in Budapest with Rózsa and Zsuzsu. It's important to remember that Rózsa was not Jewish. Lajos was not one to question authority, so when the Nazis finally came in 1944, he wore the yellow star as required. And when he was called to report, he went. The family begged him not to do it, but he went anyway. As with so many others, he never returned.

These words echo through the multitude of stories from the Holocaust, stories that have and continue to come in various forms from diaries, to movies, to literature – both non-fiction and fiction. In Geraldine Brooks' novel *People of the Book* (2008), for example, there is a passage describing the Nazi takeover in Belgrade, April 1940 that sounds almost exactly like the experience of Lajos Kaminer:

> After a few weeks, the arrests began. In early summer, Lujo was ordered to report for transport to a labor camp. Rashela wept and pleaded with him not to answer the summons, to flee the city, but Lujo said he was strong, and a good worker, and would manage. He took his wife's chin in his hand. "Better this way. The war cannot last forever. If I run away, they will come for you." Never a demonstrative man, he kissed her, long and tenderly, and climbed aboard the truck.[36]

The characters in this book lived and died much as the real people that were caught up in the madness. At some point, Lajos Kaminer sent a postcard saying he would be home soon. But he did not come home and was never heard from again.

Twenty years later, attempts to bring closure to his fate resulted in an official notice from the Budapest Central Court that Lajos Kaminer, taken away October 19, 1944 to destinations unknown could not be traced, is considered deceased, and his official date of death is given as November 15, 1944.

*****

In sunny California, besides the fates of his siblings, Curtiz was concerned about my grandmother Fränzi Vondrak and their son Michael who were also still in Europe. Michael was half-Jewish, and even though the lineage is meant to come through the mother, in these times, anyone with family ties to Jews was in danger.

I am still impressed with the effort Curtiz made to continue supporting them and to keep alive Fränzi's dream that at least her son would eventually come to America. Michael was lucky to have dedicated parents who both tried their best during the war years. What neither of them could foresee was the tragedy into which Fränzi's dream and Curtiz's supporting efforts would plunge my father as a young adult.

On a mild spring day in Vienna, 1944, Michael received the order to report for duty with the Organization Tott (OT), the German civil engineering outfit that had by this point in the war become a quasi-military labour force. Reluctantly, with great apprehension, Fränzi prepared her son for this assignment. She knew it was senseless to resist.

The three months he was with OT were a dark time for the young man of nineteen. In a small black sketchbook he recorded the events and his impressions in the form of a letter to his sweetheart Ada, the woman who would be my mother. Much of the narrative focuses on how it felt to travel day after day by train and to witness bombing attacks that he miraculously escaped. He writes little about the work itself; there is one reference to repairing train track that had been damaged by bombing. As the Allies were advancing, this may indeed have been the main assignment of his *Hundertschaft* (Division of One Hundred) that he was assigned to. Even though this was forced labor for thousands of part-Jews like

Prison Militaire de Paris

Michael, the Reich did in fact pay the workers. I have a salary slip for Michael Vondrak dated 13.9.44, with a note "for April, May" and stamped Saarbrücken on the back, for 137.50 Reichsmark.

During his ordeal, Michael suffered anxiety attacks that saw him in and out of sick bay. In Paris, he finally managed to see a doctor and spent several days in a darkened room in hospital. But only a military doctor could release him, so he was sent back to the troupe and shunted around the countryside again until they were back in Paris with apparently lots of free time. He commented on the fashions and even had the opportunity to buy a silk shawl for Ada and a lace camisole for his mother. It may be that he also had time to sketch. Eventually, he managed to get back to Vienna.

The OT experience stayed with Michael for a long time. Some years later, he created a set of three ink drawings: the Prison Militaire de Paris, the Cathedral at Nantes, and a scene with soldiers dancing with local girls. These drawings evoke the stark simplicity of wartime. He would remember when, how and why he created this art, but unfortunately, I can no longer ask him: Michael VonDrak passed away January 13, 2016 in Seattle. I found these drawings among the stacks of his artworks that had been stored – unseen for years – at his daughter Felicia's.

Fränzi was aware that her son was seeing my mother Ada Metzner. The two young people lived less than ten blocks apart in the 18th District. It was one of the luckier parts of Vienna to be as allied forces converged on the Austrian capital. This north-western corner of the city was not bombed, and neither were the dreaded Russians a threat here. Eventually, it would be part of the American sector. Nevertheless, everyone that could leave Vienna did so, and Ada's mother did the same. Ada's sister was already working as a pharmacist in Berlin, her brother Detlef was a musician in the army. This left my mother, the youngest, alone in the apartment on Cottagegasse.

They met in the small park where the statue of the actor Josef Kainz as Hamlet holds the skull. I can only imagine that my father spoke the line, "Alas, poor Yorik" to attract Ada, but she told me that they fell into easy conversation right away. They talked, they walked, they fell in love. She wanted to finish her term at seam-stress school, but as soon as it was over she put some potatoes into the little carrier of her bicycle and rode out into the country to join her mother.

The remaining time of the war, until things were organized in Vienna, Michael and Ada did not see each other. After becoming involved with a secret organization to help Jews escape Austria, he joined his mother in Tirol where she was staying with her niece Elly. His assignment was to meet the fleeing people on the train somewhere west of Innsbruck. Then, with his knowledge of Italian, he helped to connect them with smugglers near the border with Italy.

For her part, Ada was called on to join the *Arbeitsdienst* (Labour Service), a six-month mandatory work service imposed by the Nazis, ostensibly to combat youth unemployment. One of her assignments was on a farm, helping a woman with small children whose husband and oldest son were serving in the army. The poor woman lived in constant fear that they would not return.

The Post-War Years

As the war in Europe wound down, on the other side of the world in Hollywood, Curtiz kept a wary eye on events, and he kept on working. Slowly, he came to know the circumstances of his loved ones, but he knew their suffering was not over. It was still his priority to help in any way he could. Finally, in the spring of 1946, correspondence between Curtiz and Fränzi resumed.

The first letter dated April 2, 1946 was apparently routed through the American military in Vienna; it bears a stamp from Austrian Censor Station Number 84. On May 23, there is also a full page letter written in English to Michael, now twenty-one.

I am aware that Michael – and perhaps even Fränzi – suspected it was Desider Pek, Curtiz's secretary, who actually wrote the letters and typed them up for a quickly scrawled *Miska*. There is no doubt that Pek edited the letters for grammar and spelling, and the two men probably discussed the options and advice given. However, the actions promised and delivered are proof enough for me that Curtiz cared enough to make them happen.

These post-war letters directed Fränzi and Michael to inquire about obtaining entry visas for America, at least for Michael if not both of them for the time being, and that Michael should use his rightful access to Czech citizenship (through his mother's parental heritage). Officially, Czechoslovakia was America's enemy but the Czech troops had "fought with us against the Nazis. They are our allies. Here a Czech is seen as a friend but Austrians are still 'Germans' because there were so many Nazis there." [37] The necessary affidavit would be sent immediately, the letter promised, but in actuality, it took some time to arrive.

As well, there is direct mention of the American officer Lieutenant Wilkerson who was instrumental in forwarding Fränzi's letter in the first place, and who would continue to help. His brother was an actor at Warner Brothers. Through Lt. Wilkerson, Curtiz and Pek would try to send parcels of food to augment the slim rations that people were receiving in Vienna.

Curtiz promised that if Michael wished to continue his studies once he was in the US, he would be enrolled in Art School. He should practice his English and strongly consider enlisting in the US Army or Navy, for then all doors – including fast-track citizenship – would be open to him. This last bit, though pragmatic, I don't believe was truly Curtiz's advice. His abhorrence of war, gained from his own experience in World War I, would appear to preclude this way of thinking.

Curtiz also told Fränzi about the fate of his own family – one brother, two sisters and their husbands most likely lost, and mother having died in Hollywood. Catching up on four long years, he reminded her, "As you can see, we have all suffered." [38] As he obtained information about what was happening in Budapest and what was left of his own family, Curtiz – along with Pek, who also had relatives stranded there – made every effort to support as many as possible.

In Budapest, the situation was much different than in Vienna. Much of the city was destroyed after the Red Army's two-month siege to drive out the German Nazis, and the Russians eventually occupied all of Hungary. While the powers that be wrangled over territory and political advantage, it became increasingly difficult for ex-patriots like Curtiz to communicate and send much-needed supplies to family.

*****

With all this evidence of Curtiz's efforts to help Fränzi and Michael, and the explicit goal to bring his son to America after the war, it is interesting to speculate how those feelings percolated through his work in directing his films. During the filming of *Night and Day*, the Cole Porter story, in the summer and fall of 1945, the war in Europe was all but over. But according to James Robertson, battles largely caused by the actor's demands continued between Curtiz and Cary Grant. [39] However, I believe that the decidedly tense scenes between the father and son characters on screen also relate to Curtiz's personal struggles with the uncertainties of being a father. As it turned out, there would soon be tense scenes between him and his son Michael Vondrak.

Curtiz's other son Michael Forster did not create tense scenes with his father, even though he worked at Warner Brothers as an extra after graduating from UCLA in 1943with an engineering degree. In fact, Forster had stayed as far away from Curtiz as possible, joining the army as soon as he could. He received training as an X-Ray technician but saw no active service. As Germany's defeat became the expected outcome, the army took advantage of Forster's knowledge of German to train him as an interrogator of prisoners of war. He did serve in that capacity behind the advancing American lines and later on, in Czechoslovakia. When everything was more or less over, Forster decided to continue his studies at the University of Grenoble, France.

*****

Had Curtiz taken a good, hard look at his kids at the end of World War II, he would have seen four young adults trying to make their own way in life. His involvement in their lives increasingly included *their own* decisions, not his, and not their mothers'.

Not only his children and family, but also his entire career became increasingly unsettled in the years following World War II. Since 1926, he had worked for Warner Brothers under contract, and with appropriate increased salary and benefits, but otherwise directly obligated to the studio bosses. For some time, Curtiz had thought of striking out with his own production company, and now seemed to be the time to take the plunge. There was a lot of speculation, much wheeling and dealing, but after his current contract expired, Michael Curtiz Productions Incorporated became a legal entity in May 1946. The corporate structure, with Curtiz holding 51% and Warner Brothers 49% of the shares, ensured an ongoing relationship with the studio while giving him more freedoms in the business end of things and a direct percentage of profits. For example, while Curtiz would select the projects and oversee casting, the studio remained partially responsible for production costs. [40] Curtiz writes to his daughter Kitty about these developments with pride.

> As you can see from the stationery, my production unit has been organized, although the funds necessary for making the pictures have not been deposited as yet. I'm just as busy as though I'd be making a picture, because I have to prepare two stories at the same time.
>
> … The local papers were full of notices concerning the new company, and all I hope is that I'll be making just as many good pictures as I have done it under the <u>direct</u> Warner banner. [41]

But there were also concerns: "we're still not settled with all the details of forming the company," he wrote to her November 2. The first film he had planned to produce was delayed because of overwhelming preparatory work and a lengthy strike by the set builders.

> So, I decided to make a mystery story, titled "Unsuspected." I wanted to come out with a real big production like "Victoria Grandolet" but under the circumstances there was nothing else for me to do but compromise. I'm without a picture for months, and you know I can't stand any idleness.

"Victoria Grandolet" never did become reality, but *The Unsuspected* became a success for Michael Curtiz Productions Incorporated.

The new business venture also had an effect on his relationship with Bess Meredyth. They were living together again, at a new address 4300 Noeline Avenue, and Bess became his story editor. Even her now twenty-eight year old son John Meredyth Lucas was hired as a writer, "making it a family affair" [42] In a letter to Kitty, Bess writes that they are "busier than bird dogs. I've been working on two or three scripts at a time – and every night – we have story conferences here at the house." [43] In another letter, she elaborates:

> Poor Mike is working like the deuce because it is three times the work and ten times the responsibility having his own unit. He not only has to direct the picture, but has to be responsible for all the business end of it and all the people working for him. [44]

His next film, *Romance on the High Seas* may be best remembered for introducing Doris Day as the Hollywood star she would become – one of the best results of Curtiz having total control for casting. Vernon Scott quotes Curtiz:

> I was preparing to shoot [the film] when Betty Hutton, the star, became pregnant. So I looked high and low for a replacement until a shy, freckled little girl walked into my office. I was impressed with her simplicity and lovely voice, so Doris got the role. [45]

Some years later, Day showed her appreciation in a sweet way by naming one of her favorite dogs Michael. When he found out, he took the gesture "in the spirit in which it was intended – as a compliment" [46]

Of all the business tasks that he took on as head of his own production company, scouting for new talent was probably the least onerous for Curtiz. He had always done it, as far back as 1921 when he and his then-wife Lucy Doraine spotted Walter Slesak for *Sodom and Gomorrah*. He would do it again famously in 1952 when he signed the already established singer Peggy Lee to act in *The Jazz Singer*. Lee had turned down other offers to act, but Curtiz persuaded her to take on the challenge. "If a girl can sing a song with the warmth she has, ... she can do the same thing on the stage – if somebody will show her the technique. Connecting the heart and the brain at the same time – that is the technique." Curtiz was patient with her because he could feel her potential. "I have no patience with anybody who has no talent," he said. "Peggy has tremendous talent" [47]

As head of his own production company, Curtiz could also offer employment without first having to get permission from the Warner Brothers bosses. In *Romance on the High Seas,* for example, his brother David (Dezsö Kertézs) has prominent billing as Second Unit Director. David and his brother Gabor (now using the name Gabriel or Gabe) finally made it to Hollywood from their Tijuana exile in 1940, at a time when it was still easy for them to get a job at Warner Brothers with nothing more than a letter of recommendation. "Dave became a cutter, and Gabriel a third assistant," Curtiz explains to Kitty in his letter of March 30, 1946. They worked their way up despite some resistance from the Film Editors Union, and now that Curtiz had his own production company, they were free and clear.

While employed by the studio, David held a position in the Special Effects Department with a weekly salary of $200 and with the proviso that if he were requested to work in another part of the studio where a higher salary is paid, he would get that increase.[48] After *Romance on the High Seas* where he is actually named special effects director, and several films where he is credited with montage, he is most often billed as second-unit or assistant director.[49] It's interesting to note that for the majority of his film credits, he uses the alternative name David C. Gardner. His name had, of course, been Kertész, which in Hungarian means gardener.

When Michael Curtiz Productions came into being, David took over Curtiz's private affairs from Desider Pek, and Curtiz's youngest brother Gabriel also part of the family team. Pek had been an intimate partner in Curtiz's correspondence with my grandmother, and he had become quite involved with the affairs of Kitty, now Mrs. Karl Eberson. Curtiz himself may not have been aware of subtle problems arising with the change in how these matters were handled by his brothers.

As an example, whether it was carelessness or calculated disruption, there was a mix-up about who exactly answered Kitty's 1946 Christmas cards, but the incident was only a shadow of things to come. Pek writes to Kitty about this in detail January 19, 1947. Within the year, the birthday telegram to Kitty in November

1947 is signed "MIKE AND DAVID." And then suddenly Pek was more or less out of the picture.

In September, November and December, 1947, it is David and not her beloved Miska who wrote to my grandmother Fränzi – the first letter handwritten, the next two typed on Michael Curtiz Productions Inc. letterhead. David explains that Curtiz, who is too busy, has told him what to write. But the feeling wasn't the same for her or my father Michael. The direct contact was missing.

Then in 1948, letters regarding final plans for Michael's voyage to America were from David (January) and – surprisingly – Pek (February, March and May). They present a startling contrast: David's is rather negative and businesslike whereas Pek's are personal and reassuring. Some unexplained intrigue seemed to be afoot. Indeed, when young Michael arrived in Hollywood later that spring, things were not very pleasant for him, as he told me himself.

*****

But my father's emigration plans were not the only topic where Pek had been involved as Curtiz's confidant. In 1947 there was a tricky situation about whether Curtiz really went to Palm Springs when he was supposed to be in New York. The newspapers reported it was New York but as she did not see him there, Kitty questioned it. In a long letter to her, Pek revealed the cover-up and offered this explanation: Margaret Ettinger, "Mike's publicity woman (also one of the members of the Board of Directors of Curtiz Productions) ... knew where Mike was going to go and she wouldn't have given her prominent aunt what they call a bum steer."[51] Given that Ettinger's aunt was none other than Louella Parsons, the famous columnist, what was printed about Curtiz's whereabouts was expected to be believed.

Louella Parsons, long-time movie writer for the *Los Angeles Examiner*, was also a good friend of Curtiz. She had already been instrumental in hushing up details about Kitty's attempted suicide in 1939, so it wouldn't be unusual to change a few details about her friend's doings now, or at any time for that matter.

Rosemary DeCamp, in her *"Tales from Hollywood"* alludes to his reputation. "He evoked a great deal of gossip. Stories of his sexual prowess were rife, but I never knew anyone who admitted first-hand knowledge."

One such story supposedly involved Elizabeth Taylor's mother Sara. "Everybody seemed to know of the affair between Curtiz and Sara Taylor; it's difficult to imagine Elizabeth also wasn't aware." [52] This one never made it into the papers either. A friend in the right place?

In telling my grandfather's story, I have for the most part stayed away from whatever gossip might be available about his sexual escapades. Despite the certainty that they happened regularly, not much can be proven. His attitude was cavalier. Curtiz may not have put much importance on extra-marital sex, if we consider what John Meredyth Lucas says:

> Mike had a European attitude about marriage. It formed a
> stable home, provided comfort but was not expected to con-
> fine one's pleasures. Such adventures, Mike claimed, had no
> effect on men. [53]

I could say it was a different time – definitely before the #MeToo movement which is wholly justified, of course. I could say people in his business had and still have different opportunities. Whatever I could say, readers could rightfully object, one way or another. I fully acknowledge the mayhem and personal trauma that Curtiz's sexual behavior caused for others. Therefore, despite the allure of Sex Sells, I prefer to tell his story on the basis of reliable facts and reputable evidence.

****

Within a two-month time span in 1947, at the age of sixty-one, Curtiz became a grandfather twice without his knowledge. Becoming a grandparent is an important event in anyone's life, as it provides hope for the future. He would have several more unknown grandkids before a full five years later, Curtiz actually experienced that feeling himself. In early 1952, Bess's son John Meredyth Lucas and his wife Joan had a baby girl, Elisabeth. A photo reproduced in his book has the caption, "John watches as Mike holds granddaughter Elizabeth MacGillicuddy Lucas (1953)." [54] The joy on grandpa's face is genuine!

John and Joan named their middle boy Michael – another Michael! And their youngest is Victoria. Although Meredyth Lucas was not Curtiz's natural child, the two had a good father-son relationship, as attested to in plenty of detail in *Eighty Odd Years in Hollywood*. I am indebted to this would-be uncle for many details that can be shared only by a family member. Curtiz did not formally adopt John, and this prevented his children from becoming heirs in the Estate of Kitty Curtiz.

Curtiz's daughter Sonja Dalla Bonna had married Jack Hill in 1946, and on May 16, 1947 she gave birth to Christina Frances Hill in London, England. It's unlikely that Sonja informed Curtiz; her children told me it was only much later that she took up correspondence with him. Curtiz would eventually meet Christina and two more grandchildren by Sonja, giving him at least a brief chance to feel like a grandfather. That three of the Hill children, my cousins, had the opportunity to meet Curtiz and I did not is one of those regrets that I carry with me. Even though Curtiz was far more involved with my father Michael than with Sonja, the circumstances were so very different.

My father had married Ada Metzner in February, and I was born July 9, 1947. My grandmother Fränzi, her dream to get Michael to the United States now almost a reality, did not inform Curtiz about Michael's marriage to Ada and a child on the way. Two letters of Curtiz sealed the fate of my little family. In January, he was already preparing the Affidavit, and asked only for some last-minute details:

> Here is the important thing: what did you (you or Michael) indicate about our relationship? Did you indicate at the consulate or at the UNNRA office that Michael is my son or that you both are "relatives"? I want to make sure to prepare the Affidavit accordingly. If I write something else that what you wrote down, you will not get a Visa. I will prepare the Affidavit to show that I will take responsibility for both of you, so you can both come, but it is possible that only Michael can come alone. [55]

I wonder what, if anything, she replied to his handwritten postscript: "Where is Michael now? He should continue to learn English and I would be happy if he were to write me a few lines." In fact, Michael was attending the Kalaus School of Art and making sure that my mother had milk and food. He would walk for blocks to the American authority and stand in line to get staples and food stamps for perishables. On the way home he'd buy milk at the corner store. He did the same for his own mother and grandmother.

Curtiz's next letter is dated June 4, 1947 and it would have arrived in Vienna just before I was born. My father was living with my mother at her family apartment, so Fränzi would have to decide when and how to tell her son the news.

> Enclosed I am finally sending the Affidavit that I've promised you for so long. ...
>
> THE AFFIDAVIT IS FOR YOU BOTH BECAUSE I WANT TO BRING YOU BOTH HERE. I have declared Michael as my son and you as a relative. ... Let me know what they tell you at the American Consulate, so I can send you the ship fare tickets and the necessary money.

There is a hint in this letter that my father may have some difficulty regarding his citizenship and the political situation, and Curtiz could only hope that things go smoothly. But Fränzi would have had to give Michael the letter Curtiz had written to his son.

> It is easier for me to write English, and I hope you haven't forgotten what you've learned. I was very sorry to learn that you're not feeling well and trust your condition has improved sufficiently to be enabled making the trip. Would like to have you both here, my dear son, and pray to God that you both will get the American Visas....
>
> There's so much I'd like to say, but one can't "enclose" any feelings in a letter like this, and all I can say now is that I'm very anxious to see you both in America. I know you two will be happy over here, because this great country gives everybody an opportunity to make a living and find freedom and liberty at the same time. ...
>
> I received the card on which you painted a section of Vienna, and I must say you're a talented boy. If you want to study art over here, I'll have you enroll in a school where you can develope (sic.) your ability. That little painting – Vienna in moonlight – ist really a wonderful work, and I'm proud of you.
>
> Well, my dear son, I'm closing my letter. Please write me. May God bless you both.
>
> Lovingly;

[signed] Miska

I find it impossible to imagine how my father reacted, what he and my mother talked about when they read this letter. For Curtiz, my mother (and soon I) did not exist: we were not mentioned in the Affidavit that Curtiz had prepared. How could his plan go forward?

What happened is that the unspoken lie was allowed to continue, and at some point over the next few months, a decision was made that Michael should go to Hollywood a single man. This idea culminated with a divorce in which my mother perjured herself by admitting to a viable ground for divorce: refusing to follow her husband in emigrating to America. It was a preposterous and vicious lie that must have broken their hearts. My mother had gone along with it, had kept it secret from her own mother and sister, for the sake of Michael and the promise of reconciliation in the U.S. as soon as possible.

My aunt recalled the day in November 1947 when my mother came home crying. Meta asked what was wrong, and when Ada told her of the court proceedings, she was stunned. She was angry at her little sister for letting it happen. Ada's blind trust was not rewarded; her naïveté cost her the marriage for good.

In the spring of 1948, when Michael reached Hollywood everything went according to plan at first. In a letter to his mother, he describes his arrival with excitement:

> I arrived in Los Angeles at 3:30 on May 25 [by train]. Uncle Desje [David] picked me up and we drove straight to Papa who was just working. After a few minutes he came to me and arranged some work for me for the first three weeks. ...
>
> I thanked Uncle for all he had done for me and you. He took me to The Imperial, a rooming house at 2119 N. Beachwood Drive, Hollywood, not far from his place, and I had a bath in my room. At 7 o'clock, Uncle came and took me to dinner. ...
>
> I dressed tip top to meet Papa – white shirt and blue tie, and he was surprised how I had grown. [56]

One of the first things my father did was to go to the recruiting office for the American military. The fact that it would take two and a half years should not have come as a surprise, but it was just one of numerous things that helped to unravel the whole venture.

Eventually, Michael told his father about Ada and me, his wife and child in Vienna. Curtiz was outraged. Apparently he said, "You should have told me. I would have brought you all over." I believe it was a huge blow to him that Fränzi and his son had deliberately not told him the truth. From then on, the relationship between Curtiz and his son deteriorated. For Michael, depression set in, and the situation soon became intolerable. Without his father's support, he was on his own.

Michael tried desperately to return to Vienna, but it seemed that fate threw a wrench into every way he turned. Within two years, he ended up depressed and sick in Philadelphia while my mother eked out a living in Vienna, and I as a toddler was oblivious to the tragedy. My parents never saw each other again.

*****

Now that his children were living their own lives – riding their own emotional and financial roller-coaster, so to speak – Curtiz was freed from providing financial support. Despite the losses suffered within his Budapest family, at least they were accounted for or their fate was known. This must have given him a measure of peace. Nevertheless, difficulties with his career and in his own personal life showed no signs of slowing down.

The total output of Michael Curtiz Productions Inc. was only four movies that were actually released: *The Unsuspected* (1947), *Romance on the High Seas* (1947), *My Dream is Yours* (1947) and *Flamingo Road* (1948). Within two years, Curtiz's dream of independent film making was ending. It may be true, as Robertson suggests, that he lacked administrative ability. There may also have been some backroom politics that doomed the company. In December 1948, Curtiz abandoned his production unit and signed a new seven-year contract with Warner Brothers. [57]

Only four years and eleven pictures into this new commitment – *The Boy from Oklahoma* filmed in 1953 being the last – the contract was abandoned, and a year of legal wrangling threatened to spoil the long working relationship between Curtiz and Jack Warner. In a heartwrenching letter, Curtiz details the good, the bad, and the ugly. This paragraph sums it up:

> I could go on and on, dear Jack, because I thought these eleven pictures would be like life insurance for me. I never dreamed I would be battling over my financial reward with

Obringer or in a court action against the studio with which
I spent twenty-six years and for whom I made eighty-seven
pictures. This is my life's work, dear Jack, and I am sorry
that my memories of it are spoiled by these unpleasant conferences, just because I want my rights and a little financial
return on these long years of work. [58]

Finally, on August 3rd, 1954, an agreement was reached, and Curtiz
walked away from Warner Brothers with some satisfaction and a
chance for new beginnings.

PART VIII

THE LAST TEN YEARS

As we get older, we tend to become more attuned to the idea of life fading away. I have watched friends and family members going through that process, either directly or as one of those left behind. One way or another, we all have to face mortality. I believe that in the last ten years of his life, my grandfather would also have felt the shadows cast by such awareness. Both in his personal life and his work, he endured mini-tragedies that wore him down.

Curtiz's relationship with the people closest to him – wife Bess Meredyth and daughter Kitty – continued on a precarious track. The couple's separation, never the clear break of divorce, kept Curtiz in financial if not emotional limbo with Bess. After their brief separation in 1936, they re-united; they worked together during the heydays of Michael Curtiz Productions Inc. and they likely found a way to live relatively separate lives together for years. People do that.

For Curtiz and Bess, this worked for a long time, but in 1960 they separated for good. And it actually got into the papers. Louella Parsons writes about a formal separation in her column:

> The thirty-year marriage of famous writer Bess Meredyth and well known director Michael Curtiz is over.
>
> I have known about this separation for four months, but both of them are old friends of mine so I promised not to say anything until a property settlement was reached. This has now been done, with Mike making a very generous settlement on Bess which includes their beautiful estate in Encino.
>
> … There will be no divorce. [1]

In other words, this was a business deal. The personal arrangement of living separately but still together would continue at least
for a few more months. The noted property settlement is also
mentioned in Curtiz's Last Will and Testament, executed a year
later. In the Will, two further clauses bequeath to Bess monies that
Paramount Pictures and Formosa Productions, Inc., may still owe
him under specified employment agreements.

In a letter to Kitty, Curtiz confirmed the rumors about him
moving out. If they could have lunch together, he wrote, he would
"tell [her] personally everything that is happening to [him]" [2] A
few months later, in September, Curtiz prepared to travel to Italy
to direct *St. Francis of Assisi*. Before he left, he wrote to Kitty again:
"When I come back from Rome, I will be living at the same place
where I am now <u>alone</u>." [3]

Bess's son John was also affected by the breakup. His own
children would lose the natural grandma-grandpa presence that
they were just beginning to understand. John remembers the
event of the separation in his memoirs, adding this personal angle
to the story:

> On the morning he left, he called Ethel [the cook] into the
> dining room and told her he would not be coming back. He
> asked her not to tell Mother as he would explain it himself.
> For months he wrote her regularly from location....
>
> Finally one of his letters to her contained the news. He
> did not want a divorce but he could no longer live at home. [4]

It must have been a tremendously difficult decision for Curtiz. It's
not easy to walk away from a long relationship such as the one
between him and Bess.

✳✳✳✳✳

Kitty, the daughter Curtiz loved and was most involved
with, went through a tumultuous time during the 1950s as well.
After almost ten years of marriage, the thirty-seven year old Kitty
divorced Karl Eberson and became embroiled in a destructive
relationship with a man by the name of Yorik. For a number of
years, they lived in Washington, DC. Curtiz tried to encourage
her, and he advised her to come back "to your home where at least
you have more warmth and friendship." He enclosed $50 "to take
care of little bills" and offered to send money "for the road" if and

when she did decide to come back to Hollywood. [5] In his next letter, he addresses her personal dilemma directly. She should come home and consider getting back together with Karl.

> ... you are still young and you can establish yourself in your profession and work out your private life. It will just take a little energy....
>
> There is no use crying about mistakes and no use suffering over them. We have all made mistakes and in the end, what must be will be and it will turn out right if we just analyze the situation clearly and act accordingly. [6]

On the subject of love, he states simply, "Even if we are in love we must be just a little selfish." This glimpse into Curtiz's philosophy on life and love is precious. Kitty eventually did come back to California, remarried Karl and lived with him in her Woodland Hills house.

In the last years of his life, the relationship between Curtiz and his daughter continued on friendly terms. Quite often he apologized in brief letters for being too busy to see her as much as he – and she – would have liked. He sent her postcards from Europe while working in Vienna on *A Breath of Scandal* (1959) and in Italy on *Francis of Assisi* (1960), and he kept her apprised of his personal life as noted regarding the separation with Bess. While working on his last picture *The Comancheros* in 1961, he again wrote to Kitty from location. The last letter is short:

> I returned from Moab, Utah last week and am terribly busy on this picture. I should be free in about three weeks.
>
> I hope I can get together with you then, perhaps for lunch.
>
> Love, Mike (jl) [7]

Joyce, Curtiz's secretary at Twentieth Century Fox signed for him and sends her personal regards in a P.S.

What happened as her father became seriously ill is a story that only Kitty can tell in her own words. He would have been proud to know that after his death and over the ensuing years, she made quite a name for herself in the social and political circles in California. After Karl Eberson passed away in 1971, she liquidated her assets in California and returned to Europe for good. When I first made contact with Kitty in 2000, she was concerned about her share of her father's estate as allotted in his Will. By that time, it was of course much too late for her to object, so my 2002 appeal to the Director's Guild in Los Angeles on her behalf was predictably unproductive.

*****

Beginning in 1953 when he quit Warner Brothers, Curtiz both lost and gained in terms of how the work in his last ten years would continue. He basically became a freelance director after he and Warner Brothers signed the final agreement August 3, 1954. And being the kind of person he was, he immersed himself in work for almost ten more years, directing a total of eighteen more movies.

Almost immediately, he directed *The Egyptian* for Twentieth Century Fox, thereby giving some credence to Louella Parsons' original "guess that he'll sign with that studio because he had worked with Darryl Zanuck in the past," [8] He also signed with Paramount, directed seven pictures and had a personal office at that studio for some time. Under specific arrangements, he directed five more feature movies for Warner Brothers. For MGM and Samuel Goldwyn Jr. (Buena Vista - Disney) he made two. Finally, he also directed one each for the foreign companies Mirisch-Jaguar Productions and Perseus Productions.

It could be said that some of Curtiz's best work is from this period. Was it the freedom from Warners? Was it his mature experience? In his overall assessment, James Robertson notes that "Curtiz retained the ability to turn out noteworthy films..., and when the material moved him sufficiently, he remained a formidable film-maker." [9]

The Paramount production of *White Christmas* (1953) has become another cult favourite and a Christmas classic on television. For the French production company Formosa, he directed *Proud Rebel* (1957) about which Olivia de Havilland gave me some personal insights when I met her in Paris; the film is reminiscent of Curtiz's 1930's famous westerns. Anyone who loves Elvis Presley will recognize the Paramount-produced *King Creole* (1958) as one of The King's best movies. MGM's 1962 version of *The Adventures of Huckleberry Finn* remains one of the best film treatments of Mark Twain's novel. And Curtiz's last international work, Perseus/Twentieth Century Fox's *Francis of Assisi* (1961) received many accolades.

Of this short list, *King Creole* and *St. Francis of Assisi* resonate with me the most, although for different reasons. Like most eleven-year olds in 1958, being an Elvis fan was a no-brainer. Living on the farm, I could groove to his songs on the radio. At that time I was probably more intent on listening to the lyrics as a way to learn English, and I had no idea about Elvis in movies. It was many, many years later that I saw any them. Jailhouse Rock was offered on TV, but I saw King Creole only on VHS and later DVD. Much has been written about Elvis, so it's easy to find what has been said about this film. For the most part, I agree with the available material, both the positive and the negative. It's gratifying to know that Elvis himself said that his role as Danny Fisher was one of his favourites. Especially regarding what various sources say about Curtiz, I am pleased that his direction of The King is given positive assessment. As James Robertson points out, Curtiz took Elvis seriously even if his fans only wanted him to sing and gyrate. [10] I love showing visitors the production still that hangs on my wall showing Elvis and my grandfather in deep conversation; it's always a hit.

A Last Look at the Kids

In his last ten years, my grandfather's personal life still had its ups and downs. He connected with one of his Vienna children, Sonja Dalla Bonna (Mrs. Jack Hill) and her three children. His relationship with Jill Gerrard included another child and caused far-reaching confusion. Curtiz had no contact his oldest son Michael Forster although he is named in the Will, along with my father. Perhaps most important of all, while directing *The Egyptian* for Twentieth Century Fox he nurtured a budding relationship with Anitra Stevens (Ann Stuart) and she would be his final cohabiting partner. And for me and my family's part in this whole history, it was gratifying to know that while filming *A Breath of Scandal* in Europe in 1959, Curtiz met one last time with my grandmother Fränzi Vondrak.

The stories surrounding these events and developments, which are inextricably connected to Curtiz's final film output, help me to complete my own journey of having "found" my grandfather Michael Curtiz. They show me that the man behind the harsh taskmaster in the director's chair, the womanizer, and the English language assassin was ultimately a man who treasured family above all else.

The Vienna Children

Curtiz's daughter Sonja had tried to keep in touch with him, but any correspondence she might have received back was lost in that Belize hurricane. In 1955, she and husband Jack Hill took things a little further. They packed up and made a trip to California with Christina age eight, Duncan age six, and baby Celine just born that year. Disneyland had just opened, and Curtiz, who was just filming the comedy *Don't Give Up the Ship* with Jerry Lewis, gave the children $20 each to spend at the amusement park. After this meeting, Curtiz sent them Christmas cards, signing himself, "Love, Uncle Michael."

The family made another trip to Hollywood in 1960. Duncan, the cousin from that family branch who I got to know best, was eleven this time. He shared with me his experience of meeting our grandfather.

> I remember that the whole process of visiting Michael Curtiz at Paramount Studios was not a "drop by & say hello" visit. Michael was a busy man and had our day planned for us already. Certain hours he was free to be with us & others he would have us escorted around. My dad, an avid amateur photographer, was not allowed to take his camera equipment past the reception desk. This was a real blow as even snap shots of Michael and the family would be impossible. He did manage to get one shot, though, outside the studio grounds, after our Smorgasbord lunch. Granddad has his arm around my shoulder, little Celina is next to him, then Christina with Mom hiding her mommy tummy behind her daughter. I very much treasure this photograph.

> Inside Paramount Studios, I remember a receptionist escorting us to Michael's office. We spent a fairly long time together in his office and he talked to each one of us with interest. It was clear that he and my Mom were dad and daughter together as she proudly showed off her kids to him. I remember he gave each of us kids a $20 bill, which we thought was amazing. I think my allowance at the time was 25 cents a week.

> I had been looking through a huge hard cover book that was on a coffee table in front of me. It was a very high quality production with glossy pages of early cowboy days with

lots of text and pictures of Billy the Kid and other infamous outlaws. This was the type of book where in our house we would have to wash our hands before we touched it, the type of book where you would be killed by mom or dad if you ripped a page or wrote in the margins. So I was shocked to see that it had scores of pictures cut out with scissors and plenty of writing in the margins! Michael noticed the look on my face. He said simply, "Do you like that book, it's yours." Unfortunately that book was lost in Hurricane Hattie when we lived in Belize City a couple of years later. Also lost was an autographed picture of Elvis Presley with Michael Curtiz from the making of the movie King Creole. Granddad had given it to Christina.

One of my favourite memories is from the huge Paramount Studios cafeteria where Granddad had taken my family. Here we were amongst all the studio employees. About ten feet away at another round table were a whole bunch of huge tough cowboys. Now this was in the days of cowboy heroes I was a real big fan of all of them. For a kid like me these were not actors, they were the real thing. My neck was twisted sideways to look at these guys and I realized one was Davey Crocket. I felt like I was jumping out of my skin.

Granddad must have noticed my enthusiasm. He stood up quickly and said, "come with me." In a split second we were half way to the cowboys' table and my brain said maybe my granddad had enough pull to bother them. Well in the next half second a whole table of cowboys were standing at attention as Michael Curtiz confronted them. I was less than five feet tall and all these guys including Michael were giants. Michael was right in front of Davey Crocket and said "Fess, this is my grandson Duncan. Duncan this is Fess Parker." Fess Parker stuck out his huge hand and said, "Howdy, partner" in a very enthusiastic and friendly manner. I was awe struck and wondered how I would tell my friends in Calgary.

Most surprising of all, Granddad asked if we kids had any interest in being actors. He said he was making "The Adventures of Huckleberry Finn" soon, and to me, he said, "you could be in that movie if you like." Mom immediately said to him, "wait till he gets out of school at least." It was not

Hill Family photo

till later in life that realized how close I was to being an actor
if my family had said yes that day. [11]

Duncan's older sister Christina also came away with a memento,
a book about Curtiz's 1940 film *The Sea Hawk* which she cherished
all her life. For a time she and Curtiz also wrote letters back and
forth, which she thought was "quite amazing … that this busy
man would write to a young girl." She also had a postcard from
him from Italy when he was filming *Francis of Assisi*.

Sonja learned of Curtiz's death in 1962 from *Time Magazine*
and showed it to her children. Wanting only an acknowledgment
of her existence in his life, she obtained a copy of his Will, but
she was disappointed that her name hadn't even been mentioned.
Proof of lineage would come only many years after her own death,
when her children had to prove their right to be heirs in the estate
of Kitty Curtiz who died intestate and without children. As a result, not Sonja herself, but at least her children had proof that she
was Curtiz's child.

*****

Curtiz's son Michael Forster carried on with his life during
these ten years but had no contact with his father. After the war,
he "bummed around" until he took a job as a mathematician at
Douglas Aircraft in Santa Monica, California. Although he didn't
stay at that job the first time around, the experience was in the

back of his mind while trying different ways of making a living. Eventually he was re-hired by Douglas: "I now permanently joined the professional, college educated, upper middle class." [12]

Forster married Virginia Anne Johnson in 1951, and their first daughter Michelanne was born April 26, 1953. He and Anne had two boys, John David born June 2, 1955 and Paul Edward born March 29, 1960. They adopted another girl, Susan Carolyn in 1967. Michael, who already had

Michael Forster
during his working career

a degree in mathematics from UCLA, continued with his education, earning a Master of Science in Electrical Engineering from Southern Methodist University in 1957. Ten years later in 1968, while working half-time, he went back to UCLA and obtained a Ph.D. in Systems Analysis. If Curtiz was proud of his first son in 1947 when he saw him as an American soldier returning from duties in Europe, he would have been doubly proud of him twenty years later.

At the time of his Curtiz's death, April 1962, Forster was a manager at General Electric-TEMPO in Santa Barbara. It was with mixed feelings that he went to the funeral at Forest Lawn, and he remained, half-hidden, at the back of the chapel. Someone might have recognized the family resemblance, he told me. Thilde Forster, who had fought in the courts for Curtiz's first Vienna child, died in California ten years later.

Both Forster and my father are mentioned in Curtiz's Will, but not as beneficiaries. This was no doubt based on solid legal advice – it is clearly vague, and if there were any hard feelings on the part of Forster and my father, they had no recourse.

> I have in mind MICHAEL FORSTER and MICHAEL WONDRAK, but intentionally and with full knowledge I make no provision for either of them in this, my Last Will and Testament, for the reason that I have amply provided for them during my lifetime.

The fact that Sonja Hill – Curtiz was definitely aware of her married name – was not mentioned is indeed a mystery.

*****

After 1953, my father Michael VonDrak with a new way of spelling his name, with his new wife Frances and their two daughters Felicia born January 1, 1956 and Mia born September 1, 1959 respectively, established himself successfully in the Philadelphia art community. He studied at the Philadelphia Museum School of Fine Arts, taught at the Bryn Mawr Art Center, the Main Line School Night Association, and private students in his studio. He founded the Colonial Philadelphia Atelier where he taught watercolor and oil painting and his work was shown at the Philadelphia Museum of Art, the Newman Gallery and the Philadelphia Art Alliance. Although Curtiz did not provide for VonDrak in his will, there was an insurance policy; after Curtiz's death, my father and his family used the pay-out to buy a car.

*****

So much for Curtiz's now grown-up children, the ones he had dealt with since before coming to America in 1926. There was one unexpected surprise, however. For a time he had a relationship with a young woman Beth Jill Gerrard who in January, 1954 gave birth to a girl. The baby was named Deborah Michelle, but I will refer to her as Candace, the name she still goes by.

I came across Candace in my early research and was excited to have found another relative. The fact that she uses Curtiz as her last name created some questions, since he and Gerrard were never married, but it was also an immediate association. She would be my aunt, younger than me, but my aunt nevertheless. I immediately got in touch with her and found her friendly and willing to share her story. She told me that Curtiz had indeed been a father-figure to her, taking her to the studio and on other outings. As an adult, Candace also had plans to write the Curtiz story.

Beyond that, however, I knew very little until further research cast a shadow of confusion on the story of Candace and her mother. Apparently Curtiz supported Gerrard financially for a time – possibly for years – and even signed a Paternity Agreement. Eventually, however, he recanted, stating in his Will of 1961 that he had signed the agreement under duress. After he died, Gerrard took her case to court and won a settlement in her favor. And on the strength of that court decision, Candace also became a primary heir in the estate of Kitty Curtiz and now shares in the royalties paid out by the Director's Guild of America.

Several sources indicate a darker twist. James Robertson refers to an article by R. Graves, published 1983 in *Classic Images* that puts it this way:

> ... after his death actress Jill Gerrard won a paternity suit against his estate, but the court heard evidence that he had been sterilized just before his second marriage in 1929 and the accuracy of the verdict is questionable. [13]

The Associated Press, Los Angeles reported on the case, correctly naming Jill Gerrard a "former model" and including the details of the lawsuit and settlement. Further research indicated that evidence of Curtiz having had a vasectomy was given by two doctors. Finally, according to my cousin Anikó Szanto, her grandmother (Curtiz's sister, Margaret Kaminer) had told her that "Miska had a surgery that made him sterile" [14]

Obviously the truth is shrouded in mystery. What emerges out of this confusion, however, is that at least for a time, Curtiz did acknowledge and was proud to be a father-figure to this little girl. Once again, I am left with the feeling that his deepest need for family eluded him.

Anitra Stevens aka Ann Stuart

Perhaps the saving grace for Curtiz during this time of uncertainty regarding the girl Candace, was that he met the young actress Anitra Stevens whose real name was Ann Stuart. What can I say about Ann Stuart? What would my grandfather want me to say about her? That she was the last great love of his life? That he felt she understood him? That her youth rubbed off on him and gave a man in his late sixties a dose of youthful hope? All of that or none of it may be true, so I will try to stick to the facts.

In his Last Will and Testament, Curtiz provided generously for his "friend" Ann Stuart. The bequest included the ranch near Malibu, the household contents, car, and one-half interest in the rest of his estate. When I first read this document, she was a mystery person. Although I had speculated about who Ann Stuart might be, it took my trip to the Warner Brothers archives in 2002 to prove the connection between Ann Stuart and Anitra Stevens the actress.

At the archives, I found the biographical questionnaire that Ann had filled out in August, 1952. [15] Right at the top, in a large sweeping hand, Ann Stuart explains that she had chosen the screen name Anitra Stevens because she thought it would bring her luck. Ann - I will use her real name here – says she was born March 10, 1929 in Detroit, Michigan, but that she had lived in Hollywood for some time and attended Hollywood High School where she had enjoyed sports and acting in Shakespeare plays. She had always wanted to be an actress and she succeeded in getting minor roles almost immediately after graduating. For her big break in the movies she credits Michael Curtiz, who saw to it that she was cast as Yvonne in *The Jazz Singer* (1952).

Apparently, Curtiz wanted to work with her again after seeing her act a small role in *The Story of Will Rogers* that had been relegated to the "cutting room floor." [16] Did he see in Ann just another beautiful young woman, or did he see the kind of natural acting potential for which he was always on the lookout? Whether it was true or a clever front, Curtiz prided himself on his talent scouting. When a starlet introduced to him casually by the agent Paul Kohner accused Curtiz of "oogling" a beautiful blonde during the meeting, he wrote back indignantly that, "I have no interest in picking talent in drug stores. I can only discover a good actress by seeing her work." [17] Regardless, he actively sought out Ann Stuart for a guaranteed role in *The Jazz Singer*.

Another tantalizing connection between Curtiz and Ann is the fact that her father had been a circus and carnival man in his early years. With Curtiz's own early experience in the circus, this would give them something to talk about. It's difficult to know when exactly the personal relationship began between Curtiz and Ann, but her major role in *The Egyptian* would definitely provide more opportunity.

The Twentieth Century Fox film was produced by Darryl Zanuck who chose Curtiz in homage to the two men's long association and because he knew that directing a Biblical epic was one of Curtiz's abiding strong points. For some reason, James Robertson, in his otherwise detailed account of the film in *The Casablanca Man*, does not mention the role of Queen Nefertiti which Curtiz personally secured for Ann. Images of the actress available online show her almost exclusively as this character. Her filmography confirms that except for a minor role in a television episode of *The Man Behind the Badge,* she did not appear in movies again: Curtiz may have had a hand in that too.

After I "found" Ann Stuart with the help of the Director's Guild just a few years before her unexpected death in 2005, I was able to exchange a few letters with her. Her memories of Curtiz support my sense that he was indeed a loving and sentimental partner for her, but also somewhat insecure to the very end. I must admit that I had hoped for more. I asked Ann about Curtiz's personal papers, but she said that after his death, Bess Meredyth came and took everything away. Newspaper clippings shed only a sliver of light on the conflict between Ann and Bess in regard to Curtiz's Last Will. Clearly, Ann did not receive all that Curtiz intended her to have, and yet she seems to have had enough to live comfortably for the rest of her life. One source of income about which I learned through my dealings with Kitty Curtiz and ultimately her estate, was the royalties paid by the Directors Guild. As I understand it, Ann was receiving all of the royalties while she was alive. It was a goodly amount, and thus a steady income. Her beneficiaries still receive fifty percent of Ann's share of the royalties, and they will as long as Curtiz films are shown anywhere – in other words, into perpetuity.

Ann Stuart did deserve more than money, though. It was she who cared for Curtiz through his final illness. Kitty told me that Ann would let no-one near him. According to Anikó, Curtiz's nephew Paci did see him one last time when he was already bed-ridden in the home he had shared with Ann. The Death Certificate gives the date, time and place of death as April 10, 1962 at 6:10 p.m., 14155 Magnolia Boulevard, North Hollywood. Witnessing a loved one's death, especially in the home, is never an easy thing.

A Bitter Ending

In 1957 while he was working on Proud Rebel, Curtiz suffered a severe attack of appendicitis. Louella Parsons headlined her article "Rush Curtiz to Hospital for Surgery." [18] John Meredyth Lucas explains that during emergency surgery, "they detected a nodule in his prostate and biopsied it. He was told there was no problem." [19] But in fact "the biopsy was positive and the disease had already spread beyond the confines of the original site so surgery was not an option." [20] Left untreated, the cancer advanced over the years. In our times of more advanced medical practices

with prostate cancer, it's difficult to understand how people reacted to it in the 1950s. It's possible that not knowing the seriousness of his illness may have helped Curtiz continue to work. On
the other hand, it seems unfair that he was not told. His usual
cavalier attitude toward health is demonstrated when he writes
to Kitty after returning from Italy and Assisi. "I was a sick man
for a few days in Rome," he writes, "but not as sick as the papers
indicated. ... You should not worry about me as I am very well." [21]

By the end of April, Curtiz was on location in Utah for the
filming of *The Comancheros*. A freak accident in June is reported
but appears not to have affected him.

> Director Michael Curtiz and Stanley Scheure were injured
> when Curtiz fired a shot to signal 50 Indians to attack the
> film's star, John Wayne. Curtiz's aim was bad. He shot his left
> hand and the script supervisor's right leg with one bullet.
>
> Both men were treated by the location nurse. [22]

It is known that Curtiz did not direct all parts of this last film.
Both John Wayne himself and former stuntman Cliff Lyons are
mentioned as having shot some of the scenes. Back in Hollywood
two months later, both the L.A. Times and the Los Angeles Herald
& Express announced that Curtiz was admitted to hospital for
fatigue and was undergoing tests. John Meredyth Lucas elaborates, saying that an X-ray revealed that "his bones were found to
resemble lacework." According to John, the "studio was told but
nothing [was] said to Mike." [23]

Where Belongs the Heart?

My grandfather Michael Curtiz may have spent half of his
life in America, but I believe he was a European at heart. The
Austrians have a term, *Herzensösterreicher* (Austrian at heart) that
could easily be transposed to Hungarians. It applies to those in-
dividuals who left their home country and gave up their first citizenship. Retaining dual citizenship was either not an option or it
was taken lightly by many.

I remember how it happened with me and my parents. After
living in Canada for ten years my stepdad arranged for us to get
our Canadian citizenship. It was a proud moment for the family.
We could now fully take part in the privileges and responsibilities
of our adopted country. I don't remember the loss of our Austrian

citizenship even being discussed. As a teenager I was more concerned that I could go to the closest high school after moving into the city from the farm. That is why my dad also denounced his Roman Catholic religion; here we still have a "public" and a "separate" school board.

My stepdad came to regret losing his Austrian citizenship and he was disappointed years later that he could no longer get dual citizenship. The only way was to return to Austria and live there for the stipulated time, as any other immigrant. As for myself, I have become painfully aware of this situation only in the last few years. I am very content to be a Canadian citizen, but I am also happy that I can call myself an Austrian at heart. My birth country is a continuous draw, and I am fortunate to have family there still. The people and the memories are a joy.

Near the end of his life, Curtiz still had people and memories in Hungary, Austria and other parts of Europe. He still had work connections. In 1959, he agreed to make *A Breath of Scandal* with Sophia Loren, John Gavin, Maurice Chevalier, and Angela Lansbury. And it was during filming in and near Vienna that he saw my grandmother Fränzi for the last time.

My heart went out to her when, full of emotion, she told me about their meeting. He was staying at the Imperial Hotel in Vienna, and Fränzi found out about it through her friends. At first she didn't know what to do, but she finally got up the courage to go there and try to see him.

On June 13, they met in the Imperial Hotel Café. I imagine them sitting close together, she ordering a *Mélange* and he an Americano, black; she too nervous to accept a slice of *Sacher Torte* that he offered, he not going in for sweets as a rule. After a short time, they slipped into an easy conversation, and he told her, "you are the bestest person in my life." Flattery – maybe, but why? Maybe it was more sincere than he would have admitted. They both signed a postcard addressed to their son Michael in the USA.

I can't help feeling sad for what Curtiz was already going through at that time. His marriage with Bess was all but over, and although he was already living with Ann Stuart, his personal life was in turmoil over the girl Candace. He did not know that he was deathly ill. Fränzi was like a pleasant breeze from his younger years.

Just over a year later, Curtiz traveled to Europe one more time, to direct *St. Francis of Assisi*. He had the intention of going

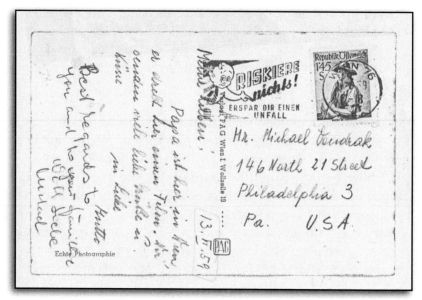

Postcard to Michael

to Vienna to see Fränzi again, but it didn't work out: From Rome, he wrote a postcard to thank her for her letter and greetings. [24] He was disappointed that the work wouldn't be finished until the new year. The weather had been bad, always raining. He sent her wishes for a Merry Christmas, With Love. When I look at the extra material on my DVD of *St. Francis of Assisi* which shows Curtiz wearing his overcoat and a hat, wandering around the rain-drenched location, I can't help thinking that he looks very tired.

As far as I know, this was the last correspondence between them. My grandmother may still have held out some hope of seeing Curtiz, however. She was already planning to travel to Philadelphia and possibly to stay in the USA and live with their son Michael and his new family. She had applied to renew her passport, which would otherwise have expired in October, 1960.

That visit finally happened two years later, only months after Curtiz's death. Ironically, she even obtained a Green Card, issued August 29, 1962, certifying that she was admitted to the United States as an immigrant. Her life-long dream realized – too late. During the six months she stayed with my father and his family, they made a trip out to California where she could at least visit his grave. There, Fränzi made peace with her Miska before returning to Vienna to live out her life. She died in 1991.

EPILOGUE

I wonder still: was Miska a hopeless romantic hiding behind the mask of a cynic? As a film director, Curtiz – more so than most people – was in a position to visualize what happens to romantics, how they are used and abused, how they fall apart. He was strong enough to prevent that by not fully revealing his own feelings even to those he lived with. Instead, he showed emotions to the world, through his films.

Do I know my grandfather better now than I did on that dusty country road in Northern Alberta back in 1962? Whatever I had heard about him or imagined then still stands. He was famous – a giant among people. He was unreachable – for me and many others who tried. But at fourteen, I could not have understood what I know now, that he was also just a man.

My work on this project has sometimes made me feel very close to him. I've imagined talking with him and hearing him prompt me to continue. I've had some vivid dreams. He has shown me what it means to be passionate about work, about family, about life.

Finding and getting to know my many relations has been one of the most rewarding results. To find previously unknown cousins right here in Edmonton, to meet an uncle in Santa Barbara and correspond with a cousin in New Zealand and an aunt in Florida – new horizons opened before me at every turn. Most of them were only too eager to share their own knowledge about Curtiz. Anikó's chart graced the wall of my study for months and is still the go-to tool for continuing our family tree. There were disappointments too, such as losing Kitty Curtiz's friendship before it had a chance. I've had to let go of things I couldn't change, information I couldn't find.

In my heart I truly believe, and I hope my book will help his descendants truly appreciate that Kaminer Manó –Kertész Mihály – Miska – Michael – Mike Curtiz was as much a man who treasured family as one who needed to make great films.

NOTES

Introduction: A Journey Begins

1. Omi is the endearing version of Grandmother in Austrian German. Fränzi is short for Franziska.
2. In the early 1990's Anikó Szanto wrote to my father after seeing his artist's website that said he was the son of Michael Curtiz. Anikó is the granddaughter of Margaret, one of Curtiz's sisters, and has been an important source of information about his family.
3. Note on names: in Hungarian, the family name precedes the first name in writing and in speech. This also applies to street names, for example Liszt-Ferenc utcá is Franz Liszt St. in German and English.
4. Picture of #12 Jokai utcá taken by me, 2000.
5. "Ich Schau Dir in die Augen, Kleines" Neue Kronen Zeitung, Krone Bunt, 6. August, 2000.
6. Manó is Hungarian for a boy's name meaning "God is with us" (Hebrew). This meaning links it to Emmanuel, but also to Michael, a common biblical name meaning "who is like God." In a June 1925 letter to my grandmother, Curtiz noted that his given names are Manuel Michael, thus my assumption that his first legal name was Manuel Mihály. Spelling of names quite often varies among records: Ignácz may also be written as Izsák, and Golde Natt also appears as Aranka Nathan.
7. Neuester Plan der Haupt- und Residenzstadt Budapest (Most Recent Map of the Capital and Empirical City Budapest) 1901. Published by Barta, Lajos
8. The names could be changed but had to begin with the same letter (in this case K) as the original.
9. K.&K. (Kaiserlich, Imperial Austrian and Königlich, Royal Hungarian) The political compromise of 1867 established the dual monarchy of Austria and Hungary. The K.& K. administration created a lifestyle that spread throughout the Austro-Hungarian Empire.

10. Hausner, Oesterreich, p. 14

11. Etel (daughter) grew up to be married twice, first to Imre Szüszü and then to Armin Hamburger. She had two children, Lászlo and Lilli. Antal (son) born January 25, 1885. Antal changed his name to Kertész (also in 1905 along with Mihály) and married Erzsebet "Erzsi" Urán. They had a son Laszlo "Laci" Kertész who lived most of his adult life in France [Anikó]

12. From here on, I will use Aranka as my great-grandmother's name, as it is the one that is given on all later records.

13. Historical Population Chart, Vienna website

Part I Childhood and Adolescence

1. Hannibal Goodwin, a New Jersey Episcopal minister, had been working on developing the celluloid film medium. He applied for patent in 1887 but was refused. Although George Eastman, a well-known name in the future movie business, gained the first commercial success with film, Goodwin remains as the inventor. (Retrieved April 24, 2005 from http://www.plastiquarian.com)

2. Marton, p. 16

3. Frazier, George. "The Machine With a Rage" True, October 1947

4. Peter Martin's article "Hollywood's Champion Language Assassin" (1947) was followed closely by his book Hollywood Without Makeup (Philadelphia: Lippincott, 1948).

5. Anikó Szanto, the granddaughter of Margit Kaminer, Nov. 2000 e-mail. Most of the information about the Kaminer family comes from Anikó Szanto, but not all names, dates and details are supported by documentation.

6. Viviani, 1974; Rosenzweig, 1982, World Film Directors, 1987; Robertson, 1993; Keim, 1999.

7. Anikó Jan 2001 e-mail

8. Anikó, Jan. 2001 e-mail noting personal communication with Margaret, 1989 and Kati Manhart (Anikó's mother), 1996

9. Letter from MC to Fränzi dated Vienna, June 4, 1925. My grandmother kept all or most of the letters she received from Curtiz throughout their thirty-five year relationship. In 1966, when she finally visited her son, my father

Michael VonDrak, she gave him the letters. I received copies in about 1998.

10. Nagy "Tendencies" para 7
11. i.b.i.d. para 7, 9
12. i.b.i.d. para 11, 12
13. Martin, *Hollywood Without Makeup*, p. 120
14. Martin, p. 121
15. A Hungarian couple Mr. and Mrs. Hajnal of Edmonton, Alberta noticed these details.
16. The 1999 film *Sunshine* written and directed by Hungarian filmmaker István Szabó, traces the fate of the Sonnenschein family through several generations beginning in the late 1800's.
17. Martin, p. 121
18. Frazier
19. Pécs is a city in the Baranya Region of Hungary, also referred to the "Gateway between Europe and the Balkans." In 1908, the population was about 50,000, mainly Roman Catholic. About 10% were Jewish. Political and social volatility here saw Pécs figuring highly in the events leading to the end of the Austro-Hungarian Empire.
20. Balint, Lajos "From Kertesz to Curtiz" Filmvilag, 1966. V.1) This article was translated from the Hungarian by Emil Sandi (2005).
21. Balogh, 78
22. Balint, i.b.i.d., para 5
23. Balint, i.b.i.d., para 3
24. Balint, i.b.i.d., para 3
25. Balint, i.b.i.d., para 6
26. Balint, i.b.i.d., para 3
27. Burns, Bryan. World Cinema: Hungary, p. 2
28. Lukacs, John, Budapest 1900 p. 128
29. Marton, The Great Escape 26, p. 27

Part II Life and Work in Hungary: 1913 - 1919

1. Kertész, wrote the article "A rendezö" (The Director) in the film magazine *Mozgófénykép Hirado* in 1913. This quotation from p. 70. As an interesting note, Alexander Korda wrote reviews for this magazine after he returned from Paris, thereby helping to establish the film critic as a specialty writer.

2. Kertész, "The Director, the Actor and the Dramaturge" 1917. Second article by Kertész in *Mozgófénykép Hirado*. Both articles cited were provided by Gyöngyi Balogh and translated by Emil Sandi, Edmonton, Alberta, 2005.

3. Burns, Bryan. *World Cinema: Hungary*. Wiltshire, England: Trowbridge, 1996, p. 2

4. Canham, Kinglsey

5. Martin, Peter. *Hollywood Without Makeup*. Philadelphia: Lippincott, 1948, p. 122

6. Frazier, George. p. 136

7. Wikipedia.de

8. http://filmstarpostcards.blogspot.ca/2009/11/lucy-doraine. html Retrieved June 17, 2011

9. Viviani, Christian. *Anthologie Du Cinéma*, 1974, p. 117, (my translation from French)

10. Catherine of Alexandria was one of the most important saints in the religious culture of the late middle ages. In the Roman Catholic Church, the martyr virgin is celebrated on November 25.

11. Curtiz, Kitty. "Hunger" *Kinderzeit, Kinderfreud, Kinderleid*, 1999, p. 9 (my translation from the German)

12. Horn, Pierre L., Ed.. *Handbook of French Popular Culture*. p. 79

13. See notes 1 and 2 above

14. Another Hungarian film magazine where Kertész articles appeared

15. Another Hungarian film magazine where Kertész articles appeared

16. Wikipedia article on Michael Curtiz

17. Balint, 1966. para. 1

18. Baxter, *The Hollywood Exiles*, p. 133

19. Vajda kept his ties with Kertész when they collaborated on the script of *Sodom and Gomorrah* filmed in Vienna 1922/23

20. Meredyth-Lucas, p. 78

21. ibid, pp. 78-79

22. ibid, p. 79

23. Curtiz, Kitty. *Kinderzeit, Kinderfreud, Kinderleid*, 1999, p. 10 (my translation)

24. Balint, 1966, para. 11

Part III Kertész in Vienna: 1919 - 1926

1. The Hungarian producer Oskar Meßter was already established in Vienna before WWI. GMBH (Gesellschaft mit Beschrenkter Haftung) means Limited Company.
2. Balint, 1966. para. 3
3. Robertson, p. 152
4. i.b.i.d., p. 4
5. The German Umlaut was dropped from the name once Thilde and her son Michael were in America
6. For purposes of clarity, I am showing these and all Kronen amounts in Austrian Schillings, the currency made official in December 1924. In that conversion, 10,000 Kronen equaled One Schilling. From 1923 to 1926, the Schilling remained stable enough.
7. It would be interesting to make a full comparison study of Kertész's income and maintenance payments, but I leave that to more mathematical minds.
8. My translation from the magazine *Kino*, original source Paimann's Filmlist of 1922, p. 94
9. Fritz, Walter. *Im Kino Erlebe ich die Welt*, pp.103-104
10. ibid, p.104
11. This and all translations of the archive files are mine. Note the inconsistency in spelling; officially it is Dalla Bonna, but throughout my research materials, the variations include Dalla Bona, even Dallabona. Except in direct quotes, I have tried to use Dalla Bonna exclusively.
12. My grandmother always wrote her name as Franziska or Fränzi Wondrak, and my father was born Michael Emmanuel Franz Wondrak. He changed the W to V during his teens, and changed Vondrak to VonDrak after his first few years in the US, ca. 1953. My own birth name is Ilona Vondrak.
13. I am indebted to Liselotte Jensen, my best friend's mother, for transcribing the cursive handwriting into a form I could work with for translating into English.
14. Letter from Fränzi Wondrak to me, 24.9.1987
15. Letter from August to Anna Wondrak dated New York, October 22, 1908
16. Fritz, Walter. p. 96
17. ibid, p.96, Note 8 - Walter Fritz private file

18. Lucy Doraine, Wikipedia.de
19. Curtiz, Kitty. *Kinderzeit, Kinderfreud, Kinderleid*, 1999, "Das Kleine Glück" p. 13 (my translation)
20. Fritz, p. 101
21. www.oenb.at "Hyperinflation and Collapse of the Currency" para.1
22. At the time, 10,000 Kronen equalled 1 Schilling
23. (*Kino in Österreich*). (Wien 20 Jahrhundert and Austrian film books)
24. This and all other letters from Curtiz to Fränzi (and others) are translated by me
25. Hoppe, Ralph. *Die Friedrichstrasse*, p. 82-83
26. ibid, p.81
27. Mattl-Wurm, p.45
28. Meredyth-Lucas, John, p.34
29. Bolzano is Italian and therefore current name of Bozen, as the city was known before WWI. I will use the current Italian as it is used in English.
30. Over the ensuing years, letters from Fränzi's friends were addressed to Frau Kertész.
31. "Der Selbsterlebte Film des Regisseurs Kertesz" The Self-experienced Film of the Director Kertész" *Illustrierte Kronen-Zeitung* (Illustrated Crown News). I received the news article from the Hungarian film historian Gyöngyi Balogh. It's unlikely that Fränzi saw it as she was in Abbazia and/or Bozen at the time.
32. The conversion of Kronen to Schilling had begun at the end of 1923, but obviously the process was not yet complete
33. *Fiaker Nummer Dreizehn* (German alternative title Einspanner No. 13) English title Cab No. 13, released March 6, 1926 in Austria and May 8 in Finland (IMDb).
34. English title *The Golden Butterfly* (USA) and *The Road to Happiness* (alternative English title).
35. IMDB commentator bullybyte 2007
36. Frazier, George. "The Machine With a Rage" *True*, October, 1947, p. 136
37. Warner Brothers Archives legal files
38. Markus, Georg, *Kronen Zeitung*, Vienna, 2007

39. The *SS Leviathan* was seized from the Germans (Vaterland) in 1917. After WWI, the ship was re-purposed for passenger crossings between Europe and America until 1934.

Part IV America – The First Years

1. Retrieved from www.greatoceanliners.net/vaterland.html
2. Delehanty, Thornton. "Curtiz Recalls His First 4th; Thought Flags Were for Him." *NY Herald-Tribune*, 7.12.1942.
3. Retrieved 2010 from http://www.zazzle.com/cruise+ship+posters? (pg. 2)
4. Retrieved February 3, 2010 from http://www.dorothyparker.com/dot28.htm (para.5)
5. Strauss, Theodore. "The Blitzkrieg of Michael Curtiz," no page#
6. Higham, Charles. pp. 20/21
7. Herman, p. 43
8. Warner Bros. Pictures Inc. PAC:BM letter p.1
9. Cass Sperling's Documentary *The Brothers Warner*; Gabler, p. 123
10. Higham
11. Gabler, p. 42
12. Higham, p. 13
13. i.b.i.d., p. 16
14. i.b.i.d., p. 16
15. Gabler, p. 123
16. i.b.i.d., p. 136
17. letter to Kitty, 1940
18. letter to Michael Vondrak, 1940
19. Meredyth Lucas p. 9. He uses the term stepfather even though Curtiz never did formally adopt Bess's son.
20. Retrieved from: http://www.wsjhistory.com/babins_kosher_restaurant.htm
21. Jerome, Stuart p. 26/27
22. Will Hays letter July 26, 1926 (Warner Brothers Archives)
23. Bureau of Immigration file No. 55080/898
24. Meredyth Lucas, p. 34; Robertson, pp. 12/13; Marton, p. 68
25. Robertson, p. 13
26. Letter to Fränzi, March 1928
27. Robertson, p. 14
28. Meredyth Lucas, p. 48
29. Veigl, p. 77 (on fashion, see also article by Flusser para. 5

30. Meredyth Lucas, p. 48

31. "More Beautiful than Hollywood" *Mohezit* p. 9 (translated from the Hungarian by Terése Homann)

32. Entry on Meredyth in *Booking Guide and Studio Directory Vol. XII*

33. Meredyth Lucas, p. 11. Besides her son's book, Imdb.com is the main source for filmography and biographical information on Beth Meredyth.

34. Meredyth, Bess. In Hughes, p. 287

35. Meredyth Lucas, p. 5

36. Meredyth Lucas, p. 37

37. *L.A. Examiner,* 28 June 1928

38. *LA Examiner,* 2 December 1928

39. Meredyth Lucas, p. 57

40. Strauss, *L.A. Examiner,* 24 June, 1928

42. *L.A. Examiner,* 2 July, 1928

43. Meredyth Lucas, p 58

44. Retrieved 2010 from http://en.wikipedia.org/wiki/File:NoahsArk1929.jpg

45. "Ancients Must be Interpreted When Shown to Moderns" *L.A. Examiner,* 02 December, 1928

46. Robertson, p. 16

47. Warner Bros. legal files

48. letter July 1929

49. Meredyth Lucas, p. 52

50. Louella Parsons, *Hollywood Examiner,* 4 December, 1929. There is some confusion between this property and the beach house used in Mildred Pierce fifteen years later: "Monty's Beach House, used in the key opening scene and several others, was actually owned by the film's director, Michael Curtiz. It was built in 1929 and stood at 26652 Latigo Shore Dr. in Malibu. It collapsed into the ocean after a week of heavy storms in January 1983" (Retrieved 21/08/11 from http://www.imdb.com/title/tt0037913/trivia). Another website says the house was owned by one Frederick Rindge, Jr. (http://www.malibucomplete.com/mc_hazards_floods.php) And yet another one mentions Anatole Litvak as the owner. My efforts in tracing ownership through the L.A. County land records office have been unsuccessful.

51. *Hollywood Examiner,* 8 December, 1929

52. Meredyth Lucas, pp. 51/52

Part V The Past Not Far Behind

1. www.passengerlists.de
2. Subtitle *Das Frauenideal unserer Zeit* (The Ideal Woman of Our Time)
3. Thilde Forster's German films do not appear to have appeared in English
4. German title *Herzen Ohne Ziel*
5. The value of Austrian Schillings to Dollars is approximate, based on the exchange at that time.
6. From Court Judgment, Bezirksgericht Hietzing, 30 April, 1931
7. Curtiz letter February, 1930
8. Personal communication, 2010
9. Curtiz letter to Wienninger & Wagner, 11 May, 1931
10. Curtiz letter 13 June, 1931
11. All parts of the article translated from the Hungarian by Terés Homann
12. "Citizenship Through Naturalization" Retrieved Aug. 15, 2012 from http://www.uscis.gov/portal/site/uscis
13. Bolger, Eileen. "Background History of the United States Naturalization Process" June 18, 2003, p. 2. Retrieved www.colorado.gov/dpa/doit/archives/natinfo.htm
14. U.S. Department of Immigration file P.53141
15. Meredyth Lucas, p. 74
16. Curtiz letter 16 September, 1936
17. Curtiz letter 25 October, 1936

Part VI Life Work Liberty

1. Newspaper? 24 October, 1931 [clipping 17] (Note: Some clippings from the UCLA Library archives do not show source.)
2. Robertson, p. 25
3. Source? Will Hays, quoted in 12 April, 1933 clipping
4. Source? 30 November, 33 clipping
5. Curtiz letter, 20 April, 1933
6. Robertson, p. 34
7. Source? 10 December, 1935 clipping
8. Robertson, p. 35, 34
9. Robertson, p. 44

10. Permission granted, Warner Bros. Archive file # 1495. A glass shot glass shot is a special technique for combining actions on a set (in this case, Flynn and De Havilland at the window) with a painted background attached to a large piece of glass (the castle walls around the window). In the finished shot, we see both at once and are fooled into believing we see only one image.

11. Olivia DeHavilland personal interview, March 12, 2006

12. Warner Bros. (who?) letter to Curtiz, 7 September, 1934

13. Curtiz letter 8 January, 1936

14. Personal communication with Eva Nágy, Rosza Kaminer's niece. Budapest, 2014

15. Meredyth Lucas, p. 82

16. Meredyth Lucas, p. 89 Note: Meredyth Lucas writes Ince Sandor. This is most likely Alexander Sandor Ince, Hungarian Theatre Producer. Curtiz calling Ince his cousin may be a term of endearment; they definitely knew each other, though.

17. Meredyth Lucas, p. 90

18. *Los Angeles Times*, 6 September, 1936

19. *Los Angeles Times*, -----

20. Roland Swaffield letter, 13 June, 1939

21. Meredyth Lucas, p. 127

22. Meredyth Lucas, p. 124

23. *Los Angeles Times*, Doraine Clippings

24. Curtiz letters (to Kitty) … dates

25. Kitty Curtiz, "The Field Marshall of Film" German Magazine, date missing, p. 8

26. *Los Angeles Examiner*, 23 July, 1939

27. *New York Journal-American*, 24 July, 1939

28. Most of this material from Michael Forster, unpublished autobiography, by permission

29. Letter from Thilde Forster's lawyer, "hhm" memo courtesy of UCLA Library files

30. Los Angeles Examiner, 9 October, 1934

31. Michael Forster, p. 79

32. Michael VonDrak, personal communication, 2010

33. Matthias letter to Fränzi, no date

34. Curtiz letter, December, 1935

35. Michael VonDrak, personal communication, 2010

36. Curtiz letter, 11 May, 1936

37. Curtiz letter, 9 February, 1939
38. Curtiz letter, 6 June, 1939
39. Curtiz letter, 27 June, 1939

Part VII Wild Years Ahead

2. Curtiz handwritten letter to Kitty, undated – Fall, 1940
3. Curtiz letter, 23 November, 1940
4. Articles respectively: Elizabeth Copeland, *Richmond VA News Leader*, 17. February, 1940; Theodore Strauss, *New York Times*, 19 May, 19…; and *Brooklyn Daily Eagle*, 15 December, 19…
5. Elizabeth Copeland… article name *News Leader* date
6. Swaffield letter, 23 January, 1941
7. Pek letter, no date
8. Pek letter, 14 July, 1941
9. Michael Forster, p. 51
10. i.b.i.d. p. 52
11. i.b.i.d. p. 52
12. i.b.i.d. p. 54
13. i.b.i.d. p. 55
14. Dallabona: Vienna Archive File 1 P 27/33 314
15. Curtiz letter, June 1941
16. *New York Post*, 13 June, 1941
17. Howard Koch, p. 77
18. Harlan Lebo, pp. 64, 74, 75 respectively
19. Paul Kohner letters courtesy of the German Archive of Cinematography
20. Paul Kohner Day Letter, 29 December, 1943
21. Curtiz letter, 5 January, 1944
22. Harlan Lebo, p. 192
24. Wikipedia entry for This is the Army
25. James Robertson, p. 83
26. L.A. Tribune, 2 July, 1945, courtesy Warner Bros. Archives
27. James Robertson, p.83
28. Bob Thomas, p. 5
29. Add a note about efforts to get more info?
30. Pek letter, January, 1943
31. Details about Karl Eberson by permission of Helga von Bulow, editor of Kitty's autobiography (in the process of becoming an American citizen (August 23, 1943). He had already enlisted (13 February 1941) in the American army

32. Pek letter, May, 1943
33. Curtiz letter, 25 October 25, 1944
34. Bess Meredyth letter, June, 1945
35. Bess Meredyth letter, June, 1945)
36. Brooks, p. 58
37. Curtiz letter, 23 May, 1946
38. Curtiz letter, 2 April, 1946
39. Robertson, p. 93
40. Robertson, p. 95
41. Curtiz letter, 15 October, 1946
42. Meredyth Lucas, p. 193
43. Bess Meredyth letter, 12 January, 1947
44. Bess Meredyth letter, 27 February, 1947
45. Vernon Scott "Curtiz is Top Star Discoverer" 9 August, 1956
46. Warner Bros. Archives memo, undated
47. Warner Bros. news release, 12 September 12, 1952 by Gene Handsaker
48. Obringer letter, 4 January, 1949 [WB Archives]
51. David Curtiz filmography, International Movie Data Base (imdb)
52. Pek letter, 2April, 1947
53. Heyman, quoting Irene Dunne, p. 61
54. Meredyth Lucas, p. 72
55. Meredyth Lucas, p. 72
56. Curtiz letter, 8 January, 1947
57. Michael Vondrak letter, 25 May, 1948
58. Robertson, p. 101
59. Curtiz letter, 15 January, 1954 on Twentieth Century-Fox letterhead, courtesy Jim Robertson

Part VIII The Last Ten Years

1. *Los Angeles Examiner*, 25 March, 1960
2. Curtiz letter, 28 March, 1960
3. Curtiz letter, 2 September, 1960
4. Meredyth Lucas, p.222
5. Curtiz letter, 9 January, 1952
6. Curtiz letter, 14 April, 1952
7. Curtiz letter, undated 1962
8. *L.A. Times*, 14 April, 1953
9. Robertson, p. 143

10. Robertson, p. 123
11. Duncan Hill, 2000
12. Forster, p. 71
13. Robertson, p. 153
14. Aniko Szanto email, 7 August, 1999
15. Warner Bros. Archive questionnaire, by permission
16. Warner Bros. Archive memo
17. Paul Kohner letters
18. Louella Parsons, 27 August, 1957
19. Meredyth Lucas, p. 208
20. Meredyth Lucas, p. 226
21. Curtiz letter, 30 January, 1961
22. *L.A. Times*, 28 June, 1961
23. Meredyth Lucas, p. 226
24. Curtiz postcard, 14 December, 1960

BIBLIOGRAPHY

Balint, Lajos "From Kertesz to Curtiz" *Filmvilag,* 1966. V.1.
Retrieved 8/26/2005 from www.sulinet.hu/tart/ncikk/
ah/0/6104/casa4.htm.

Balogh, Gyöngyi. "Die Anfänge zweier internationaler
Filmkarrieren: Mihály Kertész und Sandor Korda " in
*Elektrische Schatten: Beiträge zur Österreichischen
Stummfilmgeschichte.* Filmarchiv Austria, Vienna, AT,
1999, pp. 77-100.

Baxter, John. *The Hollywood Exiles.* London, England:
Macdonald & Jane's, 1976.

Bolger, Eileen. "Background History of the United States
Naturalization Process" June 18, 2013. Retrieved Nov.
15, 2017 from https://socialwelfare.library.vcu.edu/
federal/naturalization-process-in-u-s-early-history/

Brooks, Geraldine. *People of the Book.* Viking Penguin, NY,
2008.

Burns, Bryan. *World Cinema: Hungary.* Wiltshire, England:
Trowbridge, 1996.

Canham, Kingsley. "Curtiz: Cynicism, Cinema and
Casablanca" in *The Hollywood Professionals, Vol. I.*
London, England: Tantivy, 1973.

Delehanty, Thornton. "Curtiz Recalls His First 4th; Thought
Flags Were for Him." *NY Herald-Tribune*, 7.12.1942.

Filmmuseum Berlin – Paul Kohner Collection

Frazier, George. "The Machine With a Rage" *True* October,
1947, pp. 60-61, 136-138.

Fritz, Walter. *Im Kino Erlebe ich die Welt.* Christian
Brandstätter, Vienna, 1997.

Gabler, Neal. *An Empire of Their Own: How the Jews Invented
Hollywood.* Crown Publishers, NY. 1988.

Hausner, Ernst. *Oesterreich.* Jugend & Volk: Vienna, 1986.

Herman, A book about William Wyler – his travel to Hollywood

Heyman, C. David. *Liz: An Intimate Biography of Elizabeth Taylor.* Carol Publishing Group, N.Y., 1995.

Higham, Charles. *Warner Brothers.* Charles Scribner's Sons, New York, 1975.

Hoppe, Ralph. *Die Friedrichstrasse: Pflaster der Extreme.* Berlin-Brandenburg: be.bra verlag, 1999.

Horn, Pierre L., Editor. *Handbook of French Popular Culture.* Westport, CT: Greenwood Press, 1991.

Hughes, *The Truth About the Movies,* 1924

Jerome, Stuart. *Those Crazy Wonderful Years When We Ran Warner Bros.* L. Stuart, 1983.

Keim, Norman O. *Films Of the Golden Age.* "I put all the art into my pictures the audience can stand." 17, 1999, pp. 64-71

Kertész, Mihály. "A rendezö, a szinész, a dramaturg" (The Director, the Actor, the Dramaturge) *Mozgófénykép Hirado* 1917, Vol. III, No. 51.

Kertész, Mihály. "A rendezö" (The Director) *Mozgófénykép Hirado* 1913, Vol. 15, pp. 69-70.

Koch, Howard. *As Time Goes By.* Harcourt Brace Jovanovich, N.Y. 1979

Lebo, Harlan. *Casablanca: Behind the Scenes.* Simon & Schuster, N.Y., 1992

Martin, Peter. "Hollywood's Champion Language Assassin" (1947)

Martin, Peter. *Hollywood Without Makeup.* Philadelphia: Lippincott, 1948.

Marton, Kati. *The Great Escape: Nine Jews who Fled Hitler and Changed the World.* New York: Simon & Schuster, 2006.

Mattl-Wurm. *Geschichte Wien: Das 20. Jahrhundert.* Pichler, Vienna, 1998.

Meredyth, Bess. "Beginning a Scenario" in Laurence A. Hughes, Editor. *The Truth About the Movies: By the Stars.* Hollywood, CA: Hollywood Publishers, Inc. 1924.

Meredyth Lucas, John. *Eighty Odd Years in Hollywood.* Jefferson NC, McFarland & Co. Inc., 2004.

Nagy, "Tendencies" Article about public school system in Hungary in the 1880's

Robertson, James. *The Casablanca Man.* London, England. Routledge, 1993.

Rosenzweig, Sidney. *Casablanca and Other Major Films of Michael Curtiz.* Ann Arbor: UMI Research Press, 1982.

Scott, Vernon. "Curtiz is Top Star Discoverer" *New York Morning Telegraph,* August 9, 1956

Smith, F. Berkeley. *Budapest: The City of the Magyars.* N.Y. James Pott & Co., 1903.

Strauss, Theodore. "The Blitzkrieg of Michael Curtiz," *New York Times*, May 19, 1940.

Thomas, Bob. *Joan Crawford, A Biography.* Simon & Schuster, N.Y., 1978.

Veigl, Hans. *Die Wilden 20er Jahre: Alltagskulturen zwischen zwei Kriegen.* Vienna: Ueberreuter, 1999.

Vienna; Historical Population. Retrieved Nov. 2018 from https://ipfs.io/ipfs/QmXoypizjW3WknFiJnKLwHCnL 72vedxjQkDDP1mXWo6uco/wiki/Vienna.html

Viviani, Christian. "Michael Curtiz" *Anthologie du Cinema, TomeVIII.* Paris: L'Avant-Scene, 1974, pp. 113-176.

Wakeman, John, Ed. *World Film Directors, Vol. One 1890-1940.* New York: H.S. Wilson Co., 1987, pp. 172-81.

Warner Bros. Pictures Inc. Archives, Los Angeles, CA. 2002

FAMILY TREES

Michael's Older Half-Siblings

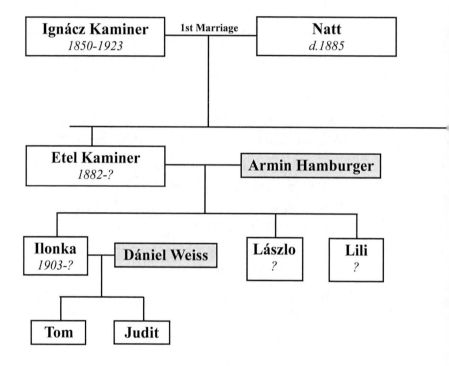

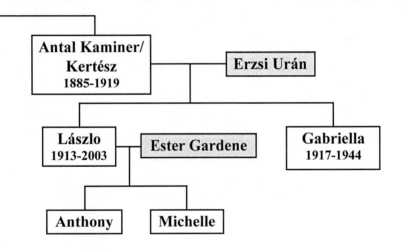

FAMILY TREES

Michael's Siblings

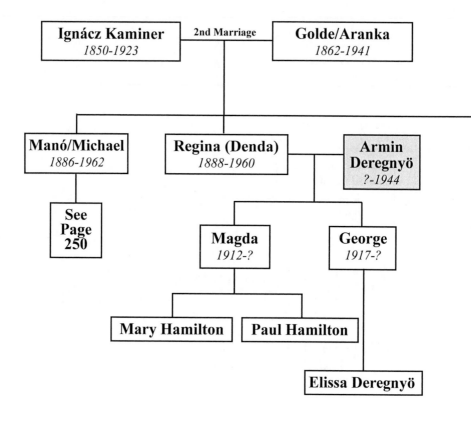

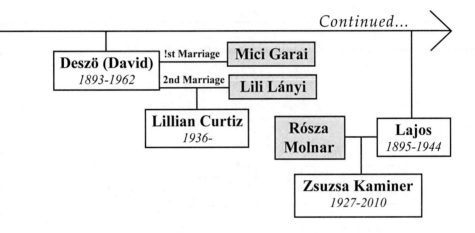

Continued...

Deszö (David)
1893-1962

!st Marriage   Mici Garai

2nd Marriage   Lili Lányi

Lillian Curtiz
1936-

Rósza
Molnar

Lajos
1895-1944

Zsuzsa Kaminer
1927-2010

FAMILY TREES

Michael's Siblings (Cont.)

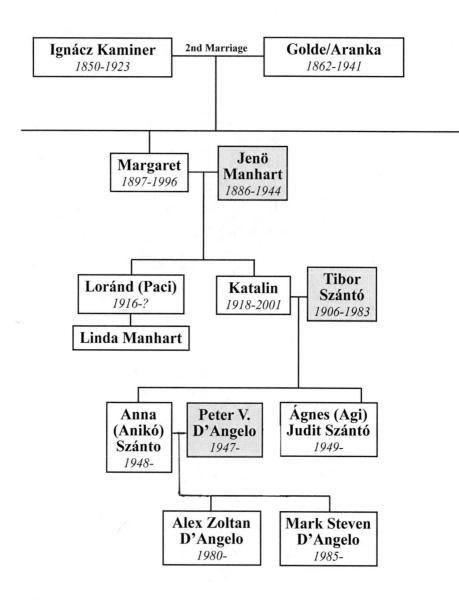

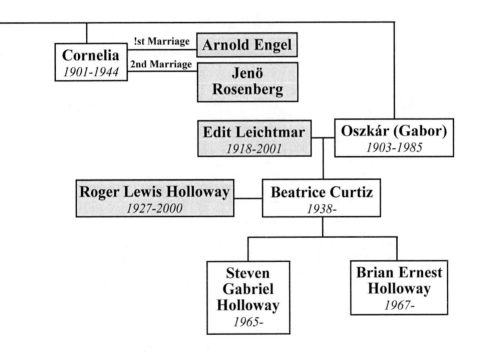

fAMILY TREES

Michael's Marriages and Liaisons

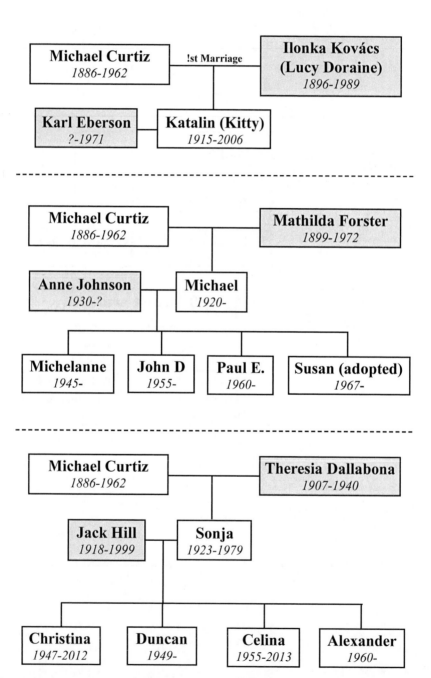

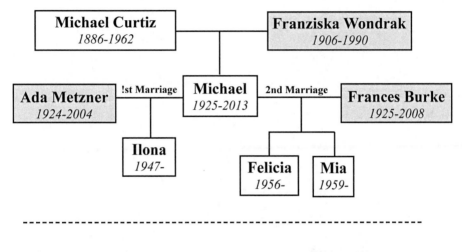

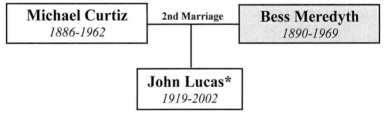

John Lucas was Bess's son from previous marriage

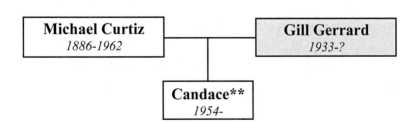

**Candace was declared MC's child by a California court after his death*

To order more copies of this book, find books by other
Canadian authors, or make inquiries about publishing
your own book, contact PageMaster at:

PageMaster Publication Services Inc.
11340-120 Street, Edmonton, AB T5G 0W5
books@pagemaster.ca
780-425-9303

catalogue and e-commerce store
PageMasterPublishing.ca/Shop

ABOUT THE AUTHOR

Ilona was born in Vienna, Austria, July 9, 1947 to Michael and Ada Vondrak. She was adopted by Ada's second husband Frank Sobernig. In 1956 she emigrated to Alberta with her parents and lived on a farm near Perryvale until 1965. From then until 2010 she made her home in Edmonton. She married Gary A. Ryder in 1972 and they have two children: Robert and Kelly. Ilona worked as a legal assistant with McCuaig Desrochers for twenty years, and after obtaining her Master's degree from the U of A, she was an English instructor at Grant MacEwan University until her retirement in 2008.

Ilona now lives in Beaumont just south of Edmonton. She loves to spend time at the family cabin at Island Lake near Athabasca and to explore Alberta's nature with the St. Albert Trekkers Volkssport and Waskahegan Trail walking clubs. The nearby Edmonton International Airport keeps her connected to Austria and the world.